The Army Officer Corps and Military Modernisation in Later Colonial India

The Army Officer Corps and Military Modernisation in Later Colonial India

Pradeep Barua

UNIVERSITY OF HULL PRESS

THE
UNIVERSITY
OF HULL
PRESS

Cottingham Road
Hull
HU6 7RX

A CIP catalogue record for this book is available from the British Library.

© **Pradeep Barua**

Published 1999

Paperback ISBN 0 85958 668 5

All rights reserved. No part of this publication may be reproduced, stored in a retrieval system, or transmitted in any form or by any means, electronic, mechanical, photocopying, recording or otherwise in accordance with the provisions of the Copyright Act 1988 without the prior permission of The University of Hull Press.

Printed by
LSL Press, Bedford, England

Contents

Acknowledgements	ii
Dedication	iii
Introduction	1
Chapter 1: A Cathartic Debate	7
Chapter 2: The High Road to Dehra Dun	37
Chapter 3: An Officer and a Gentleman	61
Chapter 4: *Wogs in the Mess*	91
Chapter 5: The Roots of Doctrine	115
Chapter 6: The Crucible of War	137
Chapter 7: The Indian Army and the Colonial Legacy	161
Conclusion	191
Bibliography	207
Index	221

To my parents

Pannalal and Ramola

Acknowledgements

A major portion of the research for this dissertation was conducted at the India Office Library (Blackfriar's Rd), and I would like to thank the members of the library staff for their patience and assistance. I would also like to thank the staff at the Army Museum, the British Museum and the Public Records Office.

A one-year fellowship from the Arms Control Disarmament and International Security Program of the University of Illinois (1992-3) enabled me to initiate the preliminary research work into this project as a doctoral dissertation. A fellowship from the Department of History, University of Illinois(Summer 1994) was instrumental in providing me with much needed financial support to conduct my research in British archives. A Olin Post-doctoral research/lecturer fellowship from the International Security Studies Program at Yale University(1995-6) allowed me to make substantial revisions to the manuscript to prepare it for publication. The final changes were completed with the help of a research grant from Research Services Council of the University of Nebraska at Kearney(1996-7).

I owe a deep debt of gratitude to my doctoral advisor Professor Blair Kling for his advice and guidance through every step of this research project at the dissertation level. I am also grateful to Professor Stephen P. Cohen, Professor John A. Lynn, Professor DeWitt Ellinwood, Professor Geoffrey Parker and Professor Paul Kennedy, for their advice and moral support on this and indeed other research projects. A special thanks is due to Professor Cohen for sharing with me his unique insights into the Indian and Pakistani armies. Additionally Professor Cohen was kind enough to allow me access to typescripts of his 1960's interviews with many ex-Indian Army British, Indian and Pakistani officers. A special thanks is also due to John Lynn, who has also been a tremendous source of inspiration and support for me in my efforts to publish this and other works.

Last but not least I would like to acknowledge the support of my family. The unstinting assistance and patience of my parents Ramola and Pannalal and my brother Sandip and their unwavering faith in me is the main reason I have been able to successfully complete this book.

Introduction

The colonial Indian army evokes strong and diverse images for different people. To some it is the very essence of imperial glory, often personified by a Kiplingesque picture of magnificently attired cavalry bearing down on marauding Pathan tribesmen as in the movie *Kim*. To others the image is more sinister, like that of mercenary troops gunning down their own people at Jallianwallah Bagh in the movie *Gandhi*. Lost in the conflicting symbolism of these images is another Indian army. An army that did not spring up with the passing of a Royal decree, or with the payment of a few Rupees to Indian peasants, rather it was an army that was painstakingly molded over a period of almost a century. During this period some fundamental changes took place that dramatically altered the character of this army, and perhaps even the nation it belonged to. This is the story of those turbulent changes.

During the first half of the twentieth century the colonial Indian army underwent a dramatic transition. What had hitherto been a predominantly glorified colonial police force was transformed into a relatively modern army, complete with its own institutionalized officer corps. This impressive achievement was the culmination of a complex, if cautious, programme of military modernization and has practically been ignored by the historiography on the colonial Indian army. The scant work that has been done tends to underplay this crucial development. This book analyses some of these neglected institutional and organizational reforms. Institutional reform refers to the development of a professional officer corps along with the training establishments that sustain such a cadre; organizational reform refers to the structural and doctrinal evolution of the colonial Indian army.

Scholars including Stephen Cohen, William Gutteridge, Andrew Sharpe, Jeffrey Greenhut and David Omissi see the slow progress made by the British to establish an institutionalized Indian officer corps as evidence of British racism. They argue that 'Indianization' (the replacement of British officers by Indian officers) was a low priority for the British because they perceived no benefit in it for British rule in India. I will show that these scholars overemphasize the influence of Indian nationalist politicians whom they credit for pressuring the British into any reform.[1] A similar view is held by Mark Houston Jacobsen who also analyses the organizational modernization of the colonial Indian army.[2] Martin A. Wainwright has distanced himself somewhat from the dependency writers by acknowledging that considerable advances were made in modernizing the colonial Indian army and the adjoining military-industries (but only during the Second World War).[3] Both Wainwright and Jacobsen, however, fail to explain British motivations for proposing radical military reform. Their mono-causal explanation of military reform being dictated by the needs of imperial defence is inadequate. Indeed, all of the aforementioned scholars appear to favour the World Systems school of dependency theory which sprang up in the mid-1970's. According to this school, the developed world forms the core of a world system economy that exploits the peripheral underdeveloped world, extracting its resources.[4] The Indian army is often seen as a resource of the periphery (India), which is being exploited by the core (Britain). The end result has been the veil of information that shrouds a unique and remarkable event in the history of colonial military modernization. Recently, however, two important works by Tony Heathcote and David Omissi have greatly expanded our understanding of the Indianization of the office corps; with a significant chapter in each book being dedicated to this subject. Omissi's book, in addition to offering one of the best single chapter assessments of Indianization, also provides significant new and detailed information on the sociological relationship between the sepoy and the *Raj*.[5]

My work seeks to analyse India as an historically specific case and not as part of a generalized evaluation of colonial military modernization. My study will demonstrate that not only were the dynamics of colonial military modernization in India a complex process of interaction of external (British) and the internal (Indian) factors, but that the role of being the modernized and the dependent partner in the relationship changed rather dramatically in the course of these reforms. I will show that in the case of the Indian army it is misleading to lump it in the 'periphery' of an imperial world system. I then seek to remove the colonial Indian army from the structures in which the modernization and dependency theorists have placed it. I seek to untangle the study of the colonial Indian army from the intellectual straitjacket that these theorists have placed it in and identify and analyze the players and actors in it. In this case the actors are the British Viceroys, Civil Servants, and the Indian officers. It is their perception of modernization and their interaction with each other, British with Indian and British with British, that ultimately determined the course of reform in the colonial Indian army.

The first chapter of the manuscript seeks to establish the organization and composition of the post mutiny (1857) colonial Indian Army on the eve of the Great War (which is also the starting point for the modernization period). This is essential in order to understand the intellectual and strategic origins of the Indianization programme. Chapter two analyses the dynamics of the organizational politics in the post-war period. The politics and debates of this period ultimately resulted in the establishment of the Indian Military Academy at Dehra Dun, thus initiating the institutionalization of the Indian officers corps.

Chapter three examines the first phase of the Indianization process - the military and social education of the Indian officer cadets at Sandhurst and the Indian Military Academy. It examines the social and ethnic backgrounds of these officers, and compares and contrasts cadet life in Sandhurst and the Indian Military Academy at Dehra Dun. Chapter four analyses the careers of the Indian officers in the Indian Army proper. It examines how the Indian officers were accepted into the army dominated by the British, and their own reactions to the treatment they received. It concludes with case studies of the types of Indian officers most likely to succeed or fail in such an environment.

Chapter five analyses the doctrinal evolution (the second leg of the modernization programme) in the post-1919 era. It examines how changing perceptions of the Indian Army at home and in England not only transformed it into a relatively modern fighting force, but also enabled Indian military doctrine to evolve in a more realistic and coherent way than its British counterparts. Chapter six examines the emergence of the modern Indian Army in the Second World War. It begins with an analysis of how Commonwealth armies led by the Indian Army and not the British Army, emerged with a winning tactical doctrine in the war. It concludes with an examination of how a professional Indian General Staff emerged from the ranks of the rapidly growing Indian officer corps during the war.

Chapter seven examines the overall impact of the modernization programme on the armies of independent India and Pakistan. Relying mainly on confidential reports of British military advisers to the U.K. High Commissioners in India and Pakistan, the chapter examines closely the performance of the officer corps of the two armies in the first half-decade after independence. In doing so it demonstrates how it was the Indian Army and not the Pakistani Army which emerged as the main beneficiary of the partition of the armed forces.

Finally the conclusion examines the evolution of the Indian officer corps in the post-independence period. It analyses how the independent Indian officer corps evolves in such a way that involve some striking continuity and discontinuity with its colonial past. Among the issues examined in this chapter are the continued doctrinal evolution of the officer corps, the ethnic, sociological and economic composition of the corps, and civil military relations. The chapter ends with a commentary on the overall effectiveness of the Indian officer corps especially, in comparison to other developing world officer corps.

Notes

1   Stephen P. Cohen, *The Indian Army: Its contribution to the Development of a Nation*, (Berkeley: University of California Press, 1971); Willaim Gutteridge, 'The Indianization of the Indian Army 1918-1945', *Race: Journal of the Institute of Race Relations*, Vol. 4., May 1963; Andrew Sharpe, 'The Indianization of the Indian Army', *History Today*, (March 1986); Jeffrey Greenhut, 'Sahib and Sepoy: An Inquiry into the Relationship Between the British Officers and Native Soldiers of the British Indian Army', *Military Affairs*, (January 1984).

2   Mark Houston Jacobsen, 'The Modernization of the Indian Army 1925-1939', unpublished Ph.D. dissertation (University of California, Irvine, 1979).

3   Martin A. Wainwright, *Inheritance of Empire: Britain, India, and the Balance of Power in Asia*, (Westport, Conn: Praeger, 1994).

4   See Immanuel Wallerstein, *The Modern World System*, (New York: Academic Press, 1974).

5   David Omissi, *The Sepoy and the Raj: The Indian Army, 1860-1940*, (London: MacMillan, 1994); T.A. Heathcote, *The Military in British India: The Development of British Land Forces in South Asia, 1600-1947*, (Manchester: Manchester University Press, 1995).

Office US Group, Rajputana Rifles, Hong Kong 1938
© Pradeep Barua

Chapter 1
A Cathartic Debate:
The Indianization of the Indian Army Office Corps, 1817-1919

The dynamics of colonial military conquest have rarely been the subject of significant academic debate. Most scholars agree that the conquest of the Non-Western world by the West was primarily a case of advanced state organizations with superior military technologies overrunning the inferior ones. The most frequent depiction of a battle of colonial conquest is that of a few well disciplined European troops holding their ground and overwhelming the hordes of the *native* armies. This scenario has also largely been accepted in India's case. Scholars such as Geoffrey Parker, Bruce Lenman, and R.G.S. Cooper attribute India's collapse to its inability to catch up with the West in terms of military organization and tactics.[1] Their analysis is based on the assumption that everything the Indians did was in reaction to the West. However, recent research has shown that the British succeeded not so much because of the inability of Indians to completely adopt the Western military system, but because of the ability of the British to adapt rapidly to the changing military situation in India.[2] It is only by acknowledging the fact that the wars of colonial conquest in India were in military terms at least a contest among equals, that one can begin to form an understanding of motivations behind the British attempts to modernize their colonial army in India.

The debate on the post-conquest era has been monopolized by dependency theorists. Many of these scholars found the affair of the so-called 'martial races' fascinating. Briefly, the 'martial races' were certain categories of peoples from the sub-continent whom the British considered to be particularly suited physically and mentally for inclusion in the Indian army. Scholars including Nirad C. Chaudhuri and David Omissi have adopted the view that the martial races were in effect a conspiracy by the British to 'divide and rule' India,[3] thus theorizing that the British employed certain minority communities like the Sikhs and the Gurkhas to suppress the larger Hindu community. Again, recent research has indicated that the martial races were the culmination of a prolonged process by the British to classify the peoples of colonial India. As a result of early anthropologists cum administrators pseudo-scientific conclusions, the British officialdom for much of the nineteenth and early twentieth century actually believed that certain Indian ethnic groups were more suited to military life than others.[4]

The belief that the Indian army was merely an exploitative tool in the hands of the British has deflected the attention of researchers from a key aspect of the modernization of the Indian army: the Indianization of the officer corps. Scant years after the revolt of 1857, the British had on their own initiative begun a process which would ultimately pave the way for the complete transformation of the colonial Indian army into a modern national army. Yet before we investigate the dynamics of this change, it is imperative that we have a clear understanding of the organization and composition of the Indian army on the eve of these reforms.

The Frontier Army

In the years of incessant fighting in India from 1750 to 1850 the East India Company army proved itself to be a major military innovator. It was not uncommon for techniques that were learnt in the Indian campaigns to be utilized by British troops in their European campaigns. Experience of the Anglo-Sikh Wars in particular greatly affected the development of British tactics. At Chillianwallah and Guejrat for example, the British used for the first time a combination of line and column infantry formations.[5] At Chillianwalla it was the stunning defeat of British Cavalry that prompted the adoption of the inversion drill for cavalry formations by entire divisions rather than by threes and twos as had been the regular practice. As one scholar has noted '...it required the Chillianwallah debacle, a far greater strain on the British cavalry than the charge of the Light Brigade, to ensure....[that] inversion was permitted....'[6] Artillery went through a similar process of reform. During the battle of Gujerat the final battle of the Sikh wars, the British in reaction to the excellent Sikh artillery deployed no less than a hundred guns, the largest artillery concentration by the British to that date. The Sikh wars convinced the British that artillery was the answer to reduce infantry casualties.[7] However, once India was firmly in British hands, the military emphasis changed from dynamic conquest or a more mundane policing effort.[8]

After the revolt of 1857, control of the Indian army passed to the crown. A commission of inquiry was appointed immediately to investigate the causes of the 'mutiny' and to propose changes in the army's organization. The chief recommendation of the Peel Commission (headed by Secretary of State for War Jonathan Peel) was that the proportion of Indian to British soldiers in India in the future should not be greater than three to one.[9] As a result of this recommendation the number of British soldiers stationed in India trebled in comparison to pre-mutiny levels, placing a tremendous burden on the British army. The Cardwell system while maintaining the ratio in favour of British troops sought to neutralize some of the pressure on Britain. In the process of a far reaching reform of the British army, the Secretary of State for War Edward Cardwell, introduced a twelve year standard service to be split between active and reserve service. According to this system, short service commission soldiers who came to India (or elsewhere in the empire) must be at least twenty years old. They would serve with the colours at least six years, after which they could return to England on reserve status.[10] In practice it was never possible to keep anywhere near an equal number of battalions at home, and units were unable to maintain regular drafts. According to Brian Bond, the home units became little more than training battalions for their sister battalions overseas. One contemporary British military critic of the system, Colonel G.F.R. Henderson, went so far as to declare that the real army was in India.[11] Ironically, the Cardwell system was ill-received in India too. The Government of India resented the expenditure imposed by the system (the cost of passage to and fro for the recruits) as well as the fact that India essentially had the job of training raw recruits for Britain. The Government of India noted 'It was no consideration for the efficiency of the army in India that evoked the short service system, and its suitability to the conditions of Indian requirements had been gravely questioned on more than one occasion.'[12]

In July 1879 the army in India comprised of 6,602 British officers, 60,341 British and 123,254 Indian soldiers.[13] That year the specially appointed Eden Commission, whose mission was to examine the army's organization and expenditures, warned of the dangers in persisting with the Presidential armies. The commission proposed the establishment of four regional corps located in Bengal, Madras, Bombay, and the Punjab. It also concluded that it was not possible at that time to reduce the army (The Presidential armies were abolished by Lord Roberts in 1895, in favour of a single army headquarters).[14]

It was under the energetic and ambitious Lord Kitchener that the Indian army experienced dramatic structural and doctrinal reforms prior to the Great War. Kitchener's primary aim was to deflect the Indian army from its increasing emphasis on internal security duties. Ever since the revolt of 1857, the deployment of the Indian army had been based more on internal rather than external security concerns. Kitchener began by forming the army into nine divisions, divided between two commands - Northern and Southern, the latter having four divisions and the former five. The regiments were re-numbered and deficient ones were eliminated. The old designations of Madras, Bombay, and Bengal that had persisted through Lord Roberts' reforms were dropped from the regimental titles. In 1905, Kitchener established the staff college at Deolali, later moved to Quetta. Kitchener undoubtedly hoped that the army would absorb the lessons of the Boer War, just as the British army was attempting to do at their own staff college at Camberley. It was his experience of fighting Boers with high powered Mauser rifles that led Kitchener to re-equip the Indian army with the Lee Enfield .303 magazine rifle. He also introduced the 2.75in Mountain Screw Gun. The screw gun fired a ten pound shell to about six thousand yards and broke up into five mule loads for transport, making it a highly effective mobile support weapon.[15] The officers of the newly created Mountain Batteries were not from the Indian army, but came from the Royal Artillery and spent several years in India. Whatever reservations Kitchener may have had about institutional military reform (Indianization), he did contribute significantly to the establishment of a small and highly trained frontier army.[16]

Although it was Kitchener who streamlined the army for frontier fighting, it had been engaged in frequent conflict there long before his arrival. With few exceptions warfare against the North Western Pathan tribes was mainly a mid-level insurgency operation. A lot of time was spent on endless patrols and garrison duties in some forgotten hill-top or valley. Prevention of an uprising was preferable to a battle. To this end intelligence was vital, and primarily gathered by the tireless political officers and their agents. Since the tribes rarely confronted the British in open battle, it became vital to guard from ambush all lines of communications (LOC) to garrisons and outpost ambushes. This often entailed the establishment of high posts to protect and support advancing troops and convoys. The 2.75in screw gun was the lynch-pin of most of these posts, the forerunners of the fire-bases found in Vietnam. Punitive offensives launched usually ranged from battalion to brigade level formations.

The unique requirements of a frontier army had an impact upon the British home army as well. At a 1906 meeting to coordinate the practices of the home and Indian armies, the majority of the Army council rejected the Army Corps formations of the British and Continental armies in favour of large divisions as seen in India, which were regarded as more flexible and better suited to the Imperial requirements of the British army.[17] The disorganized state of the North West and Afghan tribes and their lack of modern armament allowed the British to control them with a small but highly professional army.

The system of recruitment reflected both the highly selective requirements of such an army and the workings of the 'martial race' system. Soldiers already in the regiment typically brought in relatives and friends to apply for entry. After a medical examination and interview with the Indian non-commissioned officers, and the Adjutant of the regiment, they were usually placed on the 'Umedwar' or 'hopeful' list, to be called up when vacancies opened. Training of the new recruits was usually done within the regiment itself. Towards the close of the nineteenth century, as 'martial race' selection became the norm, recruiting officers would rove a particular district looking for the right kind of recruit to be presented before the British officers. The elaborate process of selection was heavily influenced by pseudo-sciences like anthropometry (race determination by physical measurements), and ultimately led to the creation of a series of recruiting handbooks which conveniently highlighted physical and mental traits of a particular 'martial race'. These handbooks which were regularly updated became the bible of the recruiting officer.[18]

The Debate

It is only within this context of a highly specialized army that we can comprehend the unprecedented reforms that the British were trying to implement in the Indian army. These reforms are remarkable not only due to their controversial nature, but also due to the fact that they were being discussed long before the consolidation of British rule in India had become a reality. The issue of the Indianization of the officer corps is not a twentieth century phenomenom, rather it can be traced back to the early nineteenth century. Sir Thomas Munro, a prominent administrator in Madras (Governor of Madras from 1819-1827), writing in 1817 on the subject of granting commissions to Indians in the army stated 'No elevation of character can be expected among men who in the military line cannot attain any rank above that of Subadar [NCO], where they are as much below an ensign as an ensign is below the Commander in Chief.....'[19] In a relatively far-sighted report that predated similar conclusions about Indian soldiers in the Great War, Munro was pointing out to the obvious lack of initiative that characterizes soldiers of colonial armies. Munro added 'Our government will always be respected from the influence of our military power; but it will never be popular while it offers no employment to the native that can stimulate the ambition of the better class of them.'[20] Here Munro was raising a political issue, by pointing out that it would be better to rule with the support of the 'better class' than with the use of force alone. In 1842 another prominent British administrator in India, Sir Henry Lawrence, concurred with Munro and stated that unless higher positions were open to sepoys[21] of '....better education, [and] superior character.....' it was quite possible that their energies and talents could be turned against the British.[22]

The views aired by Munro and Lawrence are amazing for they came at a time when British rule in India had not yet been consolidated. In 1817 the remnants of the Maratha Confederacy in Western India and the Sikh Kingdom in the Punjab were still independent of British control. The Sikhs in fact were only 'subdued' after a decade of bloody warfare in 1849. The rationale behind their views lies in the unique brand of Utilitarianism they espoused in India. Munro and his fellow Utilitarians in India believed in pragmatic government. Their common aim was to preserve as much as possible the original institutions of Indian society rather than change them completely. To this end the Munro school was prepared to support liberal measures like the admission of Indians to higher posts in the civil service and the army. Unlike such Utilitarians as James Mill, they did not believe in the ability of government to illuminate or educate the people. As far as Munro was concerned the task of government in India was paternal protection and little more. Change, if and when it came, would do so from within Indian society itself and could not be imposed from the outside.[23] Almost Machiavellian in concept, their writings on the subject, nevertheless, provided a convenient precedent for the liberal British officials and generals who in the late nineteenth century launched a concerted effort to introduce Indians into the officer ranks of the army.

The revolt of 1857 dampened further talk of reform (at least at an official level), till Sir George Chesney, first as Military Secretary and later as Member of the Military Department, took a sustained interest in this issue. On 16 April 1884, Chesney, in reference to a proposal to confer a Honorary Commission upon the Nawab of Mamdot wrote, '....it would be sound policy to open a definitive military career to natives of the higher classes giving them not only honorary commands but substantive ones.'[24] Sir George Chesney went on to propose a trial experiment with a 'native' regiment. Although this scheme was rejected by General Wilson, a Military Member, on the grounds that native princes would not take to continuous military service, it was revived in January 1885 by Chesney on the basis that the position would be open not on grounds of wealth, but to those with good birth, education, and physique. This proposal piqued the interest of the Commander in Chief General Sir Donald Stewart who, along with Sir Chesney, sent a joint proposal on 21 March 1885 to Lord Kimberly. In it they recommended the raising of two special 'native' regiments; one cavalry and one infantry, to be entirely officered by Indians (this was to meet General Wilson's plea about the painful isolation of the Indian subaltern in the British mess).[25]

Lord Kimberly reviewed the proposal on 15 April 1886 and deemed it expedient to obtain the views of senior officers, thus opening the first large scale official debate on Indianization. The outcome was a surprise. The vast majority of the soldiers polled supported the plan, while the most potent objection came from a civilian. The reasons given for supporting it and objecting to it are equally interesting. Those who backed the plan did so on political grounds and offered generalized explanations. General Sir Neville Chamberlain (no relation to the future Prime Minister) felt that British rule would benefit from incorporating Indian elites into the army. Field Marshall Lord Napier of Magdala stated that the time had come to match the civilian service in opening the higher posts of the army to 'distinguished native gentlemen of suitable character.'[26] This group backed the plan on the grounds of principle rather than fact, and their occasional dissent to the plan was based more on minute technicalities. General Sir A. Taylor, for example, objected to part of the proposal that would reduce the number of officers with new regiments below the number allowed to European Regiments.[27]

Although few in number, the dissenters on the other hand appeared to have logic on their side. Among other things they questioned if such a move would actually increase the efficiency of the army. They wondered if they [Indian officers] would lead another mutiny. They questioned if there was evidence of any demand for military employment amongst the Indians. Finally they wanted to know if British officers would ever be placed in a subordinate position to an Indian.[28]

Last minute attempts to revise the scheme were unsuccessful.[29] They were firmly put down by General Sir Frederick Roberts, who had succeeded Sir Stewart as Commander-in-Chief India. In his minute of rejection Lord Roberts declared -

> Though a policy which would improve the prospects of the native officers of the Indian army and open to men of superior military qualities opportunities of rising to positions of trust and responsibility is one which has my warmest sympathies, I am unable to support the proposal that Indian gentlemen should be appointed to the commissioned ranks of the army in the same grade as Europeans. I am convinced that however well-educated and clever an Indian may be, and however much he may distinguish himself, he would be never looked up to by the British soldier in the same way that the latter looks up to the British subaltern.[30]

Without the support of the Commander-in-Chief all hope for reform in the near future died, and the Government of India decided to drop the plan on 'financial' grounds.[31]

In 1888 Sir Chesney reopened the issue by proposing the creation of a military school, since he felt that education was the key to higher military posts. Sir Chesney had discarded the plan to advance existing native commissioned officers and had instead re-applied an earlier proposal of the Army Reorganization Committee of 1879. Although this scheme had the support of the civilian members of the Council, Lord Roberts rejected the proposal and it too was shelved during a council discussion on 13 June, 1888.[32] But to Lord Roberts' chagrin, the issue refused to die, for in 1890 Colonel Holroyd, Director of Public Instruction in the Punjab, submitted a scheme for creating a military section in Aitchison College, Lahore for native officers of good birth, who, after passing a course in the college, could be appointed to native regiments. At the same time the Duke of Connaught's Memorial Committee based in Poona put forward a similar scheme. Sir Chesney immediately supported these plans, but Lord Roberts rejected them declaring 'Once you introduce anything but regimental training, on however limited a scale, you are on the highroad to an Indian Sandhurst.'[33] As if finally to squash the issue, Roberts added that he doubted if Indian officers could be impartial like the British in handling rival claims of jealous native soldiers.

The issue of commissions for Indians arose again in 1897, this time in England. The Maharajah of Cooch Behar pleaded to the Secretary of State for India (Lord George Hamilton) that his sixteen year old son then studying at Eton be allowed to join a British regiment. Noting the War Office's opposition to such a move, Lord Hamilton wrote to Lord Elgin stating 'The War Office have destroyed their own case by admitting Dhuleep Singh into a cavalry regiment.'[34] He also pointed out to a Committee led by Field Marshal Sir Donald Stewart which had noted in December that the 'occasional' admission of sons of 'Indian Princes and Gentlemen...would be politically very desirable...'[35] In his reply in February 1898 Lord Elgin stated that he and his council felt the proposal would do little to secure the goodwill of the Indian nobility. They also believed that the men who would send their sons to England would not be among those with influence in India. Thirdly like the dissenters before them, they considered Indian custom and caste to be a major consideration to the chiefs of the strongest race (martial), preventing them from sending their sons to England.[36] Lord

Lansdowne, writing to Lord Hamilton that same, month felt that the request of the Maharajah must be turned down, for the reforms, once begun, would have no end in sight.[37]

The momentum for reform, however, was gathering pace. Sir Alfred Lyall, the (Anglo-Indian) chairman of the Political Committee was determined to make a beginning. Part of his strategy was to embarass the War Office by portraying its opposition to Indians as a policy based primarily on the grounds of colour. Lyall also addressed the fears of the War Office that reform would result in a flood of Indians; he assured them that this would not be the case, as the Secretary of State would selectively nominate only a limited number of Indians for officer training. He added '....nor is it to be anticipated that more than a few Indian youths will really desire to enter a service which offers little or no emolument, and involves long absence from their native country....' Sir Lyall cautioned the War Office about its fears that the Indians with military service would prove dangerous by stating 'The danger lies rather among those who have been educated as Europeans, and have not been employed....'[38]

Another potential problem arose when Sir Arthur Wilson, the legal adviser to the Secretary of State, pointed out that special legislation would be required to admit the sons of native Indian chiefs. The settlement of 1790 which formally placed the crown on the Hannoverians, also contained a clause forbidding any person 'born out of the Kingdoms of England, Scotland, or Ireland, or the dominions thereunto belonging...., except such as are born of English parent,' to hold office or place of trust, civil or military. Wilson added that although this rule had been relaxed in favour of naturalized persons, it otherwise remained in force.[39]

As Lord Hamilton and Sir Wilson pondered ways to sidestep this constitutional hurdle, the Secretary of State for War, Lord Lansdowne, delivered a death-blow to the latest reform attempts. Late in 1898 he came out in full support of Lord Elgin's view that those who would send their sons to England would be 'natives of advanced opinion' with a veneer of British civilization. Lansdowne considered all non-Europeans as unsuitable candidates. In the case of Dhuleep Singh Lord Lansdowne pointed out the prince had to leave the regiment as he could not pass the riding school, and that he had set a bad example for the other cadets with his extravagant ways.[40]

Lord Curzon and the Imperial Cadet Corps

After carefully studying the debate on reform, Lord Curzon, the new Viceroy, declared that most of these reform schemes had accomplished nothing simply because they lacked careful planning. Although Curzon saw some validity in Lord Roberts' contention that most native Indian officers were quite contented, he did feel that 'from [his] own experience...manifest and undeniable', he was aware of pleas from the aristocratic ranks to obtain entry into the officer corps. Lord Curzon felt that this demand grew as educational opportunities grew. He mentioned specifically the prestigious Chiefs Colleges–Mayo College Ajmer, Aitchision College Lahore, Rajkumar College Kathiawar, and Daly College Indore, and stated–

> I hold, therefore, that the problem of finding some military opening for the cadets of princely and noble families, not merely exists, but that it is yearly becoming more acute,....[41]

Curzon also brought attention to an obvious flaw in Lord Roberts argument that the move to create an Indian officer corps could prove dangerous as it would create a class of military adventurers. As Curzon noted, this belief undermined the theory of Indians being destitute of military aptitude.

TABLE 1 [42]

LIST OF NATIVE OFFICERS HOLDING BRITISH RANK IN 1898

NAME	RANK	HISTORY/UNIT
1. Nawab of Jaora	Honorary Major 27 April 1881	Central India Horse
2. Rana of Dholpur	Honorary Major 8 February 1882	Central India Horse
3. Maharaja of Cooch Behar	Honorary Major 22 February 1883 promoted to Hon. Lt. Col.	6th Bengal Cavalry Lord Kimberly said this should be done only under very special circumstances
4. Nawab of Mamdot	Hon. Lieutenant 25 March 1885	Attached to 2nd Punjab Cavalry
5. Maharaj Dhiraj Sir Pertab Singh of Jhodhpur State	Hon. Lt. Col. 21 June 1897 Hon.Col. 20 January 1898	Proposed by Secretary of State for assistance to Tirah Expeditionary Force

6. Rissalldar Major Mohammed Aslam Khan	Hon. Major 25 March 1885 Hon. Lt. Colonel 18 January 1890	5th Bengal Cavalry Recognition of services with Afghan Boundary Commission Services with the Black Mountain Expedition
7. Maharaj of Jammu & Kashmir	Hon. Colonel 21 January 1888 Hon. Major General 22 January 1896	37th Bengal Infantry For raising it For valuable services of men and state during the Chitral operations 1895
8. Raja Jai Chand Lambargaon	Hon. Major 21 January 1888	37th Bengal Infantry (Dogra)
9. Muhammed Ali Beg Nawab Afsar-i-Jang Bahadur A.D.C. to his Highness Nizam of Hyderabad	Hon. Major 16 May 1888	3rd Cavalry Hyderabad Contingent
10. Bir Bikram Singh Son of Maharaja of Sirmoor	Hon. Lieutenant 4 September 1889 Hon. Captain	1/2nd Gurkha for drill and instruction. Approved by Government of India
11. Nawab of Rampur	Hon. Captain 6 February 1895 Hon. Major	9th Bengal Cavalry
12. Maharaja of Gwalior	Hon. Colonel 21 May 1898	For assistance to Tirah Expeditionary Force, 1897-98

Curzon instead proposed the establishment of a 'Viceroy's Corps' (later to be known as the Imperial Cadet Corps) consisting of twenty to thirty young men from princely and noble families, selected solely from the four chiefs colleges. These youths would be eligible at age seventeen to twenty and be selected according to family, conduct, and knowledge of the English language. They would be brought to Calcutta and placed under a prince or noble of high birth, exemplary character, and military attainment. In Calcutta they would live a simple life in the maidan (park grounds), associate with young English officers, be taught to dress, ride, and other physical activities, then proceed to Delhi for further military drill. They would then be sent home for the summer, and those still keen could return for a definite course of military training. The nature of the commission (a key issue that would in future almost wreck the reform effort) would be left to discussion.[43]

The I.C.C.(Imperial Cadet Corps) held its first course in April 1902. It had two seasonal locations; it wintered in Meerut and spent the summers in Dehra-Dun. Curzon's unrelenting efforts to allow Indians into the officer corps have cast him as the great pioneer in the Indianization effort.[44] In reality the I.C.C. was far from a realization of that goal. The object of the corps according to the official statement was to provide -

> military training for selected members of the aristocracy of India, and of giving them such a general education in the imperial army as British officers, they may never lose their character and bearing as Indian gentlemen.[45]

The camps at Meerut and Dehra-Dun were geared more to producing educated Indian 'gentlemen' rather than Indian officers.[46] The popular perception in those days was that Indian princes and aristocratic youth were an indolent and licentious group. The I.C.C. course appears to have been designed initially at least as a disciplining camp. Great emphasis was placed on the 'moral' aspect of the cadets, character. The rules of the I.C.C. stated clearly that 'immoral' and 'unmanly' practices would be sternly suppressed.[47] It is also evident that the cadets were to represent a 'martial' standard for the rest of the Indian princely community. There are indications that the camps were little more than princely boarding schools; each cadet for example was allowed to bring with him a personal attendant and cook.[48] The ceremonial uniforms worn by the cadets were probably among the most colourful and expensive worn by any military unit in India. It comprised of a turquoise turban with a gold hang. A gold cockade and a gold ornament completed the striking headgear. The white coat had elaborate embroidery on the collar, the cuffs, the shoulders, the back, and in the front. The kumerbund (literally stomach wrap) was blue with red embroidery. The breeches were white and joined by black patent leather boots up to the knees. Solid brass spurs completed this elaborate ensemble. The cadets also received a lot of equestrian training to conduct themselves flawlessly in ceremonial parades.[49]

After the cadets successfully completed the three and half year course, they obtained a second lieutenant's commission into what was known as the Native Indian Land Forces (NILF).[50] This, however, was an extremely limited commission, for its holders could only command 'native' Indian officers and soldiers. Failing this they were assigned to the staffs of general officers.[51] This is precisely where the majority of the cadets ended up. Their inferior status vis-a-vis their British counterparts left them in a very awkward position. General Sir Edmund Barrow commander-in-Chief Southern Army noted in March 1912 that two of his I.C.C. ADC's (aide-de-camp) Lieutenant Aga Casim Shah and Lieutenant Kanwar Amar Singh (whose diary I make extensive reference to above) '....are naturally not altogether pleased with their present position and prospects.'[52] Barrow, usually a staunch opponent of Indianization, was sufficiently moved by the plight of the two Indian officers to suggest that they be given probationary postings to regiments.[53]

The first commission under Curzon's new system was granted in July 1905. Indians commissioned in this system, however, were not employed in ordinary regimental service.[54] With the momentum for the introduction of Indians into the officer corps becoming irresistible, senior officers like General Sir O' Moore Creagh, (who succeeded Kitchener as Commander-in-Chief in 1909) also called for steps to give further responsibility to native officers. Unfortunately, even Creagh's qualified suggestion was strongly opposed by General Kitchener, who in September 1908 issued a powerful memorandum. Arguing along lines similar to previous dissenters such as Lord Roberts and Lieutenant General (later Field Marshal) Sir Charles Brownlow, Kitchener's main contention was that such a policy would be detrimental to the continuation of British rule. Yet, perhaps cognizant of the majority view in favour of reform, Kitchener added -

> Nevertheless I myself do not think that we should remain for ever stationary, and completely bar against natives of India all paths for further military advancement except those now open to them; though I am convinced that we must move slowly and on well considered lines.[55]

Kitchener also noted that he did not recall meeting men of good education among Sikhs, Pathans, and Marathas that General Creagh had described. He also deemed the Imperial Cadet Corps a failure (started a year before Kitchener's arrival in 1901). Although the I.C.C. had made a promising start by filling its quota of 24 cadets in July 1902, enthusiasm for the corps and correspondingly enrollment dropped rapidly, never to reach the 24 mark again. One of the cadets Amar Singh notes that by 1904 no Rajputs (one of the vaunted martial races) were entering the corps.[56] Kitchener correctly identified the establishment of the Corps as a political move and not a military one. He proposed instead a military college to train Indian Jemadars (N.C.O.'s) as a reward for loyalty, but would not lay down anything definite for promotion. He added 'I would sweep away the racial disability, but I would not confer any absolute rights, leaving each case to be considered on its merits.....'[57]

Fortunately, Kitchener's reservations did not have the same effect as had Lord Roberts' several decades earlier. In February 1911 the War Office informed the India Office that it was willing to give two commissions to selected sons of Indian chiefs in the Household Cavalry and Foot Guards, provided they passed Sandhurst. Later that year the Indian General Staff put forward the most cogent commitment yet to Indianization by laying down a tentative guideline for the process:

a. The administration of Indians to the full rights of King's Commission is a step of greatest importance for it is on its officers as a body that an army depends for success in war. Any distinction between the two races as regards conditions of service or relative rank will militate against whole-hearted cooperation and good comradeship, and Indians should therefore, be in allrespects on exactly the same footing as their British brothers-in-arms.

b. Indian gentlemen of best birth and position alone will be suitable to hold commissions. Therefore there will be strict selection by nomination.

c. Early education must be in England.

d. Military education must be carried out at Sandhurst where a certain number of vacancies (Indian cadetships) will be reserved for Indians who obtain the minimum qualifying marks.

e. They should go through the whole curriculum at Sandhurst, the same as their British counterparts.

f. Indians for the present will be posted to the Indian army where vacancies will be reserved for them.

g. Promotion, pay, army and regimental rank will be on the same terms as those of British officers of the Indian army.

h. After obtaining their commissions Indians should be attached to a British unit in England for a year.

i. Indians will be eligible to serve in all units of cavalry and infantry of the Indian army and should not be relegated to a special corps.

j. Three senior officers of the regiment should decide if retention of the young Indians is desirable after the first three years of service.

k. Though twenty commissions a year might eventually be given it would be advisable to limit the number to ten until this scheme has proven its feasibility.[58]

The recommendations of the General Staff were largely accepted in 1911 by Lord Crewe, the Secretary of State for India. There was, however, a important exception; the establishment of a specially formed 'native' regiment in India to absorb these officers. This would ensure that Indians could not command British officers in India.[59]

During the following years the proposals were subject to constructive criticism. Major R.L. Ricketts, the commandant of the Imperial Cadet Corps, declared in 1914 that few of the cadets were educationally fit. He doubted if there was any desire among these 'top' families to go to Sandhurst. In October the same year Viceroy Hardinge noted that the Indian middle class would reject the plan for it was restricted to the ruling class. Like Major Ricketts he felt it was useless to pursue commissions for the disinterested princely classes. Lord Hardinge thought that a military academy must be set up in India along the lines of Royal Military College at Sandhurst. In a pointed note to dissenters including Roberts, Lord Hardinge stated '....it is not the British *soldier* who would be unwilling to receive orders from the Indian officer, but the British *officer*.....'[60] Hardinge received indirect support from Sir Harvey Anderson, Lieutenant Governor of Burma, who, writing in September 1915 stated 'Indian officers in this war lacked initiative to command, because they have never been taught to do so.

Therefore they must be given opportunities of advancement.'[61]

Opposition to the proposals came from the Commander-in-Chief General Sir Beauchamp Duff who, in the best tradition of Lord Roberts and other dissenters, also considered Indians as lacking any leadership ability. He feared that British N.C.O.s and men would not take direct orders from Indian officers (a suggestion rejected by Lord Hardinge). General Duff also concurred that the proposal should be dropped as it would prove incompatible with the efficiency of the army. Sir Benjamin Robertson, Chief Commissioner of the Central Provinces, expressed concern over potential problems that would arise when Indians were in a position to order British officers.[62]

In January 1917, Austen Chamberlain, the Secretary of State for India, urged the War Cabinet to come to a decision. He asked the cabinet to sanction an announcement that it had decided to accept at least in principle the appointment of Indians to the commissioned ranks in His Majesty's Army. In subsequent letters in June and July, the Secretary complained to the War Cabinet that the War Office was holding up the entire scheme by its unwillingness to concede the principle of giving Indians command over Europeans. Secretary Chamberlain pointed out the difficulties in supplying sufficient officers of a pure European descent for the Indian army and the effect the racial bar would have on recruiting. Chamberlain was convinced that the time had arrived when the principle of granting King's Commissions to Indians must be admitted. Nonetheless, in July 1917 a War Office letter to the India Office stated -

> I am commanded by the Army Council to inform you that after the most careful consideration they have come to the conclusion that to grant commissions to natives of India would entail a great risk from the military point of view, in that it involves placing native Indians in a position where they would be entitled to command European officers. For this reason the Council are not prepared to take the responsibility of advising such a step.[63]

The 'great risk' that the War Office was referring to was explained in 1918 when they noted that granting King's Commissions to Indians

> ....cannot fail to have a very harmful effect upon the recruitment of British officers for the Indian army. The measures already taken in this direction

have rendered parents and guardians and young men themselves suspicious, and it is submitted that such a sudden and large measure as the above would more than confirm their ideas on the subject.[64]

Despite the War Office's misgivings, in August 1917 the War Cabinet formally agreed in principle to the appointments of Indians to commissioned rank in His Majesty's Army.[65] The only stipulation the War Office placed was that all candidates be subject to competitive exams in a course through Sandhurst, or by nomination after service in the ranks, or in the Officer Training Course through Sandhurst (O.T.C.). Ten Indian candidates would be nominated per year.[66]

The War Cabinet's decision brought to an end decades of internal debate within the upper echelons of the Indian government and the Indian army on the question of Indianization of the officer corps. Much of this debate had been carried out within the ranks of the Liberal reformers themselves. Outright dissent in the manner of Kitchener was the exception rather than the rule, and most of the dissenters including Roberts had tried to portray themselves as conservative reformers rather than obstructionists. At times galvanizing and some times tedious, this debate symbolized a collective catharsis on the part of the Liberal reformers. Their passionate exposual of radical reform in this the most conservative institution of the British Raj, reflected the unease the Liberals felt about the indefensible nature of their total ban on Indians from the officer corps. The Liberals also shared a common belief with their Utilitarian predecessors, that good government and an efficient army could only be achieved with the cooperation of the Indians. Their reasons for believing this, however, differed radically from the radicals. Before we can delve into the reasons behind their actions, it is essential to explore the role of the Indian army in the Great War, for no-matter how convincing the arguments of the Liberals were, the British government would have paid little attention to this vexing issue had the war not revealed glaring inadequecies in an all white officered Indian army.

The Indian Expeditionary Force in France

At the beginning of 1914 the Indian army had about 150,000 men.

As soon as the war broke out the Government of India offered Britain a corps of two infantry divisions (each of three brigades, each brigade was made up of one British battalion and three Indian/Gurkha battalions) and two cavalry divisions (with three brigades, each with one British and two Indian regiments). After a brief hesitation, this offer was readily accepted in August 1914.[67]

The Indian Corps, led by units of the Lahore and Meerut divisions, disembarked in France in October 1914. They were hurriedly equipped with short Lee Enfield .303 rifles, machine guns, and field artillery (British units) before being despatched to the front.[68] The Indian corps had been thrust pell-mell into a war the likes of which it had never seen before, and the effect on the men was devastating. Unit after unit including the vaunted 'martial races' (Gurkhas, Sikhs, and Rajputs) broke and fled the horror of the trenches. The fact that neighbouring British units did not desert the trenches like the Indians made their actions all the more troubling for the commanders.

The official British exploration at the time laid the blame on the fact that heavy officer casualties had denuded the Indian units of their leadership element. The British high command believed that Indian soldiers were in effect lost without their white officers.[69] Although the opportunity for granting commissions to Indians was ripe, the reaction from the commanders was wholly negative. Both General Sir James Willocks, commander of the Indian Expeditionary Force (I.E.F.), and General Sir Beauchamp Duff, the Commander-in-Chief India, remained adamantly opposed to the move: they were convinced that the Indians lacked the ability to command, especially on the Western Front.[70]

Historian Jeffrey Greenhut attributes the I.E.F.'s destruction in France to a traumatic form of culture shock. He explains the Indian soldiers dependence on their white officers and their inability to take command by the fact that the British officers were more than mere leaders.

> They were the interpreters of totally unfamiliar environment, of a military system so completely foreign that Indian soldiers could not function without them....they fulfilled a role no uneducated peasant could hope to emulate.....[71]

Yet, culture shock and a new military system alone fail to explain the total reliance of the Indian troops on British officers. The real answer lies in the fact that the Indian troops had been thoroughly indoctrinated into a subordinate position within the army. No Indian officer wielded command over even the lowliest British ensign. As one British observer noted with regard to native Indian officers that 'their present position of subordination to British officers in the regiment is calculated to impair any initiative or leadership they may have originally possessed.'[72] Sir Harvey Anderson, the Lieutenant Governor of Burma, also noted in September 1915 that Indian officers in the war lacked the initiative to command, because they have never been taught to do so.[73] With no Indian role models who could stand alongside their white officers, Indian V.C.O's and N.C.O's had little or no self-confidence to take on any leadership role after the loss of their white officers. Although it was the debacle at Kut in Mesopotamia that captured the imagination of the British public and the postwar military reformers, it was the performance or lack thereof of the I.E.F. in France that had the most significant long term impact in the Indian army in the inter-war period.

Conclusion

The First World War was the catalyst for substantive military reform in India. However, in one aspect of this reform - the institutional - an internal debate within the Indian army and Whitehall had been resolved prior to the outbreak of the Great War in favour of the reformers. The experience of the war, and in particular the threat of the I.E.F. in France merely helped accelerate the scope and time-frame for the implementation of these reforms.

What is remarkable about this entire debate is that it appears to have been internally generated. Pressure from Indian politicians seems to have been rather muted at this stage. The only major Indian figure to have advocated such reform was Dadabhai Naoroji[74] who made an appeal on behalf of the Maharajah of Cooch Behar's son for entry into a British regiment, only to be turned down by the British.[75] The annual conference of Indian residents in the U.K., convened by the London Indian Society, under the presidency of Dadabhai Naoroji on 20 December 1898, passed a resolution demanding '....that Indians should be allowed commissions and command the Indian army in the same manner and through the same methods as are open to Englishmen, by competition and training, and by promotion for distinguished ability and gallantry in the field.'[76] Such demands appear to have been the exception rather than the rule, as most Indian politicians' main goal was to Indianize the bureaucracy. At a 1912 military conference in Calcutta which included Lord Crewe, Lord Hardinge, and General Sir Moore O'Creagh, a collective decision was reached that 'for the time being, the admission of Indians into the higher ranks of the army had become quite a secondary consideration, and that it was best to let sleeping dogs lie...'[77] The Government of India itself was more worried about what it perceived as possible attempts by Indian nationalists such as Goakhle and the native press to sow sedition in the other ranks of the army.[78]

The reform of the Indian Civil Service has attracted much attention from researchers who feel that reform was the harbinger of similar reform in the army officer corps. Indeed the Secretary of State Edwin Montagu pointed to the progress made in the including of Indians in the civil service to pressure the War Cabinet into authorizing the grant of King's commissions to Indians. He noted that it was impossible to tell an Indian he might control the destinies of Englishmen if he became a judge, but he could never expect to hold a position of authority even while defending the empire.[79]

However, closer examination of the evolution of the Indianization of the civil service and the army officer corps will indicate that the gap between the two was far less than first imagined. The East India Company's civil service was divided into two categories consisting of the 'covenanted' and the 'uncovenanted'. The first was comprised of men recruited by the company in England and sent to India to work their way up in the ranks from the bottom. They secured their contracts by signing a covenant with the company, hence the term 'covenanted'. As the administrative services in India expanded rapidly, the company signed up a number of ad-hoc administrators without a covenant; they became part of the uncovenanted service. Generally the uncovenanted officers worked in junior positions, although a few European and Eurasian officers did hold high positions. Indians held only junior positions in the provincial cadres.

By 1804 Indians began to enter the covenanted service. In 1886 the Public Services Commission, headed by the Lieutenant-Governor of Punjab Sir Charles Aithchison, essentially segregated the covenanted and uncovenanted services into the Indian Civil Service (ICS) and the Provincial Service respectively. The ICS cadre would be recruited from England after a competitive exam, while the Provincial Civil Service would be recruited separately in each of the Indian provinces.[80] Critics of the British have seen this move as an attempt to isolate Indians from the top positions in the ICS, for in practice few Indians could afford to make the trip to England to sit for the exams.[81] Indeed, there is some evidence to suggest that the British were increasingly apprehensive about a possible influx of Indians into the hitherto all white ICS. In 1900 Lord Curzon warned Secretary of State for India Lord Hamilton of

> The extreme danger of the system under which every year an increasing number of the government and odd higher posts that were meant, and ought to have been exclusively and specifically reserved for Europeans, are being filched away by the superiority of the native in the English examinations....[82]

Curzon's remarks in this context are most interesting for it was Curzon himself who over the objection of Lord Kitchener proposed the entry of young Indians into the officer corps. Curzon declared 'I would myself fearlessly lay down the proposition that India can only be held with the aid of her sons....'[83] Similarly it was Lord George Hamilton who toiled long and hard with his legal secretary in the early months of 1898 to find a way around constitutional hurdles preventing the granting commissions to Indians. It appears that the senior bureaucrats and Viceroys were Janus-faced in their attitudes towards Indianization. While they opposed it in the ICS, they were almost obsessive in their efforts to initiate it in the Indian army. Their attitude is all the more puzzling when one takes into account the fact that pressure from Indian nationalists to Indianize the army took a distant back seat to similar reforms in the ICS. If political appeasement was the goal, than surely further concessions in the ICS would have obtained far greater mileage. In fact by 1904 even the most moderate of Indian politicians including Dadabhai Naoroji were growing frustrated with the British stance on Indian recruitment to the ICS and judiciary.[84]

The British Viceroys and bureaucrats who governed India in the late nineteenth and early twentieth centuries were essentially products of a Victorian Liberal tradition. Their main goal was to form a equitable partnership with Indians in India. They hoped to imbue the Indians with British traits, especially in running 'good government' and by doing so thus turn them into good 'brown Englishmen'. This was in complete opposition to the views of the earlier Utilitarian reformers such as Munro. To achieve this aim the Liberals were willing to incorporate Indians into positions of authority with one proviso - that reform was to be initiated and controlled by the British who felt that the Indians could be over-zealous in their efforts to replace the British with below average Indian administrators and officers. The ambivalence of the reformers is in part due to the fact that most of them, like those who opposed any reforms, were heavily influenced by pseudo-scientific theories of race; Social Darwinism in particular was the intellectual vogue of their times. Even the most 'radical' pro-Indian supporters in England like Annie Besant and Keir Hardie proposed equal treatment for Indians on the grounds that they came from the same Aryan racial stock as the British.[85] Whether the Liberals admitted it or not, they were all convinced of the inherent superiority of the white race. Liberals such as John Morley acknowledged that on aesthetic grounds he would be unwilling to 'submit to be governed by a man of colour'[86] Yet Liberal reformers including Morley were willing to accept the argument that the Indians could in time catch up with the West, and welcomed individuals such as Dadabhai Naoroji into their midst with open arms. Where the reformers differed from the outright adherents of Darwinism, such as Roberts and Kitchener, was in their belief that 'civilized' western concepts like the rule of law, justice and humanity could slowly permeate the sub-continent; it was a nineteenth century Liberal vision of trickle down civilization.

Unfortunately for the British, they could not exercise total control over reform in the ICS. Political pressure both at home and in India tended to hasten most of the reforms, leading to an almost instinctive 'hold the fort' mentality on behalf of senior British ICS officers and Viceroys. This attitude has puzzled some researchers; S. R. Mehrotra states -

> The Morley-Minto reforms [Indian Council Bill 1909] were a typical product of nineteenth-century English liberalism which believed that statesmanship was mainly a question of determining how far popular demands should be conceded, but which seldom bothered to think out the fundamentals of policy, or relate it to a well-defined larger purpose.[87]

M. N. Das argues that 'The Liberal policy gradually boiled down to two aims, first to interest and inform the British public about India, and second, to please the Indians by granting reforms.'[88] In the Indian army, the pressure to Indianize was comparatively weak and sporadic, consequently the government was far more willing to experiment in this 'controlled environment'. The army's stringent requirement for total professionalism and competence also worked to aid the process of reform. It became clear early in the Indianization process that the only effective Indian officer would be one with a King's commission and the same training and status of his British counterparts. As Colonel H.D. Watson, commander of the Imperial Service Corps noted in 1914, no compromise was possible 'you must go whole hog, or not at all'[89] The debacle on the Western Front liquidated any doubts that may have persisted about granting full commissions to trained Indian officers. This also explains the War Office's curious attitude towards reform. Having fought tooth and nail to prevent any move to grant commissions to Indians, they capitulated when the die was cast and insisted that all Indians go through exactly the same system at Sandhurst as their British cadets would. If Indianization was unavoidable then no effort was to be spared to ensure that the Indian officers would match the same high standards as the British officers. Halfway measures such as the establishment of an equivalent to the Provincial Civil Service were correctly rejected as harmful to the efficiency of the Indian army. Victorian Liberalism and military professionalism had entered into a fortuitous partnership to lay the foundations for the Indianization of the Indian army officer corps.

Organizational reform would take longer to impact upon the Indian army. It continued to function as a frontier army for most of the 1920's. Yet its contribution to the war effort had changed forever its role in the perceptions of strategic planners in Whitehall and New Delhi. In the decades between the two World Wars, the frontier army would transform itself, in doctrine at least, into a contemporary army and would play a pivotal role in drafting British military doctrine in the Second World War.

Notes

1. Geoffrey Parker, *The Military Revolution: Military Innovation and the Rise of the West, 1500-1800*, (Cambridge: Cambridge University Press, 1988), p.136; Bruce P. Lenman, 'The Transition to European Military Ascendency in India, 1600-1800,' in John Lynn (ed.), *Tools of War: Instruments, Ideas, and Institutions of Warfare, 1445-1871*, (Urbana: University of Illinois Press, 1990), p.120; Randolf G.S. Cooper, 'Wellington and the Marathas in 1803,' *International History Review*, 11 (February 1989), p.38.

2. See Pradeep P. Barua, 'Military Developments in India, 1750-1850,' *The Journal of Military History*, Vol. 58, No. 4., (1994).

3. Nirad C. Chaudhuri, 'The Martial Races of India,' *The Modern Review*, No 48., (July 1930): 41-51; No 48., (September 1930): 295-307; No 49., (January 1931): 215-228; David Omissi, 'Martial Races: Ethnicity and Security in Colonial India, 1858-1939,' *War & Society*, Vol 9., No 1., (May 1991): 18. In his most recent work Omissi has moved away from this position. See Omissi, *The Sepoy and the Raj*, chapter. 1.

4. See Pradeep P. Barua, 'Inventing Race: The British and India's Martial Races,' *The Historian*, Vol 58, No 1., (Autumn 1995).

5. Hew Strachan, *From Waterloo to Balaclava: Tactics Technology, and the British Army, 1815-1854*, (Cambridge: Cambridge University Press, 1985), p.26.

6. Ibid, 68.

7. Ibid, p.125.

8. For a detailed study of the Indian Army in the first half of the nineteenth century see Douglas M. Peers, *Between Mars and Mammon: Colonial Armies and the Garrison State in India 1819-1835*, (New York: Tauris Academic Studies, 1995).

9. Report of the Commissioners appointed to inquire into the organization of the Indian army [Peel Commission], Parliamentary Papers (Commons) 1859, C.2515, V. A recommendation was also made to the effect that Indian troops not be equipped with advanced weaponry and artillery.

10. Military despatch to India No. 213, 3 August 1876, quoted in K.M.L. Saxena, *The Military System of India, 1850-1900*, (New Delhi: Sterling Publishers, 1974), pp.182-3.

11. Brian Bond, 'The Effect of the Cardwell Reforms,' *RUSI Journal*, (November 1960): 229-236; also 'Cardwell's Army Reforms,' *Army*, (April 1962), pp.108-17.

12. Military Despatch from India No.70, 25 March 1890, quoted in Saxena, pp.183-4.

13. Report of the Special Commission appointed by his Excellency the

Governor-General in Council to Enquire into the Organization and Expenditure of the Army in India [Eden Commission], Simla: Government of India, 1879, British Library/India Office Records (henceforth BL/IOR) L/MIL/17/5/1687, 5.

14 Ibid, 17,43,71.

15 The 2.75in. screw gun was venerated by the Indian army not the least because of its portability, and was even immortalized by Kipling in a poem. See T.S. Elliot (ed.), *A Choice of Kipling's Verse*, (London: Faber & Faber, 1951), pp.176-8.

16 See - Scheme for the re-distribution of the army in India, Calcutta: Government of India, 1904, BL/IOR, L/MIL/175/1741; Scheme for re-distribution of the army in India and preparation of the army in India for war, India Office, 1904, BL/IOR, L/MIL/117/5/1742; Kitchener's emphasis on the North West Frontier was based largely on his concern over Russian influence and encroachment in Afghanistan. See - Note by Lord Kitchener: Consideration of the effect of the Anglo-Russian Convention on the strength of the army in India, India Office, 21 October 1907, BL/IOR, L/MIL/17/5/1745. Kitchener was also no doubt aided in his quest to modernize the Indian Army, by an earlier War Office Survey in 1902 which noted that the main issue of a war between Russia and England, would be decided on the Indian border. See - 'The military resources of Russia and probable method of their employment in a war between England and Russia,' 22 January 1902, Public Records Office (henceforth P.R.O), War Office (henceforth W.O.) 106/48, E 3/11.

17 77th Meeting of the Army Council, No. 278, 21 June 1906, P.R.O., W.O., 163/11.

18 Barua, 'Inventing Race'. For more information on the East India Company's recruitment practices see - Seema Alavi, *The Sepoys and the Company: Tradition and Transition in Northern India, 1770-1830*, (New York: Oxford University Press, 1995).

19 Quoted in Government of India despatch No. 57., 3 August 1917. BL/IOR, Barrow Collection, Mss.Eur.E. 420/9, 60-61.

20 Ibid.

21 The word 'sepoy' refers to Indian soldiers and is derived from the Persian word 'Sipah' meaning soldier.

22 BL/IOR, Barrow Collection, Mss.Eur.E 420/9, 61.

23 Eric Stokes, *The English Utilitarians in India*, (London: Oxford University Press, 1959), pp.1-24.

24 Quoted in notes by Lord Curzon, Curzon Collection, BL/IOR, Mss. Eur. F.111/253: 12-22.

25 Military Despatch No. 47 quoted in Mss.Eur.E.420/9, 61; Viceroy's

	Memorandum on Commissions for Native Officers 16 July 1900, Ibid, 23, 83.
26	Military letter from the government of India No. 47, 21 March 1885, 'Native Officers: reports by selected officers', BL/IOR, L/MIL/17/5/1721, 1,3.
27	Ibid, 7.
28	Ibid, 2-14; BL/IOR, Mss.Eur.F.111/253, 84.
29	Taking into account the dissenetrs rationale, Lord Kimberly asked for a fresh proposal incorporating a response to these questions. Sir Donald Stewart (no longer Commander-in-Chief but holding a seat on the India council) sent another despatch on 15 April 1886 to India via the Secretary of State. BL/IOR, Mss.Eur.F.111/253, 84.
30	Lord Roberts Minute 29 July 1886, BL/IOR, Mss.Eur.E.420/9, 62.
31	Government of India despatch No.139, 12 August 1887, Ibid, 62.
32	BL/IOR, Mss.Eur.F.111/253, 85.
33	Lord Roberts' Minute 27 May 1890, BL/IOR, Mss.Eur.E.420/9, 63.
34	Letters regarding Commissions in British Army for Sons of Native Indian Chiefs and Gentlemen, August-November 1897, BL/IOR, Mss.Eur.F.111/253, 36.
35	Ibid.
36	According to Hindu custom travel abroad would `pollute' the high caste Hindus like the Brahmins.
37	BL/IOR, Mss.Eur.F.111/253, 37.
38	Ibid, 38.
39	The only precedent was in 1857 in the Ionian islands under British rule. Then a act had been passed empowering persons born on the island to receive commissions in the army. Ibid.
40	Ibid.
41	Ibid, 86-87.
42	Note for His Excellency the Viceroy by P.J. Maitland Military Secretary, 26 April 1900, BL/IOR, Mss.Eur.F.111/253, 54-6.
43	Memorandum by His Excellency the Viceroy upon Commissions for Native Officers, 4 June 1900, Ibid, 87.
44	Lloyd I. Rudolf, Mohan Singh, and Susanne Hoeber Rudolf, 'The Diary of Amar Singh', unpublished typescript in University of Chicago Library, DS485.R26R36., 1976., V. 1, p.445.
45	Ibid, 468.
46	Only towards the end of their course-work at Meerut/Dehra-Dun did the cadets receive any instruction in tactics, topography, and fortifications. *Ibid*, p.1073.
47	Ibid, p.469.

48 Ironically rule no. XVI g. stated that "no extravagance would be permitted", Ibid, pp.471, 473.
49 Ibid, pp.468-477.
50 *Indian Army List*, July - October 1906, pp.153-155.
51 Ibid, 79. See also fn. 30.
52 Letter from General Officer Commanding Southern Army General Sir Edmund Barrow to Military Secretary Major General Sir M.H.S. Grover, March 1912, BL/IOR, Mss. Eur. E. 420/9, 2.
53 Ibid, 3.
54 The first officer was given a sort of honorary reserve post. Cabinet Papers and notes by Curzon 1916-18, BL/IOR, Mss.Eur.F.111/442, 6-7.
55 Memorandum from General Kitchener 9 September 1908, Birdwood Collection, BL/IOR, Mss.Eur.D.686/31, 2.
56 That very year the total enrollment fell to 14. 'Diary of Amar Singh', p.471.
57 Ibid, pp.4-9.
58 Curzon paper on admission of Indians to the major ranks of the army, sent to Mr Chamberlain and returned, 17 July 1917, BL/IOR, Mss.Eur.F.111/442, 11-12.
59 Ibid, 12.
60 Ibid, 15.
61 Ibid, 18.
62 Ibid, 17-19.
63 Letter from War Office to India Office, 5 July 1917, Ibid, 33-37.
64 Note on proposal of Government of India to grant at once a large number of temporary King's Commissions to Indians, 1918, Ibid, 38.
65 Extract from War Cabinet Minutes No. 203., 2 August 1917, Ibid, 42
66 Telegram No. 828., Secretary of State to Viceroy, 5 April 1918, Ibid, 47.
67 See Telegram No. 112 from Secretary of State for War Lord Kitchener to Field Marshal Sir John French, 27 August 1914, P.R.O., W.O. 33/173.
68 W.O. to GHQ France, 29 August 1914, W.O. 33/713; War Diary Lahore division, P.R.O., W.O. 95/39 Ibid, 4-9 11. The I.E.F. was totally unprepared for its new role as an Imperial Strategic Reserve. See J.O. Rawson, 'The Role of India in Imperial Defence beyond Indian Frontiers and Home Waters, 1919-1939,' Oxford, unpublished D.Phil. (1976), pp.6-9.34.
69 See views of Haig's Chief of Intelligence - Brig. Gen. John Charteris, *At GHQ*, (London, 1931), p.66.
70 See Jeffrey Greenhut, 'The Imperial Reserve: The Indian Corps on the Western Front 1914-1915,' *The Journal of Imperial and Commonwealth History*, Vol. XII., (October 1983), No. 1: 66-67; and Gregory Martin, 'The Influence of Racial Attitudes in British Policy towards India during the First World War,' Ibid, Vol. XIV., (January 1986), No. 2: 1002-104.

71 Greenhut, p.69.
72 C.R. [?] to Lord Crewe, No. 266, 25, Commissions for Indians, Indianization, 1915-1942, Col. 430. BL/IOR, L/MIL/7/19006.
73 BL/IOR, Mss.Eur.F.111/442, 18.
74 Dadabhai Naoroji, fondly known as the grand old man of India was thrice president of the Indian National Congress, in 1886, 1895, and 1906. In 1893 he became the first Indian to be elected to the House of Commons, as member of Central Finsbury.
75 Lord Lansdowne to Lord George Hamilton 20 February 1898, BL/IOR, Mss.Eur.F.111/253, 37.
76 Report of the Annual Conference of All Indians Resident in the U.K. printed in *India*, 30 December 1898.
77 Report on 1912 Conference, BL/IOR, Mss.Eur.F.111/442, 13.
78 M.N. Das, *India under Morley and Minto: Politics behind Revolution, Repression and Reform*, (London: George Allen & Unwin, 1964), pp. 97,108.
79 Secretary of State for India to War Cabinet 1/8/1917, BL/IOR, Mss.Eur.F.111/442, 22.
80 B. Spangenberg, "The Aitchison Commission; an Introduction," reprint of *Report of the Public Services Commission 1886-1888*, (New Delhi: Concept Publishing Co, 1977).
81 Ibid.
82 Curzon to Hamilton 23 April 1900, BL/IOR, Mss.Eur.F.111/159, 24.
83 BL/IOR, Mss.Eur.F.111/253, 87.
84 Dadabhai Naoroji speaking before the London India Society on 1 June 1904 exhorted Indians 'to claim unceasingly their birthright, and pledged rights of British citizenship, of self-government....' India, 10 June 1904, p.282.
85 Annie Besant, *Speeches and Writings*, (Madras, 1921), pp.267-8; Keir J. Hardie, *India, Impressions and Suggestions*, (London, 1909), p.102.
86 Quoted in Stephen E. Koss, *John Morley at the India Office, 1905-1910*, (New Haven and London: Yale University Press, 1969), p.125.
87 The reforms introduced by Lords Morley and Minto doubled the number of Indians in the provincial legislative council giving them a non-official majority. S. R. Mehrotra, *India and the Commonwealth 1885-1929*, (New York: Frederick R. Praeger, 1965), p.53.
88 M.N. Das, *India under Morley and Minto*, p.69.
89 Private Letter Col. H.D. Watson 30 March 1914 to Major Wigram, BL/IOR, Mss.Eur.F.111/442, 13.

Chapter 2
The Highroad to Dehra Dun:
The Institutionalization of the Indian Officer Corps 1919-1947

When the guns finally ceased thundering in 1918, 60,000 Indian soldiers had fought and died for regiment and empire in blood-soaked battlefields from Europe to East Africa. The scale of their contribution can be judged from the fact that the Indian army earned no less than 9,200 decorations including 11 Victoria Crosses. Indeed, by November 1918 India had despatched 1,302,394 men - France 138,000, Mesopotamia 657,000, Egypt and Palestine 144,000, and smaller contingents to Aden, East Africa, Gallipoli and Salonika. Additionally India supplied 170,000 animals (mainly mules and horses), 3,700,000 tons of supplies and rations for a million men.[1] By contrast all of the Dominions together could only send 978,439 men.[2] A thankful British government recognized this sacrifice; Prime Minister David Lloyd George, supported by Austen Chamberlain and the War Cabinet, decided unanimously in favour of India's inclusion in the Imperial War Conference in March 1917.[3] Four months later on 20 August 1917 Mr E. S. Montagu, the Liberal Secretary of State for India, made a historic statement to the House of Commons -

> The policy of His Majesty's Government, with which the Government of India are in complete accord, is that of the increasing association of Indians in every branch of the administration with a view to the progressive realization of responsible government in India as an integral part of the British empire....[4]

As S.R. Mehrotra points out, the declaration of 20 August 1917 'marked a definite repudiation of the concept of "the two Empires" - the concept that there could be, under the British flag, one form of constitutional evolution for the West and another for the East, one for the White races and another for the non-white.'[5] Montagu's statement represented a fundamental shift in British policy, it marked the beginning of the transition from Empire to Commonwealth.

In accordance with the August 1919 statement to the Commons, the

Government of India moved to make representative and self-government in India more a reality. Mr Montagu and Viceroy Lord Chelmsford established a Central Indian Legislative Assembly. This move was essentially building upon the Government of India Act of 1909 which had made the Viceroy's Legislative Council and the Provincial Legislatures into partial representative bodies. Indeed it is not surprising that Montagu played a chief role in this process; as Under Secretary for State in 1910 he had defended the Indian Councils Act as a great opportunity for Indians to vent their grievances, and deemed the Act an effective counter to the Congress. With these latest reforms Montagu hoped to entice 'moderates' to break from the Congress. The reforms were directed in part to meet the aspirations of educated Indians, loyalists, moderates and 'all those Indians who believed in the advance of self-government.'[6] The new Central Assembly was to have 100 of its 145 members elected from a small pool of Indian voters, with the remainder being nominated by the Viceroy. An Upper House called the Council of State was established consisting of sixty members, of whom a majority were nominated. The experimental nature of these bodies was evident by the fact that the British kept a number of 'reserved subjects' - the armed forces, police, and judiciary as inviolate from the legislation of these bodies.

This fact, however, did not deter the fledgling Indian Parliament from expressing its views on the 'banned' subjects. In the first sitting of the Legislative Assembly in early 1921, Sir Sivaswamy Aiyer tabled no less than fifteen resolutions on the Indian army.[7] Two of these resolutions called for the Indianization of the officer corps; Sir Sivaswamy Aiyer suggested that 25% of the King's commissions granted annually should be given to Indians.[8]

This chapter analyzes the dynamics of the postwar debate on Indianization that ultimately led to the establishment of the Indian Military Academy (I.M.A.) at Dehra Dun. I will begin by examining the official discourse on the subject, focusing specifically on the numerous committees that investigated the issue of Indianization between 1919 and 1932. I will also analyze the reactive discourse from the Indian politicians and determine if they had any real effect upon the Government's/Army's Indianization policy as has been purported by researchers including Stephen Cohen. I will then describe the establishment of the I.M.A. at Dehra Dun, and the role played by this institution in molding the senior leadership of the post-independent Indian Army. The chapter will conclude with an in-depth analysis of organizational politics which played such an important role in determining the relationships between the Indian Army and the Indian government, and the Indian Army and the British Army. The true explanation for the prolonged opposition to an Indian Sandhurst lies not in an embedded racism in the British controlled Indian Government and Army, but rather in an understanding of the inherent tensions created by intricacies of the above described relationships.

A Decade of Committees

During the course of his famous speech to the Commons on Indian self-government, Montagu had also announced the decision of His Majesty's Government to

> ....remove the bar which has hitherto precluded admission of Indians to commissioned ranks in His Majesty's army and steps are being taken respecting the grant of commissions to nine Indian officers belonging to Native Indian Land Forces who have served in the field.....The Secretary of State and the Government of India are discussing the general conditions under which Indians should in future be eligible for commissions. In due course the Army Council will be consulted with a view to introduction of a carefully considered scheme toprovide for the selection of candidates for training them in duties which will devolve upon them.[9]

The response from the Indian army was quite amazing. In 1921 Lord Rawlinson, the new Commander-in-Chief of the Indian army, convened a Military Requirements Committee (chaired by himself), to promote a radical scheme that would completely Indianize the officer corps in only 30 years!! Rawlinson proposed 25% of the seats at Sandhurst be reserved for Indians. This was exactly what Sir Aiyer had asked for in his resolutions; Rawlinson also agreed to a 2.5% annual increase to accelerate the process. He proposed the opening up of Engineer, Supply, and Artillery wings to Indians.[10] The British Government, not surprisingly, vetoed this enormous first step into

Indianization. The Military Secretary to the India Office, reiterating the traditional arguments of the pre-war 'dissenters', proposed instead the establishment of a separate Indian Dominion army which would exist and develop alongside the existing Indian army. As this new Dominion army evolved, it would assume the responsibilities of the Indian army, eventually replacing it.[11]

In 1922 Rawlinson convened yet another committee, this time taking caution not to involve himself in its proceedings. The committee, led by Lieutenant General John Shea, rejected the 'Aiyer' proposal on the grounds that it would prove too complicated in practice. Alternatively the Shea committee proposed a three stage plan. In the first stage (14 years) the British Indianized one regiment per group of cavalry, one battalion per group of infantry, and a corresponding proportion of other services. A total of 81 commissions were to be granted every year. In the second stage (14 years) 7 cavalry regiments, 40 infantry battalions, 3 pioneer battalions and 6 pack batteries would be Indianized. During the third and final stage (7 years) all recruitment of British Sandhurst officers would be halted and the remainder of the army would be Indianized. In this manner it was theoretically possible to Indianize the army within thirty-five years. An important part of the Shea Committee's report called for the immediate establishment of an Indian military college. This college was to be the sole avenue of entry by Indians to the commissioned ranks of the Indian army. The college was to have two wings, one for cadets from the Prince of Wales Royal Indian Military College (PWRIM),[12] and from colleges and universities; the second for selected holders of the Viceroy's Commission. Addressing General Cobbe's crucial proposal for an Indian Dominion army, the Shea Committee noted 'In absence of a conscious, mature and homogenous national spirit in India the moral factor most essential to the creation of a `Dominion' army does not exist....'.[13]

However, even Shea's scaled-down Indianization plan proved too ambitious for the British Government to accept. Viscount Peel, the Secretary of State, felt more inclined towards a much smaller effort involving four units in the 'first stage'. Ultimately a consensus was reached for 8 units to be Indianized. They included 5 battalions of infantry, 1 pioneer regiment, and 2 cavalry regiments.[14] The adoption of the 'eight unit' scheme was an acknowledgement of earlier worries about problems that might arise when Indians were in a position to wield command over British officers. As Joint Secretary to the India Office Military Department noted in a lecture to the Imperial Defence College in October 1931, there was clear evidence that British officers were reluctant to take orders from Indians. He noted '....whether right or wrong does not concern us; the fact is that it existed and had to be faced.....'[15] The British instituted the 'eight unit' scheme to ensure the continued recruitment of British officers, which was essential to the efficiency of the Indian army.

In avoiding this pitfall, the British, unfortunately, stumbled into another, namely the inevitable negative side-effects of establishing segregated units within the army. The Governments in Whitehall and Delhi were basically duplicating the negative segregation of the ICS (Indian Civil Service) into provincial (lower) and federal (higher) categories for Indians and British respectively. They ignored the astute advice of earlier reformers like Colonel H. D. Watson to avoid such harmful half-way measures.[16] This became apparent in June 1923 when the Commander-in-Chief, Lieutenant General Sir Alexander Cobbe, appointed a committee headed by the Chief of General Staff, General Claud W. Jacobs, to report on the progress made by Indianization. The Jacobs' Committee noted that the British perceived the eight Indianizing units as inferior, and that in the four years since Indianization had been in effect, no Indian officer from Sandhurst had opted for the eight units.[17]

In fact, the report of the Jacob Committee was wholly negative. The committee reported that the results up to 1923 indicated that Indianization was not likely to succeed and that it was wise to restrict it to a small portion of the army. They noted the tendency of Indian officers to gravitate towards men of their own 'class'(caste), a move which threw serious doubt on the officers' impartiality and ability to command the respect and obedience of the men. The committee also remarked on the possibility of discontent in the ranks if the Viceroy's Commissions were abolished.[18] The committee felt that the presence of British officers was essential to ensure the success of any Indianizing programme. It advised care be taken in assigning Indians to non-Indianizing units, so as not to further perturb British parents who wondered if their sons would have a viable future in a rapidly Indianizing Indian army.

Such doubts, the committee noted, had resulted in the decline in the numbers of young British officers opting for a career in the Indian army.

The Jacob Committee reserved the most damaging criticism for the Indian officer candidates themselves. The committee revealed that there was a 60% attrition rate in the four years of Indianization! Of the 25 cadets sent to Sandhurst, 10 failed the course, 2 died, 2 resigned after receiving commissions, and 1 was deprived of his commission, thus leaving only 10 successful candidates or a mere 40% success rate. To explain these astonishing figures the committee pointed out the lack of an Indian equivalent of the British Public Schools. The committee highlighted the fact that with the exception of the PWRIM at Dehra Dun, there was no 'Public School' in India. The committee also opined that in order to obtain officer grade material, Indian entrants to Sandhurst should enter a competitive exam similar to their British counterparts. The committee concluded with a warning -

> The impatience of the Indian politician, who will not understand that the safety of India may be endangered by too great rapidity in Indianization, and who will constantly press for speedier methods.There must be no question of yielding to his pertinacity in years to come, until such time as it is conclusively proved that Indianizationwill succeed.[19]

The British, although determined to stand their ground against the Indian nationalist politicians, had to concede the fact that the present system of nominating Indian cadets to Sandhurst was unsatisfactory. As moderate Indian politicians of the National Liberal Federation pointed out, at this pace it would take two hundred before the entire Indian army was Indianized![20] In June 1925 the Indian Government, following the recommendation of the legislative assembly, appointed a committee of ten Indians under the chairmanship of the Chief of General Staff Lieutenant General Sir Andrew Skeen to investigate the requirement of an Indian equivalent to Sandhurst. After an exhaustive investigation the report was presented to the government in November 1926.[21]

The Skeen Committee first analyzed the performance of Indian cadets at Sandhurst. It noted that since 1918, 243 applicants (including 16 Indians educated in England) had applied for 83 vacancies at Sandhurst reserved exclusively for Indians. Of the successful entrants 18 were still undergoing training, 44 had graduated (2 subsequently resigned their commissions), 2 died and 19 failed to qualify. This represented a failure rate of 30%, much better than the 60% failure rate reported by the Jacobs' Committee. However, when compared to the 3% failure rate of British cadets, it was still quite shocking. The report explained that until quite recently the educated Indian middle classes had been barred from military service as a result most educated Indians were generally ignorant of the possibility of a career in the higher ranks of the army. The committee laid great stress on the fact that the weak educational system in India placed Indians at a disadvantage to British cadets from the Public School system, who were physically and mentally much better prepared for Sandhurst. The committee also noted the emotional and financial burden Indian parents had to incur to send their sons to Sandhurst. Lastly the committee branded the 'eight unit'scheme as an invidious form of segregation which would ultimately result in the failure of Indianization.

In its recommendations to the government the committee called for an immediate increase of 10 vacancies at Sandhurst, making for a total of 20 vacancies. This would be followed by an increase of 4 per year till 1933, at which point an 'Indian Sandhurst' with a capacity for 100 cadets would be established. This number would be increased by 12 every 3 years, while the vacancies at the 'real' Sandhurst would be reduced to 20 per year. The committee expected that by 1952 fully half the total cadre of officers of the Indian army would be Indians. It recommended that the PWRIM at Dehra Dun be expanded and that additional similar schools be established since it was the only school in India comparable to the English Public School. The committee strongly recommended that the selection of candidates be as widely based as possible and that the candidates be selected only after passing a examination and being interviewed by a board similar to that which interviewed British candidates for Sandhurst. For reasons given above, the committee also recommended the abandonment of the 'eight unit' scheme. It recommended that Indian King's Commissioned officers be made eligible for posting to any unit in the Indian army just like their British counterparts. The committee felt that the establishment of an 'Indian Sandhurst' was unavoidable not only because of the difficulties facing

Indians who were sent to Sandhurst, but also due to the fact that Sandhurst itself could not accommodate greater numbers of Indian cadets without losing its character as a British academy. Lastly, the committee insisted that the King's Commission granted to cadets of the 'Indian Sandhurst' must be of the same status, authority and precedence as the King's Commission granted to cadets trained at Sandhurst.

The Indian government's reaction to the Skeen Committee's proposals were mixed. On the one hand the government acknowledged grave defects in the system of nominating Sandhurst cadets, the high expenses to Indian parents and the lack of adequate educational facilities in India to prepare young Indians for entry into Sandhurst. On the other hand the government was reluctant to scrap the 'eight unit' scheme until the present 'experiment' proved successful and there was a continuous supply of good officers. The government also came out against the proposal for an Indian military college on the grounds that such a college inaugurated prematurely in 1933 could not be comparable to Sandhurst. The government felt that as long as Sandhurst could accommodate Indian cadets there was no need for an Indian military college. In one respect, however, the government revealed itself further advanced in reformist thought than the Skeen Committee. The government saw Indianization as part of the eventual formation of a Dominion army - 'Our aim if we can obtain sufficient officer material, is the eventual creation of a *Dominion* army, that is, an army manned and officered throughout by Indians, comprising of all arms in which Indians desire to serve and to bear commissioned rank.'[22]

The reaction from some members of the 'old guard' to the Skeen Committee's proposal was highly negative. Sir Michael O' Dwyer, the former Lieutenant-Governor of the Punjab (1913-19), writing in the London *Evening News* compared the Indian Empire to

> ... a great edifice which is held together by the 'steel frame' of a few thousand British officers. Remove or weaken that steel frame and the whole edifice collapses, bringing down not only India's 320 millions, but the British Empire ... Surely if Britain has to play the piper in British blood - it should call the tune. Let us hope that the Viceroy and the secretary of State for India will see to that in handling these amazing proposals.[23]

The opinions of O'Dwyer and others undoubtedly influenced Indian nationalist politicians and present-day scholars who have criticized the Indian government for obstructing the Skeen Committee's proposals.[24] In reality the government had, as we have already seen, committed itself to the total Indianization of the Indian army. Dissenters to Indianization were in a minority at this time, and most of them like O'Dwyer were either retired or in too powerless a position to have any effect on the policy. The Indian government, however, was determined to see the process through as carefully as possible with minimal degradation to the army's efficiency.

By 1927 the dust raised in the furor created by the Indian Sandhurst Committee Report had begun to settle, and the dialogue on reform began to proceed more smoothly. One of the main worries had been that British officer recruitment to the Indian army would dry up if the pace of Indianization was increased. Indeed, early indications appeared to point in that direction. Between 1818 and 1923, an average of 60 British cadets annually applied for entry into the Indian Army. Soon after the publication of Lord Rawlinson's report the numbers began to fall; in 1923 there were only 45 applicants, in 1924 there were 37, and by 1925 there were only 34. However, by 1926 as the actual effects of the schemes became apparent the numbers rose to 44 and continued to increase to 50 and 68 for 1927 and 1928 respectively.[25]

In 1928 the British Government appointed a Parliamentary Commission under the Liberal barrister Sir John Simon to evaluate the impact of the Montagu-Chelmsford reforms. The all-British commission was not only soundly rejected by Indians, but its voluminous (17 volumes) proposals made little headway with the governments in Britain and India. The Simon Commission devoted considerable attention to military reforms, with Indianization playing a major role. Sir Simon, aware of resentment generated amongst Indians by his all-British commission, involved a number of Indian notables including Sir Zulfikar Ali Khan and Sir Hari Singh Gour to assist him in his inquiries into the Indian military. The minutes of the meeting between the Indian non-official members of the commission and senior army and government officials gives us a first hand insight into the vast gap in understanding that divided the British and Indians over the Indianization issue.

In the course of the commission's inquiry into the workings of the Indian army, Sir Hari Singh Gour stated that 'Indians think that the Indian army can be Indianized in one generation, in twenty-five years.....'[26] Sir Gour also felt that the 'scrupulous' selection process left out many candidates who might prove to be successful. To this remark Major General Kirke accused Sir Gour of advocating quantity over quality. The interview with General Kirke was one of the few opportunities Indians had to put their views on Indianization before those in the army and the Civil Service directly connected with the reforms. To nationalists such as Sir Gour, Indianization was but one of many steps necessary for the British to take in order to enable India to achieve self-government. They perceived the British as slowing the entire process by the foot-dragging, and even doubted British sincerity in their efforts. To the British executors of the reform schemes including General Kirke, Indianization was the crucial element in India's advance towards dominion status. They were determined to see that the process resulted in a professional and competent cadre of Indian officers capable of taking over the reigns of command from the British. The 'radical' demands of Indian politicians like Sir Sivaswamy Aiyer and Sir Gour only enhanced their determination to keep the Indians at arms length from the entire process, and this in turn fueled the suspicions of the Indian nationalists about British reluctance to Indianize the army.

By 1930, at the same time the Round Table Conferences were about to begin, the Government of India conceded that the conditions were ideal for the establishment of an Indian military college. At the conference a sub-committee on defence passed a resolution demanding that

> in order to avoid delay the Government of India be instructed to set up a committee of experts, both British and Indian (including representatives of the Indian States) to work out the details of such a college.[27]

The Indian government complied and a committee was duly established under the chairmanship of the Commander-in-Chief General Sir Philip Chetwoode.

The committee's report reinforced the many positive aspects of Indianization that were increasingly becoming apparent. It noted for instance the marked improvement in Indian schools, in the direction proposed by the Skeen Committee (Public School orientation). The committee also noted

> the material success achieved by Dehra Dun College (PWRIM) has been so great that we consider it should be gradually expanded up to a total capacity of two hundred and fifty to three hundred cadets.....[28]

The committee urged that the PWRIM be enlarged as soon as possible to act as a feeder to the Indian Military College. The success of the PWRIM is not surprising as the

> college was designed to provide the necessary preliminary training for entry to the RMC, Sandhurst, RMA, Woolwich and the RAF College, Cranwell.[29]

The PWRIM came under the direct control of the Commander-in-Chief India, thus ensuring high standards and adequate funds to provide the best trained candidates for Sandhurst. Furthermore it was set up specifically to deliver a public school education on English lines for unmarried Indian and Anglo-Indian youths.[30] The PWRIM also provided excellent experience in establishing an integrated military school representative of all the diverse ethnic and religious groups in India. For example, in the school

> special care was taken that no food is served in the mess which could in any way offend the religious susceptebilities of any student.[31]

It would take subtle yet vital touches like these to make the Indian Military Academy more of a home to Indian officer cadets than the RMC, Sandhurst, had been.

The committee determined on a course three years in length for the Indian Military College. Applicants aged between 18 and 20 years could enter the college. Most of the 60 vacancies were to be allotted by open competition in the form of an entrance exam. Officers graduating from this college were the equal in every way to British officers entering the Indian army from British colleges. The generally positive note of the Chetwoode Committee is surprising given the fact that Chetwoode in his private correspondence expressed his dislike for a separate Indian Sandhurst. He also indicated that he had little confidence in Indian-officered units, and felt that the 'eight units' should not be considered part of the army.[32]

In a conciliatory step towards Indian nationalist politicians, the Chetwoode Committee included in its non-official ranks Sir Sivaswamy Aiyer, the most virulent critic of the governments' Indianization policy. It was no surprise, then, that the committee's recommendations failed to gain Sir Sivaswamy Aiyer's, approval who filed a separate minute (along with G.R.R. Rajwade another non-official Indian member of the committee). The dissenting report (which appears primarily to have been the work of Sir Aiyer) was primarily an outburst of pent-up frustration at perceived British stonewalling on Indianization, reviewing as it did the entire history of the acrimonious debate from the perspective of the side-lined Indian politicians. Unbeknownst to Sir Aiyer, many of the points of debate he sought to raise with his minute of dissent had already been resolved by the secretive official debate on the subject. Inclusion in the Chetwoode committee, albeit in a non-official capacity, provided the indefatigable Indian legislator a rare attempt to join in the official discourse on the Indianization of the Indian army, and he was determined to make his case.[33]

The Indian Military Academy

The Chetwoode Committee had recommended three possible sites for the location of the Indian Military College: Satara, Mhow, and Dehra Dun. After some deliberations Dehra Dun became the site of choice. It was already the location of the highly successful PWRIM; furthermore, the army could avail of the ready-made facilities of the empty Railway Staff College, which had been completed in 1930, but closed almost immediately due to the financial crisis imposed by the Great Depression. The facilities of the Railway Staff College and its surrounding 155.3 acres of land were acquired for Rs. 21, 17, 597 on 1 April 1932. The former Railway College proved to be an excellent choice for the Indian Military Committee. Chetwoode Hall (which is still the heart of the academy today) was formerly the Dormer Hall of the Railway College, an imposing and unique structure sunk several floors below ground level; it was used to demonstrate model train movements to the railway's students.[34]

The infant academy soon became the focus of gifts from well wishers far and wide. The most impressive is probably a champion company silver cup trophy from Sandhurst which was presented by the Chief of Imperial General Staff Sir Montgomery-Massingbird at Sandhurst in December 1933.[35] These gifts helped build the corporate identity of the new institution; indeed the unique rituals and traditions that characterize such institutions the world over were well in the making in the Indian Military Academy (IMA) soon after it was opened.

The IMA sought to emulate Sandhurst in all ways except one - the duration of its course. The Chetwoode Committee had recommended a three year course for the IMA instead of the eighteen month course at Sandhurst. The army settled for a two and half year course. This was in recognition of the fact that academic preparation would be needed at the IMA itself to make up for the deficiencies of the Indian school system. In all other respects, the IMA followed Sandhurst; the entrance exams held on the third Monday of October for instance were conducted by the Federal Public Service Commission (India), similar to the system in England. The format of the exam also closely mirrored that of the Sandhurst entrance exam. The exam was divided into four parts, the most important of which was the Interview and Record Test. While the IMA curriculum reflected greater academic emphasis than Sandhurst, the annual exam system was very similar. One exam was held at the end of the term; the entire course was comprised of five terms over a two and half year period. It was comprised of two main sections, General Military Education and Detailed Military Education. As at Sandhurst the Company Commander's grade and remarks on each cadet were recorded at the end of each term and reviewed by the Commandant.

The IMA was open to competition for unmarried candidates who were British subjects of Indian domicile, or a subject of a State in India (princely States). Applications were usually routed through the local Collector, the Deputy Commissioner, or local Police Officer. Students from the PWRIM had to send their applications via their principal, indicating the special status this school enjoyed over its civilian counterparts in India. A total of 30 vacancies would be opened every half year, 15 by open competition and 15 to Indian army cadets.[36]

Between October 1932 and May 1941, there were 16 regular or 'pre-war' courses. Of the 693 cadets who were admitted, 535 were commissioned, giving a success rate of 85.72%, a remarkably high number when compared to the Indian Sandhurst cadets. The first 5 of the 16 courses have been recorded in the annals of the IMA as :

1. Pioneers   -   1 October 1932 to 22 December 1934.
2. Immortals   -   1 March 1933 to 4 June 1935.
3. Invincibles   -   1 October 1933 to 21 December 1935.
4. Stalwarts   -   1 February 1934 to 3 June 1936.
5. Bahadurs (braves)   23 August 1934 to 29 December 1936.

These five courses, and the Pioneers in particular, represent the elite of the Indian officer corps in pre-independent India. Not only did they have to set an example for future generations, but they were also the products of a rigorous process of selection and a comprehensive 1.5 to 2 years training course. The Indian officers coming out of the Officer Training Course (OTC) during the Second World War received only a fraction of the attention and care lavished upon the pre-war cadets by their British mentors.

The onset of the Second World War drastically changed the nature of the training at the IMA. Between February 1940 and January 1946 there were no less than 49 'war courses' at the academy. They included 8 courses for British cadets (fresh from schools in Britain) taught between October 1941 and October 1943.[37] The 'war courses' were run for Indians and Europeans residing in India. The general duration of these courses was six months. In all, no less than 3,887 cadets, (Indian and British) were commissioned during this period. Out of a total of 4,744 cadets entering the 'war courses', 3,013 were commissioned reflecting a relatively low attrition of 14.31%.[38] In addition to Dehra Dun three additional accelerated Officer Training Courses opened up during the war, at Mhow, Bangalore and Belgaum. The latter was originally reserved exclusively for British cadets but did train four to five mixed batches of British/Indian cadets towards the end of the war.[39]

The IMA proved invaluable to the British war effort in the Southern hemisphere. Without the academy's invaluable work in churning out Emergency Commissioned Officers (ECO's), it is doubtful if the Indian army could have maintained the massive formations it had on the Burma front. That the academy was well up to this task is proven by the fact that no less than 727 British cadets were sent directly from England to Dehra Dun to receive their emergency commissions.[40] In reality any significant doubts that the British might have had about the viability of the IMA had been dissipated by the excellent crop of officers that emerged from the five pre-war courses. As the concluding chapters of this book will show, it was on the shoulders of that group of Indian officers that the burden of command would fall in the post-independence period.

Organizational Politics

In the previous chapter I analyzed the motivations of generations of Liberal British reformers in promoting Indianization. It was evident that intellectual background played a major role in determining their ambivalent approach to reform. To a degree this is also true for the British reformers of the inter-war period. Yet, there remains a serious gap in our understanding of the dynamics of reform during this period. Despite the fact that the British governments in India and England had committed themselves to the introduction of Indian commissioned officers, by the close of the First World War constant roadblocks were thrown up at every stage of the reform process by senior officials both in England and in India. The continued reluctance of the British War Office to reform may come as no great surprise, but the opposition of senior officials within the Indian army and the Civil Service's military bureaucracy is something of a mystery. A partial explanation can be found in the fact that greatly increased pressure from the Indian nationalist politicians had made the British more cautious. Not only had Indian nationalist politicians, including Sir Aiyer, become more vocal about Indianization of the officer corps, but they could voice their grievances in the new highly visible legislative houses created by the Montagu-Chelmsford reforms.

The Indian legislators, however, had absolutely no control over the army. The military continued to be the sole responsibility of the Viceroy and his hand-picked council. At no time could the Indian politicians have dictated to the army, even on the minutest aspect of military administration, let alone forced it to accelerate the pace of Indianization. Although senior officers publicly expressed great concern over the pressure being applied by the Indian politicians, their internal correspondence shows a very casual disdain of the efforts of the Indian legislators. Take, for example, a private letter to Sir Alexander Cobbe, the Headmaster of PWRIM, from Sir Philip

Chetwoode, in which he noted that
> a lot of nonsense was talked by Moonje, Gidney, etc., etc., but we got everything we wanted out of them without using the official majority at all......[41]

Chetwoode and his fellow officers were secure in the conviction that the Indian nationalist politicians had no power to interfere with the Indianization process. The reaction from the press in Britain to Indianization was also generally neutral, if not favourable. The India Office information officer pointed out that with the exception of 'peculiar....*Daily Mail* propaganda.....No similar report has appeared in any [other] newspaper'.[42] The reaction of the British press seemed to indicate a sense of guarded optimism among the British public that Indianization of the officer corps was not necessarily a hindrance to the career of British officers in the Indian army. Perhaps more important, was the fact that from 1924 onwards the performance of Indian cadets was showing remarkable improvement, as shown below:

TABLE 2[43]

Table showing annual number of Indian cadets admitted to the RMC, Sandhurst, since 1918, and numbers granted King's Commissions after successfully completing a course there:

YEAR	No. OF VACANCIES	No. ADMITTED	No. COMMISSIONED
1919 (half year)	5 Sandhurst	5	-
1919 (half year)	10 Sandhurst	10	-
1920	10 Sandhurst	10	1
1921	10 Sandhurst	9	6
1922	10 Sandhurst	8	3
1923	10 Sandhurst	12	6
1924	10 Sandhurst	12	10
1925	10 Sandhurst	10	11
1926	10 Sandhurst	11	7

1927	10 Sandhurst	15	6
1928 (half year)	5 Sandhurst	3	14
1928	10 Sandhurst 3 Woolwich 3 Cranwell	3 Sandhurst	-
1929	24 Sandhurst 6 Woolwich 6 Cranwell	9 Sandhurst	11 Sandhurst
1930	24 Sandhurst 6 Woolwich 6 Cranwell	22 Sandhurst 2 Woolwich 6 Cranwell	3 Sandhurst
1931	24 Sandhurst 3 Woolwich 1 Cranwell	23 Sandhurst 4 Woolwich 1 Cranwell	20 Sandhurst

Why then did these officers attempt to slow if not stop the pace of reform? The answer to this question lies not in the nascent Indian nationalist politics of the period, but within the British and Indian military establishments.

Organizations react instinctively against any external force that is seen to impinge upon their independence and authority. Nowhere is this reflex-action more apparent than in military organizations. Specialized knowledge of military administration and functions are often the sole preserve of the military itself. This exclusive knowledge gives the military a considerable degree of autonomy from civilian authority, and, as Max Weber points out, the military bureaucracy will go to great lengths to keep this knowledge to themselves.[44] This is precisely what seems to have happened with regard to the Indian army during the inter-war period. In the last chapter we learned that it was senior officers of the Indian army who acquiesced, indeed, assisted in the efforts to secure commissions for Indians. Their participation in this reform was eased by the fact that this decision was primarily political in nature, with no military rationale to oppose it. In fact the experience of the First World War had revealed crucial weaknesses in an all-White officered Indian army (see above). During the inter-war period, however, the implementation of the Indianization policy became an internal matter for the army, at least as far as the military bureaucracy was concerned. Senior officers including Field Marshal Sir Claud W. Jacobs, the Military Secretary at the India Office, London, and the Deputy Chief of General Staff General, Sir Walter M. Kirke, resented what they perceived as dangerous interference by the British Civil Servants and politicians to hasten the pace of Indianization. General Kirke characterized this haste as being 'purely political'.[45]

Inter-service rivalries also promoted organizational secrecy and reticence towards reform. This was the primary cause of the British military's reluctance to wholeheartedly back the reforms. The British Air Ministry, for instance, was reluctant to admit Indian cadets to the Royal Air Force (R.A.F.) academy at Cranwell, for it feared that this might be the first step towards the establishment of an Indian Army Royal Flying Corps, independent of the R.A.F.[46] This inter-service rivalry was indicative of a far deeper and profound division between the British and Indian armies. The post-1919 Indian army was to all intents and purpose completely independent from the control of the British Home army, a reality that many senior British army officers refused to acknowledge.

Addiscombe to Dehra Dun

Ironically, the establishment of the IMA had turned back the clock to the pre-1857 period when the East India Company's armies were independent of the British army. This independence was largely due to the fact that the East India Company (E.I.C.) trained most of its cadets at its own military academy in Addiscombe. A brief survey of the history of this academy will help us understand the institutional reluctance the British army had towards an Indian Sandhurst. In the first decade of the nineteenth century the E.I.C. military establishment found itself in an awkward situation. Its ever expanding armies had just vanquished the armies of the Maratha Chieftan Sindhia, but the E.I.C. was unable to obtain enough officers to command its growing forces. Since 1798 the E.I.C. had made do with an arrangement with the Royal Military Academy at Woolwich to train 40 artillery and engineer cadets at a time. The arrangement was only partially satisfactory for the Company, for its cadets took second place to British army requirements. As the E.I.C.'s requirements for additional officers grew it became obvious that the limited openings in Woolwich were inadequate. The Company's problems were exacerbated when the Master General of the Board of Ordanance prohibited Professors from Woolwich from tutoring E.I.C. candidates for entry into the academy.[47]

The E.I.C.'s problems actually predated those faced by the Indian Government in the inter-war period when it sought to increase the pace of Indianization. Its solution to these problems was also remarkably similar to those adopted by the Indian government in the inter-war period; in 1809 the Directors of the company authorized the establishment of a military seminary to train its cadets. That year the company acquired the house and premises at Addiscombe Place near Croydon, formerly the residence of the late Earl of Liverpool, comprising a mansion and 5.7 acres of land.[48] The Addiscombe Seminary proved such a success that by 1813 the company reserved all officer appointments in its artillery and engineers to Addiscombe students, and in 1816 the seminary opened its gates to infantry and cavalry officers of the company.[49] Addiscombe now combined the functions of both Woolwich and Sandhurst, the latter having been opened in 1813 to train cavalry and infantry officers for the British army.

Given the great number of ground forces maintained by the E.I.C. in India it was entirely possible that in time the Addiscombe Military might have surpassed the Woolwich and Sandhurst academies in the number and quality of cadets it produced. This was not, however, to be the case, for following the 'Mutiny' of 1857, the Company's armies were taken over by the Crown, and the decision was made to shut down the Addiscombe Seminary. The official reason was that the existing facilities at Sandhurst and Woolwich were adequate for future needs, but there can be little doubt that the British army and Sandhurst in particular were glad to see the demise of this highly successful rival.

The potential rivalry a sister military academy might represent may help explain the institutional opposition of the British army towards an Indian Military Academy. Such an academy, would, and did, eventually stop any involvement Sandhurst might have with the training of officers of the Indian army. This in turn would diminish the influence of the War Office in the Indian Army, which, again, is precisely what happened. The British Army's guarded opposition to the IMA suggests that it, unlike the British

Government, was unable or unwilling to recognize the fact that the Indian army was inexorably headed towards becoming a Dominion army. The attempts by the British Army to maintain a facade of control over its Indian protege thus formed the final obstacle on the high-road to Dehra Dun. Nevertheless, for reasons discussed above the decision to establish an IMA became a reality in 1931, and once the die was cast the British army, including Sandhurst, spared no effort to help the IMA get off to a good start.

How did educated Indian youth react to the new opportunities presented to them by the opening up of the RMC, Sandhurst, and later the IMA? What were the influences that helped mould the character of these future commanders of the post-independent Indian army? These are important questions that must be answered, for no matter what was sanctioned at the official level, the success or failure of the entire Indianization plans ultimately lay in the hands of these young men.

Notes

1. *Statistics of the British Military Effort in the Great War*, (London: HMSO, 1922), pp.68-9; See also *India's Contribution to the Great War*, (Calcutta: Government of India, 1923).

2. See CAB 24/70 G.T. 6341 and 'Statistical Abstract of Information Regarding the Armies at Home and Abroad, 1914-20,' W.O. 161/82.

3. Sir Charles Petrie, *The Life and Letters of the Right Honorable Sir Austen Chamberlain*, (London: Cassell, 1940), Vol. II., pp.73-4.

4. Government of India, Home Department, Political Notification No. 2111, BL/IOR, L/MIL/7/19006, 110.

5. S. R. Mehrotra, *India and the Commonwealth 1885-1929*, (New York: Praeger, 1965), p.106.

6. P. G. Robb, *The Government of India and Reform: Policies Towards Politics and the Constitution 1916-1921*, (London: Oxford University Press, 1976), p.262.

7. These resolutions were primarily in reaction to the Esher Committee Report in 1920 which enquired into the administration and organization of the army.

8. See K. A. Nilkanta Sastri (ed.), *a Great Liberal: Speeches and Writings of Sir P.S. Sivaswamy Aiyer*, (Bombay, 1965), pp.327-42; See also India, Legislative Assembly, *Debates*, Vol. 1, part 2 (1921), p.1753.

9. Telegram from Secretary of State to Army Dept, Simla, 20 August 1917, BL/IOR, L/MIL/7/19006, 110.

10. Proceedings of the Committee appointed by the Government of Governor General in Council to examine the Military Requirements of India (short title) Military Requirements Committee, Simla: Government of India, 1921. 2 Vols, BL/IOR, L/MIL/17/5/1773.

11. Indianization of the Indian army, Lt. General Alexander Stanhope Cobbe, India Office Military Dept, 14 September 1921, BL/IOR, L/MIL/17/5/1774.

12. The PWRIM was established by Lord Rawlinson and formerly inaugurated by the Prince of Wales on 13 March 1922. Its purpose was to train Indians for entry into Sandhurst.

13. Indianization of the Indian army: Report of a Committee appointed by his Excellency the Commander-in-Chief India, Delhi: Government of India, 1922, BL/IOR, L/MIL/17/5/1778, 1-12.

14. Papers of Stuart Kelson Brown 1920-1931, Indianization 1924-1925, BL/IOR, L/MIL/5/844, 31.

15. Mr S. K. Brown, a long time proponent of Indianization, served as Joint Secretary to the Military Dept from September 1924 to 1934. See his Lecture on Indianization given to Imperial Defence College 15 October

16 1931, BL/IOR, L/MIL/5/857.

17 See Chap I.

Progress in the Indianization of the Indian Army: Report of a Committee appointed by His Excellency the Commander-in-Chief in India, June 1923, Simla: Government of India, 1923, (Secret), BL/IOR, L/MIL/17/5/1779, 4.

18 18.The VCO or Viceroy's Commissioned Officer comprised of three Indian ranks above the non-commissioned ranks; it included the *jemadar* (equivalent of a King's Commissioned second-lieutenant), the *subedar* (equivalent of a King's Commissioned lieutenant), and the *subedar-major* (equivalent of a King's Commissioned major). These ranks provided a link between the British KCO fresh from Sandhurst and the sepoy, 'whose language, customs, and outlook were utterly Indian.' The VCO ranks 'also provided an outlet for ambitious and able Indian sepoys, although they were not promoted beyond the regimental level.' See Cohen, *The Indian Army*, p.43. With the advent of the KCIO, it was felt that the VCO ranks were redundant and should be abolished.

19 Ibid.

20 Mehrotra, *India and the Commonwealth 1885-1929*, p.172.

21 *Report of the Indian Sandhurst Committee, 14 November 1926*, [Skeen Committee], (London: HMSO, 1927).

22 Despatch No. 38 to His Majesty's Secretary of State for India 13 October 1927, Birkenhead Collection Mss.Eur.D.703/38, 4; also Recommendation of the Government of India, Home Department, Political Notification No. 2111, BL/IOR; n the Report of the Indian Sandhurst Committee, n.d., BL/IOR, L/MIL/17/5/1787. Lord Irwin felt that the Indian Army like the country must eventually attain Dominion status and the 'eight units' would form the nucleus of such an army. Irwin to Sir William Marius, Governor of U.P., 18 April 1927, Irwin Papers, Irwin Mss. Eur.Mss.C 152/21.

23 Cutting from *Evening News* 7 April 1927, 'The Defence of India: "Indianization" and the Future', by Sir Michael O' Dwyer, BL/IOR, Mss.Eur.D.712/14.

24 Cohen, Mehrotra, and Jacobsen.

25 Memorandum by War Office on certain questions asked by the chairman of the Indian Statutory Commission [Simon Commission], 20 June 1929, Simon Collection, BL/IOR, Mss.Eur.F.77/54, 25.

26 Interview (in camera) with Major General W. M. St. George Kirke Deputy Chief of General Staff and Mr Mackworth Young Secretary to the Army Department (n.d.), Kirke Collection, BL/IOR, Mss.Eur.E.396/18, 131.

27 *Report of the Indian Military College Committee, July 15 1931*, (London: HMSO, 1931), p.1.

28 Ibid, 18.

29 Regulations for the Prince of Wales Royal Indian Military College Dehra Dun (1934), Delhi: Gocernmennt of India Press, 1938, BL/IOR, L/MIL/17/5/2285, 1.
30 Ibid, 2.
31 Ibid, 7.
32 See Chetwoode's notes on Indianization for Major General S.F. Muspratt, Military Department, India Office, 26 September 1932, (Templewood Papers), Hoare Mss., Eur.Mss.E240/57a.
33 The only significant opposition Sir Aiyer had to the committee's plans was to its restriction of the number of vacancies for the Indian military college that would be available to open competition. See Minute by Sir P. S. Sivaswamy Aiyer and Major-General (Honorary) Raja Ganpat Rao Raghunath Rao Rajwade, 2 July 1931, BL/IOR, L/MIL/17/5/2285, 75-108.
34 B.P.N. Sinha and Sunil Chandra, *Valor and Wisdom: Genesis and Growth of the Indian Military Academy*, (New Delhi: Oxford and IBH Publishing, 1992), pp.95-6, 130.
35 Ibid, p.133.
36 Regulations respecting Admission to the Indian Military Academy in Dehra Dun and for the first appointments to His Majesty's Land Forces, 1931, Published by the Manager of Publications Delhi: Government of India Press, New Delhi, 1937. BL/IOR, L/MIL/17/5/2284, pp.1-2.
37 General Gul Hassan Khan (Pakistan Army) who joined the I.M.A. in January 1941 recalls that during his first term at the academy, the course proceeded at a leisurely pace seemingly unaffected by the war. It was only when he returned from a two month break after the first term that he and the other cadets of his course were given a dose of concentrated training and passed out at the end of the year. General Gul Hassan Khan, *Memoirs*, (Karachi, Oxford: Oxford University Press, 1993), pp.9-10.
38 Sinha and Chandra, *Valor and Wisdom*, pp.155-59.
39 Lt. General S. K. Sinha, *A Soldier Recalls*, (New Delhi: Lancer International, 1992), p.42.
40 Ibid, p.158 Ibid, p.133.
41 Extract from personal and private letter from Sir Philip Chetwoode to Sir Alexander Cobbe, Simla 21 August 1931, BL/IOR, L/MIL/5/885, 97.
42 Ibid, 96-105.
43 Of the 157 cadets admitted to Sandhurst, 98 were commissioned, 23 resigned or were removed for various reasons, 2 died and 34 were still under instruction. See BL/IOR, Mss.Eur.E.396/18, 15; and BL/IOR L/MIL/5/857.
44 H. H. Gerth and C. Wright Mills (eds.), *From Max Weber: Essays on Sociology*, (New York: Oxford University Press, 1946), pp.233-5.

45   Copies of Important Papers. DCGS India 1929, Kirke letter September 1928, against Indianisation of Armoured Car Companies. See also letter from Field Marshal Sir Claud W. Jacobs to Kirke 26 May 1927. In this letter regarding the Indian Sandhurst Committee Report, Jacobs declares his intention to '....take both my gloves off and...fight that report to the finish....'. BL/IOR, Mss.Eur.E.396/13.

46   Admission of Indians to Cranwell, Air Ministry Letter 9/1/1929, BL/IOR, L/MIL/5/849.

47   A Diary of Addiscombe, BL/IOR, L/MIL/9/357, 1.

48   John B. Gent (ed.), *Croydon Old and New*, (S.Croydon, Surrey: Southern Publishing, Brighton, 1975), p.7; Ibid, 4.

49   Military Seminary Committee Report, 6 July 1814, BL/IOR, L/MIL/1/10 No.39.

Chapter 3
An Officer and a Gentleman
The Socialization of the Indian Officer Cadet 1919-1945

In 1925 Mr S. K. Brown, the Joint Secretary to the Military Department, India, remarked that the 'future of Indianization in the army lies in the hands of the Indian officers themselves....'[1] Indeed, no analysis of the modernization programme can be complete without a direct examination of the role played by the Indian officers in ensuring the success or failure of the Indianization effort. In the previous Chapter I revealed that one of the ultimate aims of the British was the creation of a professional national army, so that India could move ahead to take on the status of a self-governing dominion within the empire. Contrary to popular belief, Indianization was never meant to be a half-hearted attempt to mollify Indian nationalist politicians. The evidence suggests that Indianization was not a matter of political expediency to be achieved at any cost. Military efficiency remained a priority in this reform, and had it become obvious over a period of time that the Indian officers were not up to the task, it is quite likely that the entire reform process would have failed.

Had the Indian officers proved inept, the British could have exercised two options: in the first, they could have scrapped the programme altogether; in the second case, if this was not politically viable (as seems the more likely) they would have rushed through the Indianization process regardless of the cost to military efficiency. In either situation India would have ended up with a 'headless' army after independence, the all too common legacy of most newly independent colonies. So in the final analysis the Indian officers alone would dictate the outcome of the ambitious Indianization programme. This chapter analyzes the first phase of the Indianization process, the training of the Indian officer cadets.

The Direct Commissioned Officers
The first Indians to obtain commissions in the Indian army were officers of the N.I.L.F. (Native Indian Land Forces), and formerly of the I.C.C., who had seen service in France.[2] The announcement was made in a

speech to the House of Commons on Indian self-government by the Secretary of State for India, Mr Edwin Montagu.[3] These nine Indian officers were the first to face the consequences of the new Indianization policy. One of these officers was Kanwar Amar Singh.[4] After being commissioned into the N.I.L.F. on 4 July 1905 he served as an extra aide-de-camp to various British Generals, and was a N.I.L.F. captain (4 July 1914) and aged 39! when he received his King's commission in 1917. After receiving his King's Commission Amar Singh served briefly in the staff of General Knight in Bombay before joining the 16th Cavalry (Gardner's Horse) in June 1918. Between September 1920 and March 1921 he reached the high-point of his career as acting major in temporary command of the regiment. He ended his career with this regiment in Waziristan in 1923. Amar Singh's departure from the regiment was not a happy one, as his diary indicates it came about as a result of a negative annual confidential report from his superior Colonel Mears. Indeed much of the diary is replete with examples of tension with British officers – subordinates and superiors. The tension seems to have actually escalated after Amar Singh received a King's Commission. The most galling incident took place on St. Patrick's Day in October 1919 when a British subordinate, a Lieutenant Wilks, blatantly disobeyed Amar Singh's orders, leading to a very heated exchange.

Scholars including DeWitt C. Ellinwood have identified the I.C.C. and these 9 K.C.I.O.'s [Kings Commissioned Indian Officers] in particular as the 'first chapter in [the] Indianization of the Indian Army....'[5] So it is not surprising then that the entire Indianization programme has subsequently been portrayed in a negative light. According to Lloyd I. Rudolph (one of the editors of Amar Singh's diary), the army's reaction towards the first nine Indian K.C.I.O.'s represented a

> backlash within the Indian army against the politicians' notions that Indian officers could, by a stroke of the pen, be made equal to British officers....If liberal policy could not be blocked politically it could be resisted through bureaucratic sabotage.[6]

It is misleading, however, to identify the I.C.C. or the nine K.C.I.O.s as the first step towards Indianization. The granting of the King's commission to these officers appears to have been a purely political move.

The measure was a limited one, and in no way was it connected to the mainstream effort to create an Indian officer corps. As for the experiences of Amar Singh, there can be no doubt that he and the other eight Imperial Cadet Corps, K.C.I.O's were subject to varied forms of racial prejudice. But their main problem appears to have been the awkwardness of their official position, as highlighted by Amar Singh's experiences. The King's Commission had given him the right to command field formations, which he did, albeit briefly. Unfortunately, neither Amar Singh or his cadet corps colleagues had passed through Sandhurst to obtain their commissions. So it was not surprising that British officers, even subordinates such as Lieutenant Wilks, resented the authority and rank bestowed upon Amar Singh. In his case the problem was exacerbated by the fact that he had served as an aide-de-camp throughout the war and had seen no action. Therefore it was the lack of professional training and not 'bureaucratic sabotage' that ended his career. He and his fellow cadet corps officers were the unfortunate pawns of a political statement, and as such his experiences cannot be considered to be the norm by which the Indian army's reaction to Indianization can be measured.

Take for example the career of Major General Rudra. Like Amar Singh and the eight cadet corps officers he, too, served in the Great War and was commissioned in 1918. Yet unlike these officers Rudra went on to serve with distinction, ending his career in the independent Indian army with the rank of Major General. What was it that differentiated Rudra from the cadet corps K.C.I.O.s? To begin with Rudra joined the British army and not the Indian army. He was studying in Cambridge when the war broke out, and joined the Universities and Public Schools Brigade. He left with the brigade for France in November 1915 and took part in the battle of Mons. In April 1916 his unit (16th Middlessex) joined the 29th Gallipoli Division. Since Rudra did not qualify for a commission, he along with others joined the 2nd Battalion of Royal Fusiliers in the 29th Division and took part in the Somme bloodbath. In 1918 Rudra's name finally went up for commission. He and another Indian K.A.D. Naoroji, grandson of the grand old Indian nationalist politician Dadabhai Naoroji, were selected and sent for an officer training course to Berkenstead, the Inns of Court, where they joined the 17th OTC Battalion. Just before their training was due to complete the armistice was declared in November 1918.

Soon afterwards, Rudra and Naoroji were sent to General Sir Herbert Cox, Military Secretary at the India Office. Cox was greatly impressed with their war experience, his opinion no doubt aided by the happy coincidence that he had served as commander of the 29th Division at Gallipoli. Although Cox tried to obtain commissions for Rudra and Naoroji, the War Office refused saying that the two must go to Sandhurst first. Both Rudra and Naoroji had already completed most of the OTC course at Berkenstead and therefore refused requesting instead to be discharged. Fortunately, the War Office relented and the two sailed to India to join the Indian Army along with the first fifty Indian officers. This group included K. M. Cariappa the first Indian Commander-in-Chief who was the last officer to be commissioned with this group.

The key to Rudra's success appears to have been his brief stint in the OTC course in England. Also being a veteran of the Great War with tremendous experience in some of the bloodiest battlefields of the Western Front no doubt strengthened his case. As far as the War Office and the Indian Army were concerned, Rudra was a genuine candidate for a King's commission. Unlike the I.C.C. officers Rudra was not tainted by having belonged to what essentially amounted to a princely boys club. The fact that Rudra did not come from royal Indian stock obviously did not hamper his case. Unlike Amar Singh, Rudra 'earned' his commission in much the same way as many of his British colleagues had done, and not via political machinations. This no doubt made pre-Sandhurst K.C.I.O.'s like Rudra far more acceptable to their British subordinates, colleagues and superiors in the Indian Army.[7]

There were, of course, exceptions to this rule, the most notable being K. M. Cariappa, who became the first Indian Commander-in-chief of the army. In 1920 he was one of only six military trainees at Dally College, Indore, out of sixty to qualify for a commission. A cadet school had been opened at Dally college in October, 1918, with accommodation for 50 cadets. The plan was to train cadets for the Indian Army. The Indore cadet school had been opened as a temporary measure to meet the exigencies of the war. The very same year 10 vacancies per year were allotted to Indians at the Royal Military College (R.M.C.) Sandhurst, and the cadet school was closed within a year. In all 49 cadets were admitted to the Dally/Indore Cadet School (including Rudra and Cariappa) and 39 were granted commissions. After the Dally cadet programme was shut down, Sandhurst became the only avenue for Indians to obtain a commission in the army for more than a decade.[8]

There is little doubt that Cariappa was exceptionally talented. Despite the fact that he lacked 'via Sandhurst' credentials, he was the first Indian officer to graduate from the Staff College, Quetta, the first Indian to hold a Grade II (Staff) appointment, the first Indian to command a battalion, the first Indian to be appointed an army commander.[9] Cariappa, however, is the lone star among direct commissioned officers of the pre-Sandhurst and pre-Indian Military Academy (I.M.A.) group. The vast bulk of these officers, about 50 in number (see data from Rudra above) came nowhere near matching this patrician Kodava (inhabitant of Coorg).

The most important contribution to the Indian officer corps, especially that all important group that formed the core high-command element of the Indian Army from the late 1950's to the late 1970's, came from the graduating classes of Sandhurst and the pre-war I.M.A. courses in the 1920's and the 1930's. A detailed study of their careers in these formative years is essential in order to obtain an understanding of the mind-set of the post-independent Indian Army officer corps. The following notes examine the contrasting experiences of the Indian officer cadets at Sandhurst and the I.M.A. Dehra Dun.

Boys in the Square

For much of the 1920's Indian candidates for Sandhurst were selected to sit for army entrance exams. Thus there was no open competition to enter this first entry phase. Some months before the exam, the Government of India informed local governments and administrators of the date fixed for the examination, and provided a press release stating the same. Applicants were usually asked to forward their names in the first instance to the Deputy Commissioners of their districts, who in turn would forward applications to the Deputy Commissioner, who in his turn would forward them to the local government. At any stage either of the three officials could reject an applicant. In some instances education authorities like the Prince of Wales

Royal Indian Military College (P.W.R.I.M.) were permitted to send names directly to the local government.[10]

According to paragraph 4 of the 'Provisional Regulations respecting Admission of Indian Gentlemen to the R.M.C., Sandhurst, England, 1925' -

> The general rule in selecting candidates should be that selections should be made from the communities which furnish recruits, in proportion to the numbers in which they can furnish such recruits. Regard should also be had to the claims to consideration of candidates from the educated middle classes.[11]

The appropriate authorities were specifically instructed to generally select candidates from the communities furnishing recruits for the army. This emphasis on the selection of candidates from the so called 'martial races' was the reason behind opting for a 'selection' process rather than a system of open competitive exams, and it would form the corner-stone of the recruiting policy for the next five years.

Candidates who filtered through to the local government level or were selected by the principal of the P.W.R.I.M. were called in for an interview by a Provincial Selection Board, presided over by the Governor. After this hurdle the candidate's name was sent to the Government of India and he was permitted to sit for a competitive entrance exam. This exam was comprised of a written test, a medical test, and an oral examination. It was administered by two senior military officers, and an educational officer. Finally the Viceroy himself participated in the process and selected candidates whose names were recommended to the Secretary of State for India for admission into Sandhurst.[12]

This daunting road to the gates of Sandhurst reflects not only the desire of the army and the Government of India to secure the best possible candidates, but also a desire to find the 'right type' of Indian cadet. This requirement envisioned an ideal Indian candidate of "martial race" stock, good breeding and other imperceptible social skills. Perhaps no candidate more so than Koodendera Subayya Thimmaya exemplified this ideal candidate. Like Cariappa, Thimmaya too hailed from Coorg – a bonafide if somewhat obscure "martial" district. The son of a wealthy coffee planter, Thimmaya (or Timmy as his friends knew him) attended school at St.

Joseph's College in Conoor. He and his brother were the first Indians to attend the school. They spent six years in a harsh boarding school environment run by Irish brothers, just the sort of upbringing that would garner the welcome attention of the Sandhurst recruiters. Nevertheless, after a particularly brutal punishment that resulted in lacerated knees from having to crawl on broken glass, Thimmaya and his brother finished their schooling at the more contemporary Bishop Cotton's School in Bangalore. Here too the two brothers were pioneering trail-blazers for other Indians.

When Thimmaya finished schooling in 1922, the P.W.R.I.M. was being opened, and he was perceived to be 'right type' for the college. According to his biographer, 'by this time his English was perfect. English manners were second nature to him. He was five feet nine, physically hard, and a good athlete.'[13] Thimmaya became one of 32 cadets in the first class at the P.W.R.I.M. The majority of the cadets in Thimmaya's batch, unlike him, were all connected to the military. Apparently the P.W.R.I.M. at this early stage was following the government's dictum of selecting candidates with a martial background. It also could have been that the P.W.R.I.M. provided the only opportunity for sons of the V.C.O.'s and the other ranks of the Indian Army to give their sons the required education for entry into Sandhurst. Whatever the case it was apparent that educational ability was not the primary criterion for entry into the P.W.R.I.M. Thimmaya's grades had been too low for entry into Oxford or Cambridge, but not the P.W.R.I.M. At Bishop Cotton's School Thimmaya had passed out with a mediocre academic record, but at the P.W.R.I.M. he found himself at the top in scholastic ability.

After his 18 months at Dehra Dun, Thimmaya went to Simla to sit for the Army Entrance Exam. The entire process was quite daunting. A British officer was attached to small groups of candidates to observe them minutely and report on their personality and 'deportment'. Any slip-up would result in termination of the exam for the unfortunate candidate. Thimmaya got through the written and oral exams quite easily even though he was unable to speak a word of Urdu in the oral language test. He was then interviewed by the Chief of General Staff, General Sir Claude Jacob, who, fortunately for Thimmaya, was able to recall seeing him playing excellent cricket at the P.W.R.I.M., thus bringing the interview to a successful conclusion. The next all important step was the final interview with the Viceroy himself. At the Viceroy's request Thimmaya launched into a lecture on his native Coorg and its coffee-based economy. The Viceroy stopped him in mid-speech with a question 'What games do you play?' Thimmaya replied 'Hockey, cricket, football, tennis, and squash'. He was through to Sandhurst.[14]

Thimmaya's progress through the entrance exams and the all-important interviews appears to have been quite smooth and even cursory. His westernized social graces, excellent communication skills and his scholastic ability appears to have carried him through. The fact that he was a highly successful graduate from the P.W.R.I.M. greatly helped his cause.

A casual glance at the list of 67 cadets admitted to Sandhurst between January 1919 and September 1924 indicates that the Government of India was strictly adhering to its 'right type' of Indian cadet. The vast majority of the entrants came from the Punjab; they included Sikhs, and Punjabi Hindus and Muslims.[15] It is also interesting to note that Anglo-Indians, who were so greatly over-represented in the exclusive Indian boarding schools such as Doon and Bishop Cottons were conspicuous by their absence. Only one – Herbert Arthur Francis – seems to have entered in September 1924, and was removed in 1926 for falling below the 'lowest standard' and for possessing a most 'unpopular personality'.[16]

It was this initial group of Sandhurst cadets that provided the bulk of the dismal reports that the Jacob and Skeen Committees made to the Government of India. A significant number of these early cadets appear to have been the sons of ex-Indian commissioned officers, or other ranks of the army, and they quite simply lacked the necessary education and mental adaptability to get through Sandhurst. A rare exception was Ayub Khan, son of Risaldar Major Mir Dad Khan Bahadur. Nevertheless, by the mid-1920's the Indian government was beginning to widen its recruiting base for Sandhurst cadets, and the educated middle class was the main beneficiary.

One such less than 'ideal type' of candidate was Jayanto Nath Chaudhuri (yet another future army chief) the son of a most 'un-martial' Bengali barrister in Calcutta. Chaudhuri, however, was somewhat fortunate in that he sent in his application while studying in England. He was called in by the India Office in London and interviewed by a 'small, bald, bright-eyed

Field Marshal'. During the interview Chaudhuri 'admitted to a comparatively undistinguished academic record and not much skill at sports', but got in nonetheless![17]

By 1927, however, entry into Sandhurst by interview selection had stopped. Henceforth all candidates sat for the same entrance exam for Sandhurst, Cranwell, and Woolwich as did the British candidates. In Exam 1, there were four sections:

1. English, 100 pts
2. General Knowledge, 100 pts
3. Interview and Record Test, 400 pts
4. One of the following: a. Modern language including oriental, b. General History, c. Elementary Maths d. Every Day Science, 100 pts. Exam 2 was also optional. The candidate could select one topic from Languages, Maths, Science and other subjects, 300 pts.

To secure entry into Sandhurst a candidate had to earn a minimum of 35% in the Interview and Record Test. To get into the Royal Military Academy (R.M.A.) Woolwich a candidate required a minimum of 40% in lower maths and physics or chemistry. The interview test with 300 pts was the most important part of the exam. The format, indeed, was quite similar to the Army Entrance Exam, the only difference being that the Indian candidates now went through exactly the same examination process as their British counterparts, with their papers being set and graded by Civil Service Commissioners in England.[18]

Those Indians who were fortunate and capable enough to survive the intense two year Sandhurst course were subjected to a remarkable process of indoctrination. Not only were the Indian cadets transformed into army officers, they were also given a good dose of elitist British socialization. Even highly Anglicized cadets like Thimmaya and Chaudhuri were jolted by the culture-shock of Sandhurst. The first shock the Indians had to endure was the ten week introductory course to which all Sandhurst cadets were subjected. During this period the cadets spent most of their free time drilling on the square, and were collectively referred to as 'Boys on the Square'. Their uniform for this ten week period was a coarse fatigue suit of brown denim, which nevertheless had to show gleaming buttons and razor-sharp creases! In case the new cadets forgot their lowly status, they were subject to constant abuse, first from the Sergeant Major, and then from the senior cadets. Once through this harrowing ten week period, the cadets lost their uniforms and gained a degree of respectability. They also settled down to absorb the more serious aspects of learning to become an officer and a gentleman. The 'on the square' period was a particularly good time for weeding out non-Western cadets of an aristocratic upbringing who were unwilling to subject themselves to iron discipline and ritualized abuse. Chaudhuri recalls a 'Mister Ali' of Egyptian noble stock who stalked off the square and Sandhurst enraged at the treatment he was receiving.[19] To most successful Indian cadets the ten week initiation and the subsequent military education they received was not a time of bitterness. Indeed, they remember it with a degree of awe and respect for their teachers; the raucous sergeant majors in particular. These incredibly loud and abusive soldiers who insisted on being called 'staff' and not sir appeared to have a good idea of the problems Indian cadets faced. S. D. Verma who joined Sandhurst in 1927 remembers feeling particularly dejected during his first term when he, the only Indian in his squad, was the least coordinated during drill. His flagging morale received a tremendous boost when the sergeant instructor noting his depression approached him and told him that he was learning drill the right way, from the bottom up, while the 'johnnies' who thought they knew everything would have to discard a lot of their misconceptions about drill.[20]

Coloured Men and White Women

Unfortunately, nearly none of the Indian alumni of Sandhurst recalled their stay in England with fondness from a social standpoint. For most of them, their very first contact with the British after stepping off the boat was a very cold formal affair. The Indian government and the India Office had arranged for every small group of Indians at Sandhurst to have an official guardian, usually a retired ex-Indian Army officer. The role of these guardians was more negative than positive. Instead of offering constant support and encouragement to the Indian cadets, they were there primarily to ensure that they did not get into trouble. Thimmaya took an instant dislike to his guardian Colonel Sturgess upon their first meeting. He recalls Sturgess as being more concerned about the cadets' ability to handle their finances and their morals than about the obvious emotional and cultural dislocation they were enduring.[21] The attitude of the official guardians often led to considerable friction between them and the parents of their charges. A glimpse into this tense relationship is available in the exchange of letters between a Colonel Stooks, the guardian of cadet Bilimoria, and Mr Bilimoria, the cadet's father. Instead of offering the faltering Bilimoria Jr. support and encouragement, Stooks immediately asked Mr Bilimoria for his permission to remove his son from the college. The ensuing exchange of angry letters finally resulted in Stook's stepping down as guardian to cadet Bilimoria.[22] Stooks indeed seems to have been generally disliked by most of the Indian cadets in his charge. In confidential talks with sub-committee members of the Indian Sandhurst Committee, at least three Indian cadets complained that Colonel, Stooks in addition to showing no sympathy for the cadets, never acknowledged their greetings, never shook their hands, and even made one of them wait in the rain for half an hour for a meeting.[23] Only cadets like Chaudhuri, who were fortunate enough to have British family friends nominated as their guardians in England, managed to experience warm British hospitality.[24] Most Indian cadets were stuck with their official guardians and had only themselves to rely upon for emotional support and social activities.

Under these circumstances it is not surprising that most Indian cadets formed tight-knit groups. To many of them this was their first experience as foreigners, and a sudden awareness of being 'Indians' came to the fore. By the time Chaudhuri entered Sandhurst in 1926, a tradition had developed whereby senior cadets would watch over each other and the new Indian cadets outside of Sandhurst. Indian cadets apparently had to maintain certain standards. Servants for instance, had to be tipped an astronomical five shillings weekly instead of the normal half-crown.[25] If an Indian GC (Gentleman Cadet) went to the movies he was always expected to buy the most expensive balcony seats. Snobbish and silly at first glance, these 'rules' of behavior appear to have been an attempt to carve a niche of respectability amidst a sea of subtle racial ostracism. The fact that many of the earlier batches of Indian cadets came from very wealthy princely families may also have contributed to this tradition.

Of greater interest, perhaps, is the tradition whereby Indian cadets generally avoided the Sandhurst end of the term dance. Chaudhuri feels that this custom had something to do with the taboo of 'coloured men and white women'.[26] Chaudhuri's official guardian, also a retired Indian Army colonel, who in addition to his other duties 'was also responsible for seeing that none of them [Indian cadets] took home a European wife.'[27] Indeed nowhere was the British hostility towards Indians on a social level more apparent than in their attempts to keep the Indian cadets away from white women. Years later, Thimmaya would recall the affront he and other Indian cadets felt when their official guardian Colonel Sturgess treated them as if they were all degenerates waiting only to be unleashed so that they could fall upon the unprotected womanhood of Britain.[28] When Thimmaya began to correspond with an English girl he had met at a community charity dance near Reading, Colonel Sturgess began to intercept and read letters from the girl addressed to Thimmaya. In fact Thimmaya's volatile relationship with Sturgess came to an end over a fracas that developed between the two after Thimmaya danced with a European girl while on a holiday in Switzerland.[29] The highly unpopular Colonel Stooks was also accused by at least one Indian cadet of banning Indian cadets from the dance floor.[30]

There can be little doubt that the relentless efforts by the British to separate the Indian Gentleman Cadets from white girls is evidence of racial prejudice and stereo-typing on the part of the British. Somewhat more ambiguous was the attitude of the Sandhurst authorities towards Indian cadets with regard to the college's sports activities. Indian cadets, no matter how much they excelled in a sport, could not participate in inter-battalion matches or prestigious match-ups with other colleges. One senior Sikh cadet, Sant Singh, was an outstanding hockey player, described by the local press as 'that dexterous red-bearded Indian....the most brilliant player we have seen in years'. However, at the time of picking players for the prestigious matches against Oxford and Cambridge, Sant Singh's name was dropped. In fact, he was never chosen to represent the college for any major game.[31] S.P.P. Thorat who was an excellent marksman was not allowed to take part in the rifle championship despite putting his name down to compete.[32] When another Indian dared to query as to why he was being dropped from a team, he was told that 'these minor sports had a social aspect.'[33] The real reason for their exclusion was never explained to the Indian cadets (see below), and these actions only served to convince the Indian cadets that they were victims of blatant racism.

Another form of discrimination practiced in Sandhurst against the Indians was in the appointment of Cadet Corporals, Sergeants and Under Officers. Only cadet Ayub Khan got promoted to the rank of Honorary (not actual) Corporal.[34] These ranks, especially that of Cadet Under Officer, carried great responsibility and authority, correspondingly conferring great respect on the deserving cadet. According to Chaudhuri -

> As the average British cadet went through his three terms at the R.M.C., all but a few real incompetents got promoted....This same convention regarding promotion unfortunately did not apply to foreigners.[35]

Thimmaya held the opinion that the discrimination against the Indians in sports was partly 'political' and partly 'snobbery'. He noted that in the past, Indians had earned 'blues' in sports and rank in the cadet corps. However, with the arrival of Gandhi and the Congress party, the British began to fear the prospect of Indian officers leading an uprising against them. So they sought to discourage the Indians as much as possible.[36] Thimmaya does not offer any evidence of this to his biographer, and it is doubtful if this was a primary motivation. Whatever the reason (see below), it only served to alienate the Indian cadets even further, and make them feel like outsiders and 'colonials'.

This discrimination against the Indians does not seem to have been transferred into their military education at Sandhurst. Although some evaluating officers frequently referred to 'the right type of Indian cadet' in their reports, there is no evidence to suggest that they were anything but professional and impartial in their judgments.[37] In 1926 the sub-committee of the Indian Sandhurst Committee questioned the Sandhurst authorities about the performance of Indian cadets in comparison with their British comrades. The latter, including the commandant General Corkran, felt that while Indian cadets compared quite well with the British cadets in general education and conduct, they lagged behind in leadership ability. They attributed this to 'the natural diffidence of Indians when as boys they are among a class of a different race.' However, the authorities were certain that with time this characteristic would wear off. This appears to be borne out in the case of at least one Indian cadet. S. P. P. Thorat who joined Sandhurst in

1925 recalls -

> In the beginning I suffered from a sense of inferiority complex vis-a-vs the British cadets. Never having mixed with Europeans in my school and college days in India, I was diffident about my ability to compete with them. Gradually I overcame this failing.....[38]

General Corkran also added that the same criticism could probably be made of a handful of 'British boys if you put them in a Indian Sandhurst.'[39] Corkran and his staff vehemently rejected any suggestion that the staff of the college were less sympathetic to Indian cadets. When asked if Indian cadets got along well with their British colleagues, the answer was yes provided they entered into the 'spirit of the R.M.C.'[40] Individual company commanders at Sandhurst who were interviewed by the sub-committee also declared Indian cadets to be on par with the average British cadets. Some of them (Thimmaya's name is mentioned) were considered to be 'very good'.[41] A review of the confidential reports of the Indian cadets who failed to get commissions shows that the most commonly cited weaknesses were lack of leadership ability, initiative, self-confidence, academic ability and communication skills.[42]

It is possible that the Sandhurst staff was trying to paint a encouraging picture for the Indian sub-committee members (M.A. Jinnah, Phiroze Sethna, and Zorawar Singh). Nonetheless, the evidence suggests that on a professional level the British appear to have been quite fair in their dealings with the Indian cadets. Thimmaya, Chaudhuri, and other successful Indian graduates of Sandhurst have attested to this in their memoirs.

A Touch of Class ?

The ambiguous nature of the discrimination the Indians at Sandhurst were put through can be attributed to the fact it was to a large extent class-based and not solely racial. Up until the mid-1850's recruitment to the British officer corps was essentially the sole preserve of the aristocracy and the landed gentry. The system of purchasing a commission via nomination by either the Commander-in-Chief, Sandhurst, or the Master General of Ordnance, Woolwich, and the extremely low pay ensured this. When the system of nomination and purchase were eventually abolished and competitive exams introduced, the aristocratic stranglehold on the system was loosened. However, the army was more than a little relieved to discover that almost all the entrants came from 'good homes'.[43] By happy coincidence, or as a result thereof, the army found itself drawing most of its new officer candidates from the rapidly expanding British public school system. The public schools provided the necessary socialization for the sons of the affluent British professional class to stand alongside the traditional aristocracy. A few elite British schools (approximately 23 in number) including Rugby, Eton, Harrow and St. Paul's supplied the majority of the officer cadets to Sandhurst and Woolwich right up to the Second World War. According to Maurice Garnier, in 1947 fully 65% of all Sandhurst entrants originated from a public school, and no less than 88% of them became cadet leaders. Even as late as 1957 53% of all cadets came from public schools, and 67% were cadet leaders. However, the number of elite public school cadets had dropped dramatically, so that by 1957 only 28% came from the elite schools, but a relatively high 44% were cadet leaders. By 1957 23% of the cadets came from the elite public schools and only 29% were cadet leaders.[44] An examination of the data on senior British Army officers from the rank of Lieutenant General upwards, shows that between 1870 to 1959 an overwhelming 90% came from the propertied and 'newly' elite professional classes. About 40% came from the old ruling class, mainly land-owning. Merely 3% of all senior officers came from a middle class background. None came from a working class background.[45] According to C. B. Otley -

> The great majority of [senior] officers studied had undergone a privileged minority education, an education lying wholly outside what might be called the 'state' sector. A handful of great boarding schools, produced a legion of army generals.[46]

The public schools and Sandhurst and Woolwich were part of the socialization effort to bring first professional and later even middle-class cadets up to the same level as the aristocracy. Research from the late 1960's and early 1970's of middle class British officer cadets reveals that the staff of Sandhurst felt that ideologically little had changed, and that the socialization of the middle class entrants was well under way.[47]

It is within this context that we must evaluate the attitudes of the British staff and cadets towards the Indian cadets. The Indian cadets who went to Sandhurst came from a markedly different social and educational background than that of their British colleagues. To begin with, the Indian officer corps did not evolve out of an old aristocratic tradition as did its British counterpart. It originated, instead, from a largely professional background – lawyers, government officials, doctors, etc. As a result of the nature of the colonial Indian Army, the traditional Indian elites, the princely class, and the great zamindars (land-lords), never had a great interest in the army. Barred from service as officers, few were desirous of serving with the rank and file. The I.C.C. and the honorary commissions granted to Indian princes were political moves by the British government to placate the Indian elites, to offer them an honorable avenue to serve in the army. When King's Commissions were finally granted to Indians, most British officers and civil servants hoped to create an Indian officer corps along British social lines.

The deliberate adoption of a process of nominating Indian cadets to Sandhurst was merely a throw-back to the British system in the pre-1850's era. The entire process was fine-tuned to ensure that the 'right type' of Indian cadets were sent to Sandhurst. As in Britain, qualifications for the officer corps were not decided by educational merit alone, but by social affiliation. On this basis the traditional elites were far more desirable than the educated Indian middle class, who were perceived by the British to be ideologically and politically unreliable. Senior British officers, like General Sir Edmund Barrow, made it clear that they were in favour of granting commissions to Indians of royal lineage. In 1912, Barrow called for the granting of field appointments to two such officers, Lieutenant Aga Casim Shah A.D.C. to General Officer Commanding 6th Poona Division, and Lieutenant Kanwar Amar Singh A.D.C. to General Officer Commanding 5th Mhow Division, saying,

> I consider both of them fit to take their place among British officers of an Indian cavalry regiment, whether in an educational, a professional or a social sense.....[48]

The real emphasis here was social for neither of the Indians had any professional military education to qualify them for a commission in the field (see above). Both, however, had impeccable social connections; Lieutenant Casim Shah, was the nephew of his Highness the Agha Khan, and Lieutenant Amar Singh came from the old Rajput Royal families of Jaipur and Jodhpur.

Unfortunately for the British the socially acceptable Indian candidate was not necessarily the best qualified, and so their attempt at social engineering failed. There are two primary reasons for this. In the first case many of the elite Indian youth selected lacked the educational and mental abilities to get them through Sandhurst. Secondly, it was the rapidly growing Indian middle class in the inter-war period that proved to be the more aggressive and well educated. As the Indian education system expanded and matured in the 1920's and 1930's the young men from the Indian professional, business and planter class began to monopolize it. The second most favoured group after the old aristocracy were the sons of Indian soldiers from the ranks. It was the poor performance of many of these cadets who made up the initial batches of Sandhurst cadets that ultimately opened the way for the Indian middle class.

If Indian cadets felt less than welcome on a social level in Sandhurst, they were in all probability confronting a class barrier alongside a subtle racial one. The British instructor officer who informed a Indian cadet that he was being kept out of a Sandhurst sports team to maintain social standards of behaviour was most probably telling the truth, and not covering up a blatant act of racism.[49] The overwhelmingly class-based discrimination practiced in Sandhurst was borne out by the fact that Indian cadets were not the only ones to feel the sting of British social elitism. British cadets, those rare ones that did not come from an 'acceptable' social background, were shunned ruthlessly by their upper-class colleagues. Thimmaya recalled the case of one such cadet by the name of Dalrymple who, despite winning the coveted Sword of Honour when he passed out of Sandhurst, was extremely unpopular amongst the socially elite cadets who rarely spoke to him.[50] Chaudhuri, too, noted that 'Among the British cadets, there seemed to exist a pattern of groups based on schools, common interests and old family friendships. It was a sort of caste system.....'[51] In the case of the Indian cadets at Sandhurst, not only were they considered socially inferior to the upper-class British, but they were also perceived as inferior 'natives'. This last perception condemned even the most aristocratic Indian cadets to some form of discrimination at Sandhurst. M.R.A. Baig, the scion of an old aristocratic Indian family (which claimed descent from a Turkish Sultan no less), and one of the few Indians to attend one of the 23 elite British public schools Clifton, recalled with some bewilderment -

> I entered Sandhurst in January 1923, and for the first time in my life encountered racial prejudice. Our position there was much the same as that of the Jewish boys at Clifton. We did not belong and were made to feel it.[52]

Baig, who had spent 13 years in England (1910 – 1923) prior to entering Sandhurst considered himself to be

> ...a young Englishman in everything except race, religion and color. To be suddenly treated like this by those who up to now had treated me as one of themselves gave me a wound from which I never recovered.[53]

The discrimination meted out to Indians at Sandhurst, therefore, arose from several different sources. The first and the most easily identifiable was racism itself. It, however, was accentuated and probably caused by an existing and entrenched class system in Sandhurst. The official guardians of the Indian cadets, the ex-Indian Army Colonels, were actually enforcing a class cum racial exclusiveness system not too different from the one practiced by the upper class British cadets. Another form of discrimination was institutional, with Indians being excluded from high visibility positions as cadet leaders and sports team members. In all probability the authorities in Sandhurst were trying to preserve the British identity of the college. They also might have been concerned about the possibility of a negative reaction from parents of current and future British cadets, if they saw too many Indians in high visibility positions like the sports team and as high ranking cadets in the corps.

An Impossible Situation

Although England itself was far more welcoming to the Indian cadets than Sandhurst, it remained an unfamiliar place for most of them. Cultural differences often resulted in acute home-sickness. Food, probably more than any thing else made the Indians – Hindu, Muslims, and Sikhs alike yearn for home. The problem was not religious sensibilities, the Sandhurst mess avoided this potential problem by serving Indian cadets mutton (goat/sheep meat) and eggs. Furthermore, many anglicized Hindus like Chaudhuri and Thimmaya had long since broken all dietary taboos back in India, while attending exclusive boarding schools. Food in England was a problem because it was extremely bland to the Indian palate – it lacked spice! Chaudhuri and his fellow Indian cadets were sustained by weekend trips to Shafi's in Gerard Street, one of only four Indian restaurants in London in 1926.[54]

Despite the fact that from the mid 1920's the success rate for Indian cadets at Sandhurst had greatly increased, the number of qualified applicants for the ten Sandhurst positions had not shown a great increase. This in turn fueled a growing fall in public confidence in India about the entire scheme. The Indian Sandhurst Committee pulled no punches in its report. Beginning with the initial application process, the committee regarded as

> ....seriously objectionable that the channel of application should be so rigidly official and that the intending candidate should have so many official stages to traverse.[55]

Regarding the actual process of sending cadets to Sandhurst, the committee acknowledged two permanent deterrents. First was the sheer cost of the whole endeavour to Indian parents. The committee noted that the cost of an 18 month course at Sandhurst to an Indian parent was Rs. 11,000.[56] If the pre-training costs at the P.W.R.I.M. Dehra Dun were added, this would add another Rs. 10,000 (serving or retired members of the Indian Army could pay substantially smaller amounts of Rs. 7,000 and Rs. 5,000 respectively). According to the report -

> It has been represented to us and we believe it to be true, that expenditure on this scale is altogether beyond the capacity of the average Indian parent belonging to the middle classes.[57]

Secondly, the average Indian parents were reluctant to send their sons to distant foreign lands. The main report and the secret sub-committee report both noted that the emotional trauma of separation was 'repugnant' to most parents and depressing to many cadets.

Noting the lack of educational and mental preparedness of Indian cadets sent to Sandhurst, the committee pointed out, ...it cannot be expected that the educational authorities will interest themselves in the special preparation of boys for the army or will introduce the changes which are certainly necessary in the educational system in the country, so long as the prizes to be gained are limited to ten vacancies in Sandhurst per annum for all of India....[58]

In the final analysis it was the necessarily limited spaces available at Sandhurst to Indian cadets which doomed that route to Indianization to failure. Although the report made no mention of it, there can be little doubt that a mere ten seats would not encourage many parents to urge their sons to go through the arduous application process. Even when the success rate of Indian cadets at Sandhurst went up, the institution could only absorb a limited number of Indian cadets. The problem was not the lack of space; the facilities could have been expanded, but as the report acknowledged -

In every educational institution there comes a time when the authorities responsible for its efficiency must set a limit to further acceptance of foreign students lest the character of the institution may be changed.[59]

The British Government had indicated to the Indian sub-committee that Sandhurst would be willing to accept a maximum of 5% of the establishment of Sandhurst (30) and Woolwich (12) as being reserved for Indian cadets.[60] Thus, the need to preserve institutional identity and not the inadequacy of Indian cadets to perform in a foreign environment resulted in a positive report for the establishment of an Indian Military Academy.

A Home At Last

Indeed, as the report had suggested, the I.M.A at Dehra Dun proved to be a vastly more friendly environment for Indian officer cadets. No longer would Indian cadets be looked upon as visiting 'natives'. This was an academy built specifically to cater to Indian needs and Indian cadets. The early batches of Indian cadets in the 1930's must have had a special bond with the college, for like them it was at an early stage of growth. All year round the cadets were surrounded by hectic building activity, as the

Sandhurst of the East began to take shape. Although the staff of the I.M.A. was predominantly English (exclusively till 1939) relations with the Indian cadets were markedly warmer. The precedent was set by the first commandant Brigadier Peter Collins (Gurkha Regiment) who worked very closely with the Indian cadets. The bonds of affection that tied Collins to the Indians can be gauged from the fact that they endearingly referred to Mrs. Collins as their 'mommandant'.[61] Mrs. Collins responded with typical affection, presenting eight coloured glass bowls to adorn the mess tables that were still bare.[62]

At the I.M.A. the Indian cadets could freely participate in all sporting and social events. The authorities at Sandhurst, probably touched by a twinge of conscience, made a gift of a magnificent champions silver cup trophy to the I.M.A. All of these activities helped build up the espritdecorps among the Indian cadets. Even though the Indian cadets at Sandhurst were proud of their links with the institution, their sense of belonging to an elite group was hamstrung by their exclusion from such crucial bonding activities. Finally the I.M.A. cadets had definite and identifiable goals of excellence to apply for. All could compete for Senior Cadet appointments as Lance Corporals, Sergeants and Under-Officers. Cadets were also eligible to compete for that greatest of prizes, the Sword of Honour. Cadet Smith Dun won the very first I.M.A. Sword of Honour in 1934.[63] Mess arrangements were a significant improvement over Sandhurst not only was the catering attuned to religious sensibilities, but the preparation of the food allowed for the more pungent and savoury proclivities of the Indian palate. In terms of cost, too, the I.M.A. was a great improvement over Sandhurst. The fees was set as Rs.800 for each of the first two terms and thereafter Rs. 750 per term. The total sum for the entire course was Rs. 3,850, a far more sustainable sum for an Indian middle class family of some means.[64]

In 1938, a government committee reviewing the performance of the I.M.A. cadets was relieved to learn that it was an unqualified success.[65] Three witnesses, Lieutenant Colonel Crawford, Major General R. D. Inskip, and Lieutenant Colonel E. E. Watson, were of the opinion that -

The young officers from the Indian Military Academy were considered

.....to be better trained than the average product of Sandhurst. Their tactical training was thorough and of a very high order and as platoon commanders they were considered superior to the old Viceroy Commissioned Officers.[66]

The Indian Government, having learned its lesson from past attempts to maintain a system of selection for Sandhurst cadets based purely on nomination, had decided to obtain candidates for the I.M.A. via a competitive exam system. The three part exam covered General Knowledge, Languages, Maths and Sciences, History, and Geography.[67] The primary emphasis, however, continued to be placed on the Interview and Record Test which accounted for a total of 500 out of 2,000 or 2,150 pts.[68] It was quite possible for a cadet to pass or fail the entrance exam based purely upon his performance in the interview test. Take the case of Lieutenant General Gul Hasan Khan (Pakistan Army).

> In March 1940, I appeared for the competitive entrance examination to the Indian Military Academy......I managed to fail, not because of ignorance in academic subjects but because I was late for my interview, which carried five hundred marks. The Board did not takekindly to it......the crux of the examination, provided one was an average student, was to hope for good marks in the interview. Six months later I appeared again and on this occasion I made certain I was not late. I passed, being seventh out of the fifteen who were not normally selected.[69]

Successful candidates like Jagjit Singh Aurora and Mohammed Attiqur Rahman usually obtained 400 plus marks in this test (460/500 and 500/500). Aurora's total score was a very low 1,087 out of 2,150, and his rank was dead last out of a total of 41 candidates who passed the exam in October 1935. There is little doubt that Aurora would not have passed the exams without having scored high marks with the interview board.[70] As in the P.W.R.I.M., the emphasis at the I.M.A. was on character rather than academic accomplishment. Whatever the interviewing formula used, it seems to have worked. A cursory glance at the post-independence Indian/Pakistani officers who made senior rank indicates that a substantial portion of the most successful ones did exceptionally well in the Interview test.

TABLE 3 [71]
List of candidates securing 400 plus in the interview test.
March 1933 to April 1939

MARCH 1933
Joginder Singh Dhillon 450/500
OCTOBER 1933
Mohinder Singh Pathania
OCTOBER 1934
Gopal Gurunath Bewoor 425/500
Jemi H.F. Manekshaw 405/500
MARCH-APRIL 1935
Niranjan Prasad 450/500
Sukhwant Singh 400/500
Krishna Lal Thapan 405/500
OCTOBER 1935
Agha Mohammed Ayub Khan 490/500
MARCH-APRIL 1936
Gurbax Singh 490/500
MARCH-APRIL 1937
Mohammed Attiqur Rahman 500/500
Mirza Sikander Ali Baig 460/500
OCTOBER 1937
Sartaj Singh 465/500
Dharti Kumar Palit 465/500
APRIL 1939
Mohammed Asghar Khan 460/500
Sahebzada Yakub Khan 500/500

In 1943, as a result of the devastating losses suffered by the Indian/British armies in 1941 and 1942, the lengthy entrance exam process was given up in favour of a faster selection process. Groups of eight candidates were kept under a Group Testing Officer. They were put through a battery of psychological tests, individual and group obstacle tests, group discussions and then a final interview. According to General S. K. Sinha during the height of the war – 1942 to 1943 – selection standards for officers had been greatly relaxed and just about anyone who applied was taken in. However, by 1944 as the allies were on the threshold of victory, the authorities became much more circumspect in their selection. Sinha recalls that in his batch of 60 applicants, only 12 were selected.[72] The accelerated Officer Training Courses at Mhow, Bangalore and Belgaum were probably opened at the same time the new wartime selection system was introduced at the I.M.A. Although there were three other Officer Training programmes during the war, all prospective candidates had to enter the via the Dehra Dun selection process.

The I.M.A. was able to produce an average of 28 officers each half-year. They were commissioned as Second Lieutenants in the Special List, Indian Land Forces for a one year period. Generally not more than two I.C.O.'s were attached to one British unit, where, after an interval of four months, they were asked to state a unit of their preference; care was taken to ensure that they were posted to Indian units as often as possible.[73]

Even before the I.M.A. went into operation, in 1931 the decision was made to expand the 'eight units' to the equivalent of a war division, along with its artillery, armoured car and other support units. More crucially Indian officers hitherto restricted to staff duties were henceforth allowed to do staff work and cooperate with other units, thus qualifying them for higher command positions.[74] The expansion of the 'eight unit' scheme to a full division was official acknowledgement of the fact that the first phase of Indianization was working. As the I.M.A. swung into high gear, more and more Indian officers began to join the army, and by 1938 the division had a cavalry brigade attached to it. In April that year, the Indian Air Force (I.A.F.), too, literally got off the ground with two flights operating from Peshawar and Drigh Road respectively.[75]

The instructors at Sandhurst and the I.M.A. had done their jobs; once again the burden fell upon the somewhat steadier shoulders of the starry-eyed green Indian Second Lieutenants to prove to the British and indeed their own countrymen in the ranks that they were fit to command. The experiences of these officers in the formative stages of their army careers amidst an all-white elitist organization must be examined in order to understand the character of the independent Indian Army.

Notes

1   S. K. Brown to Governor General of India in Council, 1925 mo? BL/IOR, L/MIL/5/844, 30.

2   They included 7 captains and 2 lieutenants. BL/IOR, Mss.Eur.F.111/442, 22-24.

3   '....steps are being taken respecting the grant of commissions to nine Indian officers belonging to the Native Indian Land Forces who have served in the Field....', See telegram from Secretary of State to Army Dept, Simla, 20 August 1917, BL/IOR, L/MIL/7/19006, 110.

4   Whose diary I have referred to extensively in the first chapter. See also – Lloyd I. Rudolph, 'Self as Other: Amar Singh's Diary as Reflexive "Native" Ethnography', in *Modern Asian Studies*, Vol 31, No 1, (1997), pp.143-75.

5   De Witt C. Ellinwood, 'The Special Experiences of Amar Singh', paper presented at Conference on South Asia, November 1994, University of Wisconsin at Madison, p.8.

6   Lloyd I. Rudolf, 'A Soldier of the Raj? Amar Singh's military career', Ibid, p.21.

7   The details of Rudra's experiences are detailed in a letter written by him to Jack Gibson, formerly head-master of the Doon School, on 9 March 1989, Mss.Eur.C.478.

8   *Report of the Indian Sandhurst Committee,14 November 1926*, (London: H.M.S.O., 1927), pp.5-7.

9   I. M. Muthanna, *General Cariappa*, (Mysore: Usha Press, 1964), p.27.

10   The Prince of Wales Royal Indian Military College (P.W.R.I.M.) was established in March 1922, specifically to prepare cadets for entry into Sandhurst.

11   *Report of the Indian Sandhurst Committee*, p.8 (note).

12   Ibid, p.9.

13   Humphrey Evans, *Thimmaya of India: A Soldiers Life*, (New York: Harcourt, Brace & Co, 1960), p.40.

14   Thimmaya entered Sandhurst in September, 1924. Ibid, p.56. An interview with the Viceroy was a awe-inspiring moment for the young officer cadets. General S.P.P. Thorat was overwhelmed by the situation that he addressed the Viceroy as 'Your Majesty', which drew a smile from the usually impassive face of Lord Reading. Lieutenant General S.P.P. Thorat, *From Reville to Retreat*, (New Delhi: Allied Publishers, 1986), p.4.

15   See list of Indian Cadets at R.M.C. Sandhurst, BL/IOR, L/MIL/9/319, 97-102.

16   Confidential Reports on Indian Cadets sent to Sandhurst under the Indianisation policy, BL/IOR, L/MIL/9/319, 29.

17   'Muchu' Chaudhuri, 'Sandhurst Revisited', *Blackwood's Magazine*, Vol. 306., No. 1847., September 1969, p.194.

18   Provisional Regulations Respecting Admission of Indian Gentlemen to the Royal Military Academy Woolwich, The Royal Military College Sandhurst, and Cranwell. (Calcutta: Government of India Central Publication Branch, 1928). BL/IOR, L/MIL/17/5/2290, 3-8.

19   'Muchu' Chaudhuri, 'Sandhurst Revisited', p.198.

20   Lieutenant General S. D. Verma, *To Serve With Honour: My Memoirs*, (New Delhi: UBS Publishers, 1988), p.6.

21   Humphrey Evans, *Thimmaya of India*, pp.59-60. General S. D. Verma's official guardian a Colonel Stooks lived in Yately some three miles from Sandhurst, and on the first Sunday of every month Verma and the other Indian cadets under Stooks charge had to bicycle over to receive their monthly pocket-money of three pounds. Verma notes "It was our money, but we had no direct control over it." S. D. Verma, *To Serve With Honour*, p.9.

22   The unfortunate cadet Rustom Manekji Billimoria, a parsee, was finally removed from Sandhurst after being described as "distinctly below average" in the official report. Letters October to December 1928, BL/IOR, S. K. Brown Collection, Mss.Eur.D.808/1, 68-77.

23   *Indian Sandhurst Committee: Report of the Sub-Committee which visited various military education institutions in England and other countries*, (Simla: Government of India Press, 1926), pp.97-104.

24   'Muchu' Chaudhuri, "Sandhurst Revisited", p.202.

25   There was a room servant at Sandhurst for every two-three cadets on the same floor.

26   Ibid, p.200.

27   Ibid, p.202.

28   Humphrey Evans, *Thimmaya of India*, p.60.

29   Ibid, pp.72-74.

30   Cadet Raza noted that as a result his holiday in Switzerland was ruined. See Raza's confidential interview in *Indian Sandhurst Committee: Report of the Sub-Committee*, p.100.

31   Humphrey Evans, *Thimmaya of India*, p.64. Sant Singh was the 49th Indian cadet to enter Sandhurst (January 1925). He retired as a General in the independent Indian Army. BL/IOR, L/MIL/9/319, 111.

32   *Indian Sandhurst Committee: Report of the Sub-Committee*, p.104.

33   'Muchu' Chaudhuri, 'Sandhurst Revisited', p.202.

34   Mohammed Ayub Khan, *Friends Not Masters: A Political Autobiography*, (London: Oxford University Press, 1967), p.10.

35   'Muchu' Chaudhuri, 'Sandhurst Revisited', p.201. This opinion is backed by

Cadet H.A. Francis who noted that Indian cadets were refused stripes on the grounds that they were incompetent. However, inferior British cadets were often awarded stripes. A point readily attested to by cadet S.P.P. Thorat who stated that British cadets inferior to him were given stripes. Cadet Raza pointed out that every British cadet who did not get restriction (punishment) managed to get a stripe. He felt that this was a deliberate policy to prevent Indians from commanding British cadets. See confidential interviews in *Indian Sandhurst Committee: Report of the Sub-Committee*, pp.99-104.

36 Humphrey Evans, *Thimmaya of India*, p.65.

37 See Confidential Reports on Indian Cadets, BL/IOR, L/MIL/9/319.

38 Lieutenant General S.P.P. Thorat, *From Reveille to Retreat*, (New Delhi: Allied Publishers, 1986), p.5.

39 *Indian Sandhurst Committee: Report of the Sub-Committee*, Annexure I, p.79.

40 Ibid, 83-4.

41 Ibid, Annexure III., p.95.

42 Ibid, Annexure IX., pp.106-16.

43 C. B. Otley, 'The Social Origins of British Army Officers', *The Sociological Review*, Vol 18., No. 2., July 1970, p.216.

44 Maurice G. Garnier, 'Changing Recruitment Patterns and Organizational Ideology: The case of a British Military Academy', *Administrative Science Quarterly*, Vol 17., No 4., December 1972, pp.503.

45 C. B. Otley, 'Social Affiliations of the British Army Elites', in Jacques Van Doorn (ed.), *Armed Forces and Society: Sociological Essays*, (The Hague: Moutan & Co, 1968), pp.88-89.

46 Ibid, p.102.

47 Maurice Garnier, 'Recruitment and Ideology', p.505.

48 Barrow Collection, Commissions for Indians: Journal of the Army, Letter from General Officer Commanding Southern Army, General Sir. Edmund Barrow, to Major General M.H.S. Grover, Military Secretary to His Excellency the Commander-in-Chief, A.H.Q. Calcutta, 12 March, BL/IOR, Mss.Eur.E.420/9, 2.

49 'Muchu' Chaudhuri, "Sandhurst Revisited", p.202.

50 Humphrey Evans, *Thimmaya of India*, p.66.

51 'Muchu' Chaudhuri, 'Sandhurst Revisited', p.209.

52 M.R.A. Baig, *In Different Saddles*, (Bombay and Calcutta: Asia Publishing House, 1967), pp.32-3.

53 Ibid, p.34.

54 'Muchu' Chaudhuri, 'Sandhurst Revisited', p.201.

55 *Report of the Indian Sandhurst Committee*, pp.14-15.

56 According to General S. P. P. Thorat who entered Sandhurst in 1924, the

total cost of education at Sandhurst including leave expenses was around Rs.20,000. The amount had to be deposited with the Government before the candidate could appear for the entrance exam for Sandhurst. Thorat, *Reville to Retreat*, p.3.

57   Ibid, p.16.

58   Ibid, p.21.

59   Ibid, p.37.

60   Ibid, Chapter 2.

61   Philip Mason, *A Matter of Honour: An Account of the Indian Army its Officers and Men*, (New York: Holt, Reinhart and Winston, 1974), p.466.

62   Sinha and Chandra, *Valor and Wisdom*, p.134.

63   Dun was also the first I.M.A. Gentleman Cadet Under-Officer, and was parade commander in 1934.

64   Regulations Respecting Admission to the I.M.A. Dehra Dun and for First Appointments to His Majesty's Indian Land Forces, 1931, BL/IOR, L/MIL/17/5/2284, 7.

65   In September 1938, the Government of India accepted a resolution passed by the Indian Legislative Assembly – it was adopted in terms of the recommendation of the Skeen Committee – that the operation of the Indian Sandhurst [I.M.A.] should be reviewed five years after its inauguration. Although the committee could not complete its work due to the outbreak of the war, its incomplete report does give an interesting insight into the quality of the cadets for the I.M.A. *Legislative Assembly Debates*, 1938, p.1525.

66   Quoted in Bisheswar Prasad (ed.), *Expansion of the Armed Forces (1939-1947)*, p.179.

67   Ibid, 4.

68   The total number of marks increased from 1,900 in October 1932 to 2,150 in October 1935.

69   Lieutenant General Gul Hassan Khan (The Last Commander-in-Chief of the Pakistan Army), *Memoirs*, (Karachi and Oxford: Oxford University Press, 1993), p.9.

70   Pamphlet of the Competitive Examination for Admission to the I.M.A., Dehra Dun and the R.I.N., October, 1935, BL/IOR, L/MIL/17/5/2282, 26.

71   Ibid, 20-37.

72   Lt. General S. K. Sinha, *A Soldier Recalls*, (New Delhi: Lancer International, 1992), p.36.

73   While on the Special List, Indian Land Forces, the Indian officers could continue to wear I.M.A. uniform. They were outfitted with camp and kit allowances of up to Rs. 670 and Rs. 100 respectively. They were also issued a revolver, compass and field glasses. Ibid, 4-5.

74   S. K. Brown Lecture to I.D.C. October 1931, BL/IOR, L/MIL/5/857.

75   Indianisation of the Army and Formation of I.A.F., (New Delhi: Government of India Press, 1938), BL/IOR, L/MIL/17/5/1800, 1, 18.

Indian Officers on Sunday Parade, Sandhurst, 1932
Prince Cherabol of Siam (Thailand) on extreme left
© Pradeep Barua

Chapter 4
Wogs in the Mess
The Introduction of Indian Officers into the
Colonial Indian Army1919-1947

On 16 March 1929 a young Indian Second Lieutenant was embarked upon his journey from Nasirabad to Jullunder to join his new Regiment, the 7th Light Cavalry. As he approached his destination, Lieutenant Chaudhuri realized 'that this was the test, the crucial posting on which the future would depend.'[1] Along with other Indian officers commissioned after Sandhurst, Chaudhuri had completed a brief 'acclimatizing' one-year stint with a British unit, the 1st Battalion, North Staffordshire Regiment in Nasirabad. Now he was on his way to join his permanent unit, the 7th Light Cavalry. The 'future' that Chaudhuri mentions was not just his own personal future in the Indian Army, but that of the entire Indianization policy. Unlike at Sandhurst and the I.M.A., the new young Indian officers were usually on their own in their new units. The pressures upon them to perform in the field were immensely greater than any they had known in the military schools. These pressures were not only due to the fact that they were isolated, but because they had finally come into contact with the rank and file of the Indian Army. Based upon the unsatisfactory performance of the I.C.C. and other direct-commissioned officers who had preceded the Sandhurst and I.M.A. cadets, the British officers and Indian soldiers had a rather jaundiced view of the new aspirants.

Often one of the first distasteful confrontations experienced by Indian officers when they joined a unit was that of blatant racism, very different from the subtle version practiced in Sandhurst. Chaudhuri recalls the Second in Command of the North Stafford's who habitually belted out epithets for Indians, such as 'wog', 'niggers', or 'nig-wigs'. When Chaudhuri politely expressed his discomfort at the Major's use of such language, the latter expressed genuine surprise, noting that he did not think Chaudhuri would mind, for he considered him as 'one of us'.[2] General S. D. Verma also recalls 'I was called a wog in my own mess....chaps five to ten years older treated me as a pariah.'[3] John Masters, a former British Indian Army officer, echoed these views in his memoirs. He notes -

Some British Regiments treated their attached Indian Army subalterns like dirt. One even made them sit at a separate table in the mess.[4]

Other British units, however, mindful of the delicate nature of the job of introducing young Indian officers into an army career, seem to have gone the proverbial extra mile to make them feel at home. Thimmaya remembered that when he first joined the Highland Light Infantry in Bangalore for his one year stint, the British officers of that unit were extremely concerned that they not cause him any offense, noting

> you're the first Indian officer we've seen. Headquarters said we'd have to handle you tactfully. We mustn't be snide about Indians in front of you. Mustn't give you beef. We want you to like it here, and we're worried we might drop some bricks.[5]

Even when the young Indian officers were posted to their permanent units, they continued to face varying degrees of resistance. S.P.P. Thorat was posted to his permanent unit the 1st battalion of the 14th Punjab Regiment in 1927, and recalled

> .....the attitude of some Britishers towards their brother officers was not what it should have been. This was particularly noticeable in their social behavior which bordered on being hostile. They made no secret that Indians were not wanted as officers. We were forbidden to bring Indian food or play Indian music even in our own rooms. Some British officers did not allow their wives to dance with Indians in the club; in short we were treated as outcasts.[6]

Some Indian officers including Brigadier 'Tony' Bhagat and General J. S. Aurora believed that the British officers actually tried to segregate the Indian officers in a seperate mess. 'Tony' Bhagat noted

> .....at one time it was proposed that the Indian commissioned officers should have a separate mess. But I think it was soon realised that that was going to make it extremely difficult for Indian officers to get the respect that they must have if they were going to command troops. So mercifully it was not put into practice.[7]

Aurora recalled that the British were determined to preserve the Anglo-Indian rituals of the mess and food became a major point of confrontation. According to Aurora -

> The Indian meals were limited to two lunches a week, and the rest of the time the food had to be British, whereas for most of us [Indians] British food did not suit our palate. Therefore we had to find ways and means of supplementing it and even having food from the Jawans [privates] messes.....[8]

At Singapore J. S. Aurora was transferred from his post as messing member when he tried to get the cook to fry the vegetables instead of boiling them every day. In Chaudhuri's unit Sunday lunch was the only occasion when Indian food was served. And he recalls the jubiliation amongst Indian officers of their sister Indianized Regiment the 16th Light Cavalry, when after a 'long struggle' they managed to introduce a 'mildly curried' vegetable dish with every meal. Like Aurora, Chaudhuri and his fellow Indian officers had to satiate their yearning for spice by taking 'substantial' samples during inspections of the troops' meals. Other gastronomic tactics used included the tradition of relying upon the culinary skills and hospitality of the wives of married Indian officers. In certain desperate situations, Indian meals were clandestinely ordered to the tent of the temporarily attached Indian medical officer who was not a member of the regiment, and hence not subject to its dietary restrictions. After the official dinner the Indian officers would converge upon their hapless host's tent to devour their curry.[9]

The Model Indian Officer

Thimmaya selected the 4th battalion, 19 Hyderabad Regiment as his home Regiment. The unit was stationed in Bagdhad and he joined it in March 1927. Here Thimayya discovered that he had to earn the respect not only of his British colleagues but also that of the Indian soldiers. Most of the men associated command ability and education almost exclusively with British/white officers. Their negative opinions of Indian leadership were confirmed with the first batch of Indian officers. However, as more capable officers like Thimayya and Chaudhuri entered the army, the Indian soldiers were quick to give them the same respect and loyalty they had given to their

British officers.[10] Thimayya himself proved to be popular with both his Indian soldiers and the British officers of the regiment. While at Bagdhad, Thimayya was the first Indian appointed assistant provost marshal of the British garrison.[11] Thimmaya was fortunate in that his first three Commanding Officers, Colonel Hamilton-Britton, Colonel Nicholls and Lieutenant Colonel Lewis treated him fairly, and were even supportive. Under Nicholls, Thimmaya was made temporary Battalion Adjutant until he passed his Captaincy exams. At a social level, too, Thimayya found that he was well received by his British colleagues. He and his French educated wife Nina (also from Coorg) were sought after company by British families.[12]

As the Indian officers gained in seniority and experience, their self-confidence increased accordingly. In late 1939 Thimmaya's Battalion was transferred to Singapore. The new CO and his Second in Command were the dreaded 'koi-hai' ('anyone there') type,[13] still locked in the 1857 mode of thought and relations between the unit's Indian and British officers reached a new low. In Singapore the CO's mishandling of the situation led to a mutiny by the Jat and Ahir companies. The situation was prevented from getting out of hand when Thimmaya had a personal meeting with the soldiers and convinced them to stop their mutiny. He then went over the head of his protesting CO to the Fortress Commander Major General Fitzsimmons to have the soldiers armed for an exercise on the shooting range. This show of trust worked, just as Thimmaya had foreseen, thus nipping the mutiny in the bud. Although Thimmaya had to transfer out of the Battalion in October 1941 due to an unworkable relation with his CO, his reputation was in no way sullied by the incident.[14] Indeed in 1942 at the recommendation of General Polk, Commander-in-Chief Eastern Command, Thimmaya (now a major) was sent to the Staff College at Quetta.[15] He graduated second in his class of 140 and chose 'combined operations' as his first choice and specified a G-2 operations appointment in the field as his second choice. As second ranked in his class, Thimmaya had every right to apply for these positions. However, no Indian had ever been appointed to this high-profile operational post, and here the British balked. Thimmaya, to his great chagrin, received the usual G-2 staff duty appointment given to all Indians graduates of the staff college. Once again Thimmaya stood his ground and refused the appointment. His luck held and he was posted as G-

2 operations in the 25th Division.[16] Thimmaya's appointment as G-2 to the 25th Division created a problem, for the divisional commander Major General Davies had been trying for some time to get his G-3 a Englishman who had not yet gone to staff college into that post. However, all G-2 appointments were made by Army Headquarters and the Chief of General Staff, Lord Auchinleck sent General Davies 'a most imperial rocket' informing him that Thimmaya was the man for the job.

Thimmaya's arrival at the 25 Div HQ was not exactly welcome, or so he thought. But after a frank discussion with General Davies, Thimmaya was relieved to know that the General had nothing against him or Indian officers.[17] Thimmaya like many other Indian officers was being overly sensitive to any perceived hostility from the British. This, not surprisingly, led to considerable misunderstanding, but his ability to communicate his apprehensions to his British superiors solved any potential problems that might arise.

No sooner had Thimmaya settled his differences with his CO, the 25th found itself confronting the Japanese at Mungadaw in Burma. There Thimmaya was promoted to Lieutenant Colonel and took command of the 8th Battalion, 19th Hyderabad Regiment. He recalls -

> I felt a marveleous thrill of pleasure at having full command of the battalion.....but then a sense of responsibility settled on my back like heavy burden.[18]

Thimmaya could not have assumed command at a worse time. For various reasons morale in the battalion was very low and little real patrolling was being done. Nevertheless Thimmaya whipped the unit into shape and organized a successful night-attack to take a well defended 400ft hill which guarded the approaches to the Mayu Range.[19] Thimmaya's handling of the battalion in action, probably a first for any Indian, was cause for great relief amongst the high command who had placed so much trust in the young Indian officer. No less a person than the corps commander himself called to congratulate Thimmaya. The corps commander noted that in the entire corps so many Japanese had never been killed in a single engagement.[20] The rewards were quick to follow; after a months' leave in India he was made temporary G-1 of the Division.[21] On Thimmaya's return, his battalion took part in a crucial battle against Japanese-held tunnels in the Mayu range. Here for the first time, three Indian battalions commanded by three Indian Lieutenant Colonels - Thimmaya, L.P. Sen and S. P. P. Thorat - took part in the same battle. Thimmaya's battalion took not only its assigned hill feature 'Poland', but also 'Pt 109' assigned to Sen's battalion, much to the latter's consternation.

The tremendous success garnered by Thimmaya came to the notice of the Supreme Commander, Lord Louis Mountbatten, who publicly touted Thimmaya as the model successful Indian officer.[22] In the ongoing offensive against the Japanese, Thimmaya's battalion along with those of Thorat and Sen were assigned to support a British commando attack to secure the beachhead at Kangaw.[23] Once again the three Indian-led battalions performed splendidly, and broke the back of the Japanese defenses.[24] After a well-deserved rest period Thimmaya returned to Burma to command the 36th brigade of the 26th Division, becoming the first Indian to command a brigade in the field (Ramri Island).[25] His brigade was the first to enter Rangoon, where ironically it captured his elder brother who joined the Indian National Army (I.N.A.) there.[26] Months later the Japanese surrendered. His last appointment in the field before independence came as commander of the 268th infantry brigade, part of the British-Indian Division assigned to the British Commonwealth Forces for the occupation of Japan. In January 1947 he returned to India to join the Indian Armed Forces Naturalization Committee.

Chaudhuri's experience as a new officer in the 7th Light Cavalry, largely mirrored those of Thimmaya. He, too, had to win the confidence of the Indian soldiers of the regiment who were not only unimpressed with the Indian officers preceding him, but were distinctly sceptical about the abilities of a Bengali officer.[27] Although his ascent up the promotion ladder was not quite as dramatic as Thimmaya's it was steady. Just prior to the onset of hostilities in 1939, he qualified for entrance into the Staff College Quetta.[28] After completing the course (December 1939 - June 1940) he was posted as GSO-3 Operations to HQ 5th Indian Division in Secundrabad. In his new posting, Chaudhuri experienced the same opposition to his arrival just as Thimmaya had. Colonel Messervy (the GSO-1 for 5th Division) informed Chaudhuri that he was being transferred to G-3 Chemical Warfare, the reason given was that

Operations had to handle a number of top secret matters and just – then he did not think it appropriate to have an Indian officer in the – post.[29]

Unlike Thimmaya, Chaudhuri swallowed his anger and pride and accepted the transfer. Later he practically filled in the more senior position of the GSO-2 Operations who was constantly drunk! During the war, Messervy himself went on to win great fame as an armoured division commander in the Western Desert and as a corps commander in Burma. Years later in 1946, when Chaudhuri (then a Colonel) was Director Armoured Corps, HQ ALFESEA in Singapore, he ran into Messervy who was General Officer Commander-in-Chief Malaya. Something about the quiet and efficient Chaudhuri must have impressed him for by then he had lost all doubts about the quality of Indian officers; after apologizing profusely for his previous actions, he promptly offered Chaudhuri a position on his staff as Brigadier in charge of administration. Chaudhuri, taken aback by the sudden and overly-generous offer declined initially, but Messervy insisted and Thimmaya soon joined his staff in Kuala Lumpur.[30]

In October 1940 Chaudhuri's division sailed for Post Sudan in North Africa where he served in various staff appointments. Although Chaudhuri did not see any action, in 1943 he was posted as instructor to the Staff College Quetta. Here too he faced resistance. General Evans the commandant of the college said

> I am unhappy to have you here. You are a junior officer and there – are many senior British officers in the course. You will have to – use all your tact to ensure that there is no trouble.[31]

Fortunately Chaudhuri got along well with all the officers, and General Evans soon had every confidence in his young Indian instructor. After his tour at Quetta, Chaudhuri was posted to the 16th Light Cavalry for operations in Rangoon, Burma, which is where he ended his wartime career.[32] He was selected by General Auchinleck to lead the Indian victory contingent in London, in March 1946. Along with Cariappa, he became one of the first Indians to be selected to attend the Imperial Defence College (I.D.C.), London. In November 1947 he returned to Delhi to become Brigadier (Plans) at Army HQ.[33]

The Black Sheep

Thimmaya and Chaudhuri represent two of the most successful types of Indian officers. Included in this elite group are others like Cariappa, L.P. Sen, and S.P.P. Thorat, to mention but a few. However, there were an equal number of less than impressive officers. Earlier we learned that the small district of Coorg in South India was responsible for producing two of the most able Indian officers - Cariappa and Thimmaya. Unfortunately Coorg also produced one of the glaring failures of the Indianization process - C.B. Ponappa.

Along with Cariappa and Thimmaya, Ponnappa, too, benefitted from the availability of excellent Catholic education. He and his brother were educated at St. Alyosis College High School (graduating in 1915).[34] In 1918 he, along with Cariappa, was called up for training at the Daly College, Indore (renamed as the Training School for Indian Cadets). He and Cariappa became two of 39 cadets who were granted temporary King's Commissions on 1 December 1919. He was then posted to Tekrit in Iraq where he joined the 116 Marathas. Ponnappa appears to have taken part in some minor actions against Arab forces and was mentioned in despatches. On 21 May 1921 he and his unit arrived in Lahore to assist the local authorities trying to suppress the Sikh (Akali) agitation. It was here that Ponnappa had his first big clash with authority. According to Ponnappa, his battalion commander Lieutenant Colonel Marsh refused him permission to get married, but he was undaunted, and corresponded with Major General Black the commandant of the Daly College cadet wing, and finally secured leave to get married. When Ponnappa returned to his unit in the summer of 1922 he discovered that Colonel Marsh had left him an adverse annual report. The Colonel noted that Ponnappa was argumentative, sulky and unpopular, and recommended that he should not be retained in the Indian Army.[35] Despite these troubles Ponnappa managed to successfully pass his Captain's exam in March 1926. The battalion was then transferred to Quetta, where Ponnappa was made Battalion Quarter Master. Here too he appears to have had a number of tiffs with the new commander Colonel Franks.

On 1 April 1933 Ponnappa was posted to the Madras University Training Corps as its Adjutant. He rejoined his battalion on 1 April 1936 and was placed on the Special Unemployed List, from 1 April 1937.[36] But for the onset of the Second World War, it is likely Ponnappa's Indian Army career would have ended then and there. When the war broke out, however, he was recalled to duty at the Maratha Regimental Centre in Belgaum. He became commander of the 11th Maratha Territorial Battalion, which spent the war as a railway protection force in India. In 1946 he was made a full Colonel and was made president of the Officers Services Selection Board. His job was to select officers from permanent commission in the Indian Army from among those who were granted temporary commission during the Second World War. Once again his actions resulted in controversy. This time he was called to Meerut to meet the Director of the Service's Selection Board, Brigadier Raza, to answer charges that he was anti-Muslim in his selection duties.[37] This serious problem seems to have been resolved in Ponnappa's favour for he soon became president of the Board himself. It is possible that the partition of India at this time may have assisted Ponnappa, for Raza opted for service with Pakistan. However, soon afterwards he was posted to Allahabad as Brigade commander of the sub-area. This was followed by a number of similar postings till his retirement in 1952, still with the rank of Brigadier.

Ponnappa's career in the Indian Army was troubled to say the least. He appears to have been in constant conflict with his British colleagues and senior officers. Although Ponnappa has claimed that the crux of the issue was their anti-Indian attitudes, it is unlikely that he did not come across a single fair-minded British officer as his autobiography seems to imply. The problem appears to have been more a question of his own personality. He appears to have been the opposite of his fellow Coorgis, Cariappa and Thimmaya, who were quite outgoing and popular with their British colleagues. Another source of the problem might have been the nature of Ponnappa's commission. It appears that with the exception of Cariappa, few of the graduates from the cadet course at Daly College, Indore had great success in their army careers. Hampered by the obviously incomplete nature of the military education they received there, most of them were forced to learn the rudiments of military and leadership skills on the job. This was a process that seems to have proved too daunting for Ponnappa. He almost consistently received votes of no confidence from his commanders. His placement on the Special Unemployed List in 1937 was a final and possibly conclusive vote of no-confidence on his record. And while Ponnappa could lay the blame for this on the door-step of the British, he has little excuse for his subsequent lacklustre performance in the independent Indian Army. His career ended within five years in the rank of Brigadier, a rank he assumed in 1947.

The lack of an effective military education was not the only cause of failed military careers. Take the case of M.R.A. Baig a Hyderabadi who claimed descent from Sultan Murad of Turkey.[38] As a result of his family connections and wealth Baig was educated at Clifton, one of the elite British Public Schools. In January 1923 he entered Sandhurst, where for the first time in his life he encountered racism (see above). He passed out in mid-1924 and was attached to the 4/7 Dragoon Guards in Bolaram (20 miles from Hyderabad) for his obligatory one year posting. After that he received his permanent posting in August 1925 to the 16th Cavalry. Baig recalled regimental life as having been quite unpleasant for real integration of the unit had never taken place, and he and his fellow Indian officers never felt that they 'belonged'.[39] According to Baig, he and the first two Indian officers of the regiment, Faiz Mohammed Khan and Sheodatt Singh, lived together in a house known as 'the native quarter'. To Baig, who had lived as an 'equal' in Britain prior to his Sandhurst years, this type of treatment was unbearable and by his own admission he was 'outraged and reacted violently'.[40]

In 1928 Baig attended the Cavalry School in Saugor for a seven month course, followed by a course at the Small Arms School in Pachamari. He returned to his regiment in April 1929 expecting to be appointed its Adjutant, and was enraged to learn that he had not been considered for the position.[41] Although he was subsequently sent to the Machine Gun School in Ahmednagar, the perceived rebuff had proved too much for the proud Baig, and he had made up his mind to leave the army. This decision no doubt aided by the fact that at Ahmednagar too, he found that Indians were being socially excluded.[42]

Some Indian officers became virulently anti-British in reaction to the racism they experienced. Thimmaya recalls a Rajput Captain, Kanwar Daulat Singh from Kotah who unlike the other Indians in the Hyderabad Regiment was quick to confront the British at every opportunity. According to his biographer -

100   The Army Officer Corps and Military Modernisation in Later Colonial India

> From subsequent conversation, Thimmaya gathered that Daulat – Singh was a intelligent man, and a fine soldier, but his anti-British – feelings coloured his whole life. When his daily work was done, – he took off the hated uniform and donned a dhoti [Indian lower- – garment]. He never touched the foreigners food. He was always doing – 'Pujas' [prayers]. He had his family with him, but kept his wife in – 'purdah'[seclusion].[43]

Daulat Singh's anti-British sentiments became so pronounced that when the battalion returned to India, he was finally dismissed after 'trumped-up charges' were brought against him.[44]

In some cases the failure of a career meant nothing less than outright desertion and becoming a 'traitor'. Mohan Singh was among the first batch of Indians to join the I.M.A. in 1932.[45] He had risen from the ranks as a VCO, and had been selected to undergo a training course at Kitchener College, Nowgong to prepare him for entry into the I.M.A.[46] Commissioned in 1934, he was attached to the 2nd Border Regiment in Ferozepur for a year, after which he was posted to the 1st battalion, 14 Punjab Regiment at Jhelum. In February 1941 his battalion embarked for Burma, and Mohan Singh was promoted to Major and given command of the headquarters company.[47] In September 1941 the battalion which was part of the 11th Indian Division's, 15th Brigade was involved in constructing defenses at Jitra near the Malay-Thai border. At this point according to Mohan Singh, he soon began to feel 'tired and depressed'.[48] When hostilities commenced Mohan Singh's battalion was entrusted with the defence of the border 15 miles north of Jitra. Contact with the Japanese was made on 9th December, and by the 11th the battalion was under heavy attack. Constant artillery, air and tank attacks forced the battalion to withdraw to a position 2 miles to the rear. Here too the battalion was subjected to heavy fire and was finally broken. Mohan Singh himself under direct fire recalls with remarkable candour

> I had a narrow escape [from a Japanese tank]. After that it did not – take me even a fraction of a second to decide my next action. I bolted.[49]

According to Mohan Singh he then began to seriously evaluate his 'position' in the Indian Army, and the 'role' of the army. He also appears to have been influenced by Japanese propaganda, for he remarked -

In contrast to the Japanese propaganda, the British had not given even an empty promise to grant us complete freedom after the war.[50]

It was then that Mohan Singh decided that the time was right to approach the Japanese for assistance to start a movement for India's independence.[51] Accordingly he established contact with the Japanese via Indian civilians, and within a year he established the first brigade of the Indian National Army (I.N.A.).

The Reason Why

Mohan Singh's experiences reflect a rather extreme reaction to dissatisfaction with being part of the British-controlled Indianization process. Yet, there is no denying the fact that just about every Indian officer had to undergo the trauma of racism at varying stages in their careers. Indian officers reacted differently to the often hostile treatment meted out to them in their units, depending on their individual personalities. Some, including Daulat Singh, M.R.A. Baig, Osman Baig and Mohan Singh, refused to accept or ignore this sort of treatment. They remained constantly suspicious of any moves made by the British, and were unable or unwilling to communicate with them. Others, including Thimmaya, Cariappa and Chaudhuri, chose to largely ignore those British officers who were hostile and sought to cultivate, instead, British officers who were friendly. These Indian officers, generally, tended to immerse themselves in their careers and pay little heed to the controversy surrounding them. Although none of the officers discussed above appear to have capitulated completely to the negative social aspects of regimental life, they did walk a fine line. According to General D. K. Palit 'some [officers] sold out to the British socially'.[52] Finally there were those Indian officers who were for various reasons proven unsuited or unqualified for the job at hand, but attribute all the blame for their failed careers to British racism; Ponnappa and Kanwar Amar Singh (see above) are two such cases. Probably the most curious 'failed' career story belongs to General B. M. Kaul. A Sandhurst graduate (from the same batch as John Masters), Kaul actually left the infantry to join the Army Service Corps (A.S.C.). According to Kaul he was trying to join the higher paying Military Police or the Border Scouts to provide for his ailing mother, but since neither of these organizations took Indians he was forced to join the A.S.C.[53] Whatever the reason for his departure, Kaul's old unit did not want him back when he tried to rejoin it later. For most, a career spent in the A.S.C. would have meant no access to higher command positions in the Field Army. But Kaul proved to be a masterful politician, and would later ally himself with Indian politicians to take his career to dramatic heights in the independent Indian Army.

There is little evidence to suggest that there was a conspiracy by the British officers of the Indian Army to destroy Indianization as most writers and some former Indian officers allege. The responses of British officers to Indianization was just as varied as their Indian counterparts, and was similarly a matter of individual personalities and opinions. Some were indeed opposed to Indianization and did all they could to hamper it without directly disobeying orders. Others like Thimmaya's first three COs and General Das's company commander Pete Rees, took an active interest in guiding the careers of their Indian subordinates.[54] Generally most British officers maintained a very professional and 'correct' attitude towards Indian officers. If the latter proved to be communicative and able, the British would respond with guarded friendliness and respect. Their attitude towards the Indian officers is best summed up by General J. S. Aurora -

> If you were somebody who fitted in, they liked you. If you were aloof or wanted to be on your own, they left you alone.[55]

Often senior British officers would hesitate to confer any operational responsibilities upon Indian officers, but would relent and apologize for their prejudice when the Indian officer in question showed himself to be equal to or even superior to his British counterpart. The Messervy-Chaudhuri story is one such classic case (above). Another such incident involves General M. N. Das who was posted to Italy during the Second World War as second-in-command of the machine-gun battalion of the famous 4th Indian Division. When he arrived at his unit, the CO flatly refused to accept Das, and he was given the choice of returning to India, or staying on with a demotion to a company commander. A lesser individual might have returned to India, but Das remained. Within a few months the CO was replaced and the new CO saw to it that Das became the battalion commander.[56] Overwhelmingly the fate of the Indian officers lay in their own hands. If they proved to be professionally incompetent or unable to adjust to the underlying racial ostracism in their respective units, their careers usually floundered. If on the other hand they were capable officers and had the ability to ignore the racist jibes, they proved to be successful.

As the Indianization programme gathered momentum Indian officers no longer found themselves totally isolated in their units. However, attitudes towards them did not necessarily soften. General Palit recalls that when he joined his unit, relations had actually deteriorated between Indians and British. He was 'aghast' to see that there was no mixing between the two and that Indians were often referred to as 'wogs'. Neither Palit nor the other Indians in his unit were ever invited to the house of either the Commanding Officer or the Second-in-Command.[57] Palit's experience was probably an extreme case, but right up to the Second World War there was constant tension between the ever increasing numbers of Indian officers and their British colleagues. It was only during the War that the situation improved markedly.

This was caused by the influx of a large number of working class non-career British officers, who appeared not to suffer from the racial and class prejudices that their well-heeled upper-class British 'brethren' of the pre-war Indian Army had so steadfastly adhered to. Years later, Palit was still somewhat amazed when he recounted how this new breed of British officers would mix freely with Indians. Not only did they communicate openly, but they also ate Indian food the traditional Indian style with their fingers, tried to learn Hindi, and even took to Indian music!![58]

The war also seems to have softened the attitudes of the old die-hard senior officers towards Indian custom and culture, particularly with regard to food. When Chaudhuri was Brigadier in charge of Administration, Malay Command on General Sir Frank Messervy's staff in 1946, the General's senior aide a, young Major John Wainwright, approached Chaudhuri with a plea for curry, claiming that he was 'browned off' with English meals. When Chaudhuri had some Indian food brought in from the Indian troops' cookhouse, General Messervy stumbled onto the impromptu feast and joined in with great gusto and relish. After that incident Chaudhuri recalls that curry was served more often at the command house.[59]

The social ostracism that Palit and other Indian officers experienced in the army must be understood in the context of the British 'club culture' that existed in India at the time. For many British the various military and civilian social clubs represented the only avenue for meeting other British colleagues and families in a social setting. They represented an oasis where the British could relax and interact with each other without having to worry about impressing the 'natives'. Thus it is not surprising that the clubs proved to be the last all-white bastions against Indian encroachment. Although most of the military clubs opened up to the Indian officers by the Second World War, the exclusive civilian clubs like the Yacht Club of Bombay, the Punjab Club in Lahore and the Bengal Club in Calcutta kept their doors closed to Indians right up to independence.[60] As Zareer Masani points out -

> The vast majority of Indians, of course, had no desire to enter European society. And the notion of ethnic segregation was by no means new in a caste-ridden society where many Brahmins would still not eat food touched by the lower castes. What made Anglo-Indian racism unacceptable was that it was practiced by foreign rulers and affected precisely those Indians who were most Westernized and had the strongest aspirations to equality.[61]

Perhaps no Indians were more Westernized as a group than the Indian officers. In their case the exclusion was all the more painful, for the club often represented their only opportunity for social activity, cutoff as they were from their family and friends. The Indian officers were in reality in much the same position as their British counterparts, but without the support system the latter enjoyed to make a military career in India socially bearable. The problems of the Indian officers were exacerbated by the fact that there were barriers to socializing with their own people. When Thimayya's battalion was posted to Allahabad, he and his fellow Indian officers found that they were barred from joining the Allahabad Club. The Indian officers then tried to cultivate ties with the leading Allahabad families, but to their chagrin were rebuffed.[62] According to Chaudhuri -

> the Indian civilians tended to keep aloof from the army, even from the Indian officers. They were in that era both shy and perhaps a little suspicious of the military community.[63]

105

In a bizarre way the outbreak of the war proved even more beneficial to the Indian officers and the Indianization programme. As the more experienced British prewar officers either became casualties or were rapidly promoted, the Indian officers who had previously been perceived as intruders in some British circles became a precious commodity. The most significant change was the disbandment of the 'eight unit' scheme. Indian officers could now be posted to any unit within the Indian Army. Without the Indian officers it is doubtful if the British could have found enough trained officers from their rapidly diminishing British officer pool to command the Indian Army. The largest professional army of the war. It was precisely such a lack of adequately trained British officers for the Indian Army in the Great War (1914-1919) that had led to the collapse of many Indian units on the Western Front.[64] Furthermore, important appointments in Operational areas also became more accessible to Indian officers. The requirements of the war meant that more and more positions in the Staff College at Quetta became open to Indian officers. Similarly, instructor appointments also became available to Indian officers. In December 1939 two Indian officers, Captains Som Dutt and Shrinagesh, became the first Indian officers to serve on the staff of the I.M.A. Captains Khalid Jan and K. C. Khanna also joined the academy in August and September of 1940 respectively. The official history of the academy notes that these appointments were 'necessitated by the exigencies of the war'.[65] The War also placed intense pressure upon Churchill to remove existing restrictions on Indian officers preventing them from punishing British personnel. In a successful argument to repeal this restriction the Secretary of State for India, Leo Amery, noted that George Washington a senior colonial officer had been 'mortally offended by being put below the youngest joined subaltern from home [Britian]....'.[66]

The extent to which relations had improved between British and Indian officers by the Second World War can be gauged by comparing two official welcoming talks given to new officers joining the Indian Army in 1927 and in 1942-43. In February 1927 Second Lieutenant Chaudhuri was returning to India aboard the *Dorsetshire* and had to attend compulsory classes on 'habits, manners and hygiene in the Orient.'[67] He remembers what was more disconcerting was the talk on how to deal with the indigenous population. The natives had to be firmly handled for familiarity would breed disrespect. Native habits and customs were declared to be incomprehensible and generally unclean. Apart from the men enlisted into the Indian Army, the locals were classed as usually dishonest..........the emphasis lay on preserving the prestige of the white man which, linked to the Empire, took precedence over everything else, official or personal.......[68]

In 1942 the Indian Government printed a compilation of 'Four Lectures by a commanding officer for officers joining the Indian Army'. Gone were the distorted and unimaginative injunctions to which Chaudhuri referred. The 1942 orientation made a concession to the growing contribution and sensibilities of the Indian officers. It noted

the I.C.O. varies in capability just as you young officers do. One brigadier wrote 'I could not wish for a better leader British or Indian' - read accounts of decorations they have, the vast majority of them have done and are doing their job well.[69]

In a pointed reference to the Indian officers in his audience, the speaker noted that while the British had often been accused of being insular with strangers, the same 'sometimes applied to you (I.C.O.'s)....' and he asked the Indian officers to 'do their best in reaching a happy understanding with the new arrivals from England.'[70] A more dramatic shift can be perceived in 1943 pamphlet for the guidance of British commanding officers, staff and regimental officers proceeding to India. This confidential note appears to have been prepared for senior British officers only. It cautioned all concerned to

be correct and courteous at all times in dealing with Indians; it is their country and, although it may take some time to know their social grades and customs, if this is remembered it will help in dealings with them......[71]

Finally the war provided the Indian officers with a setting to put into practice the skills they had learned in peacetime. It was time to prove in a most emphatic way that they had the ability to lead men into battle. The Second World War was a watershed period in the operational and doctrinal maturation of the Indian officer corps. Although comparatively few in number, enough Indian officers, particularly from the last Sandhurst batches and the 'pioneer' group of the I.M.A. served in important operational and staff positions to provide the post-independent Indian Army with a viable and competent leadership core.

TABLE 4 [72]

LIST OF UNITS SELECTED FOR INDIANIZATION BY 1938

CAVALRY:	3rd Cavalry, 7th Cavalry, 16th Light Cavalry
ARTILLERY:'	A' Field Battery (new), 1st (Madras) Field Battery, 2nd Field Battery, 3rd Field Battery, 4th Field Battery. 2nd Brigade to be formed later - followed by another Field Brigade or Mountain Brigade.
ENGINEER:	1 Field Troop. Q.V.O.* Madras Sappers & Miners. No. 44 Division HQ.Coy., Q.V.O.* Madras Sappers & Miners. No. 15 Field Coy., Q.V.O.* Madras Sappers & Miners. No. 5 Field Coy., K.G.V.O.** Bengal Sappers & Miners. No. 22 Field Coy., Royal Bombay Sappers & Miners.
SIGNALS:	4th Cavalry Brigade Signal Troop, 4th Indian Division Signals.
INFANTRY:	2nd Battalion, 1st Punjab Regiment. 5th Battalion, 2nd Punjab Regiment. 5th Royal Battalion, 5th Mahratta Light Infantry. 5th Battalion (Napier's), 6th Rajputana Rifles. 1st Battalion (Q.V.O.L.I.)***, 7th Rajput Regiment. 5th Battalion (Burma), 8th Punjab Regiment. 5th Battalion (K.G.V.O.)**, 11th Sikh Regiment. 4th Battalion (Sikhs), 12th Frontier Force Regiment. 6th Royal Battalion (Scinde), 13th Frontier Force Regiment. 1st Battalion, 14th Punjab Regiment. 4th Battalion, 19th Hyderabad Regiment.

OTHER:	Royal Indian Army Service Corps (R.I.A.S.C.) No. 6, Distribution Supply Coy, Bolarum. Two Anti-Tank Coys (mule) 3 Troops, Two Anti-Tank Coys (mule) four Troops. Indian Army Observation Corps (I.A.O.C.) partial. Indian Army Vehicle Corps (I.A.V.C.) partial. Military Farms - Army Remount Department.

*=Queen Victoria's Own,
**=King George the Fifth's Own,
***=Queen Victoria's Own Light Infantry.

Notes

1 *General J.N. Chaudhuri: An Autobiography*, as narrated to B. K. Narayan, (New Delhi: Vikas Publishing, 1978), p.58.

2 Ibid, 49.

3 Stephen P. Cohen interview (henceforth Cohen interview) with Lieutenant General S. D. Verma, Midhurst, Sussex, 28 November 1963.

4 John Masters, *Bugles and a Tiger: A Volume of Autobiography*, (New York: The Viking Press, 1956), p.15.

5 Evans, *Thimmaya of India: a Soldier's Life*, pp.83-83. Some British units, while angered by the presence of Indian officers, managed to hide their feelings. General S. D. Verma was posted to the Royal Welch Fusiliers at Quetta. It was only when he had settled into the unit that he learnt that there was a good deal of resentment about a 'bloody wog being thrust upon us....' Verma, *To Serve with Honour*, p.14.

6 Thorat, *From Reveille to Retreat*, p.21.

7 Zareer Masani, *Indian Tales from the Raj*, (Berkeley, Los Angeles: University of California Press, 1987), p.25.

8 Thorat, *From Reveille to Retreat*, p.26.

9 B. K. Narayan, *General J.N. Chaudhuri*, pp.72-3.

10 The 4/19th Battalion's companies came from North India and included Kumaonis, Jats, Rajputs, and Ahirs. See Evans, *Thimmaya of India*, pp.102-3.

11 Ibid, p.106.

12 In Quetta, Nina was the only Indian wife not in 'purdah' (veil). *Ibid*, p.146.

13 The Hindu term translated 'any-one there', about the only Hindi learnt by many British officers to order their army of Indian servants around.

14 Singapore fell two months later, Ibid, pp.171-2.

15 Thimmaya was one of 6 Indians out of 140 students.

16 The 25th Division was then training in Madras preparing for deployment to Burma. Ibid, pp.182-184.

17 Ibid, p.188.

18 Ibid, p.194.

19 Earlier a British battalion had launched a costly and ineffective day-time attack with artillery against the same position. Ibid, pp.196-200.

20 Ibid, p.201.

21 General Davies who had cracked physically and mentally was replaced by Major General Sammy Wood, who immediately asked Thimmaya to become G-1. Ibid, p.201.

22 Ibid, p.213.

23 In fact the 51st Brigade was known as the 'All-Indian Brigade'. Thorat,

24   *Reveille to Retreat*, p.64.
Of the half-dozen or so Indian officers who commanded battalions in the Second World War, only one, Lieutenant Colonel Sarvajeet Singh Kalha, was commissioned from the I.M.A., all the others came from Sandhurst. Unfortunately Kalha who was part of the first batch of Indian officers coming out of Dehra Dun was killed in action in Surabaya in 1946 fighting Indonesian insurgents. Had he survived, he may well have been the Army Chief in 1971 instead of Manekshaw. Verma, *To Serve With Honour*, p.71.

25   Prior to the Kangaw landings, Thimmaya had taken over temporary command of the 53rd Brigade replacing its sick commander. Evans, *Thimmaya of India*, 224.

26   The I.N.A. was established after the fall of Singapore by Major Mohan Singh with the cooperation of Indian civilians and the Japanese Army. Its basic objective was to liberate India from British rule with Japanese help (see below).

27   Narayan, *General J.N. Chaudhuri*, p.69. Chaudhuri himself was six feet tall and rather fair, the antithesis of the image of a typical Bengali 'babu'.

28   His nomination to the Staff college was facilitated by the close relations he had with his brigade commander 'Mo' Mayne, who later became General Sir Mosley Mayne, General Officer Commander-in-Chief Eastern Command. Mayne provided invaluable guidance to Chaudhuri in his formative years. Ibid, p.105.

29   Ibid, p.119.

30   Ibid, p.119-20.

31   Ibid, p.133.

32   The regiment was attached to the 17th Infantry Division under Major General Cowan.

33   Ibid, p.141.

34   Brigadier C. B. Ponappa, *Soldier and Citizen: and Other Writings*, (Bangalore, India: Hosali Press, 1971), p.3.

35   Ponnappa claims that 'I was the assertive type, and the British did not like my attitude.' Ibid, pp.9, 11.

36   The Unemployed List scheme was part of the British Government's effort to reduce the military budget. Ponnappa was hired as battalion commander in the State forces of Travancore, where he promptly clashed with Lieutenant Colonel Watkins the commander of the State Forces. *Ibid*, pp.18-19.

37   This had apparently been brought to Raza's notice by the Commander-in-chief General Auchinleck. Ibid, p.28.

38   Baig, *In Different Saddles*, p.2.

39   The other officers were Faiz Mohammed Khan and Sheodatt Singh who had arrived before him, and Hiralal Atal, Idris, Khalid Jan and Shiv Verma who

40   came with, and after him. Ibid, p.54.

Ibid.

41   He was informed by the Colonel that this was automatic for he had obtained a Second Class (Q-2) grade a Saugor. *Ibid*, pp.70-1.

42   Baig's younger brother, Osman, who had followed him into the army suffered a similar fate. Chaudhuri remembered that when he joined the 7th Cavalry in 1929, Osman then a Lieutenant in the unit, greeted him with the remark '.....you must be mad to join this Regiment, it is the worst bloody regiment in the Army'. Like his elder brother Osman too soon left the army. B. K. Narayan, *General J.N. Chaudhuri*, p.15.

43   Evans, *Thimmaya of India*, p.97.

44   Ibid, p.115.

45   Sinha and Chandra, *Valour and Wisdom*, p.138.

46   Mohan Singh, *Soldier's Contribution to Indian Independence*, (New Delhi: Army Education Stores, Radiant Publishers, 1974?), p.34.

The objective of the college was 'to assist officers in preparing young N.C.O.'s for promotion to commissioned ranks and in educating them up to the standard required for a platoon commander.' See note setting forth scheme for Kitchener College at Nowgong, Letter from Major General W. Kirke Chief of General Staff to General Staff 30.8.27. BL/IOR, Mss.Eur.E.396/11.

47   Mohan Singh, *Soldier's Contribution*, p.48.

48   Ibid, p.50.

49   Ibid, p.61.

50   Ibid, p.66.

51   The Japanese appear to have tortured many captured Indian officers in an attempt to get them to defect. Captains Dhargalkar and Badhwar of the 3rd Cavalry were regularly beaten and hung up in cages for weeks on end for refusing to join the I.N.A. Captain Ghanshyam Singh of 16th Cavalry went through many mock beheadings for his refusal to cooperate. However, according to S. D. Verma some Indian officers simply relented to this pressure and joined the I.N.A. S. D. Verma, *To Serve With Honour*, pp.45 -6.

52   Taped interviews with Gillian Wright, November 1987 – January 1988, BL/IOR, Mss.Eur.R.193/9. Palit along with some other Indian officers in his unit apparently forced into a tight knit group of their own by British ostracism, began to perceive any Indian officer who still went out of his way to make contact with the British as a 'toadie'. See – Zareer Masani, *Indian Tales of the Raj*, p.25.

53   Interview with Stephen P. Cohen, 19 December 1964, New Delhi.

54   See Ibid, and also Wright interview with Major General M. N. Das, BL/IOR, Mss.Eur.R.193/9. Das remembers that Rees, who was his

Company Commander, was instrumental in guiding him through his delicate first year in the Indian Army. Following the War, Rees was promoted to Major-General and became the commander of the Boundary Force which was responsible for overseeing the flow of refugees to and from the newly created India and Pakistan. Allan Campbell-Johnson, *Mission With Mountbatten*, (London, New York: Robert Hale, 1951), p.176.

55   Zareer Masani, *Indian Tales of the Raj*, p.25.

56   Interview with Major General M. N. Das, Mss.Eur.R.193/9.

57   Interview with General D. K. Palit. *Ibid.*

58   Ibid.

59   B. K. Narayan, *General J.N. Chaudhuri*, p.73.

60   One of the reasons some clubs opened their doors to Indians was because of the actions of the British officers. When S. D. Verma and other Indian officers were rejected membership in the Peshawar Club, the CO of the Regiment (16th Cavalry) decided not to hire out any horses to the club, forcing it to end its exclusion of the Indian officers. S. D. Verma, *To Serve With Honour*, p.22. Thimayya's CO in the Highland Light Infantry (H.L.I.) also tried to get the United Services Club in Bangalore to let Thimayya become a member. When he failed, the officers of the H.L.I. threatened to resign en-masse from the club, but Thimayya, who was only attached to the unit for a year, managed to persuade them not to do so. Evans, *Thimmaya of India*, p.88.

61   Zareer Masani, *Indian Tales of the Raj*, p.53.

62   Narayan, *General J.N. Chaudhuri*, p.111.

63   Ibid, p.74.

64   See Chapter 1.

65   Sinha and Chandra, *Valour and Wisdom*, p.150.

66   Amery to Marquess of Linlithgow, Mss.Eur. F.125/11, India Office, 1 September 1942 – quoted in *The Transfer of Power, India*, Vol II, p.673.

67   Narayan, *General J.N. Chaudhuri*, p.45.

68   Ibid, pp.45-7.

69   Four Letters by a Commanding Officer for Officers joining the Indian Army, BL/IOR, L/MIL/17/5/2225, 26.

70   Ibid.

71   (Not to be Published) Notes for the Guidance of Commanding Officers, Staff and Regimental Officers, proceeding to India, with a brief summary of the more important regulations and instructions applicable, (General HQ India, WO, January, 1943), BL/IOR, L/MIL/17/5/2330, 8.

72   Indianization of the Army and formation of the I.A.F.[Indian Air force], (New Delhi: Government of India Press, 1938). BL/IOR, L/MIL/17/5/1800, 21 – 2.

114

Chapter 5
The Roots of Doctrine
Modernization of the Indian Army 1919-1939

In the years preceding the First World War, critics of the Indian Army and particularly the Cardwell system had described it as an 'albatross' around the neck of the British Army. When the system was reintroduced after the war in the 1920's, a new generation of critics took up the anti-Cardwell torch. To many of them it appeared that the British Army was essentially 'regulated by the conditions prevailing on a portion of one of the frontiers of the Empires' constituent parts'.[1] The chief concern was that the Indian Army, with its sights firmly set on frontier warfare, would hamper any progress the British Army might make towards 'mechanized warfare', the buzz-word of the 'progressives' in the inter-war British Army. An older concern was that Imperial commitments, and India in particular would sap the strength of the small postwar British Army.

This pessimism about the Indian Army's ties with the British Army became the chief concern of a younger generation of British reformers including Fuller, Ironside, Hobart and Lindsay, all of whom saw the Cardwell system as a major barrier to change in the British Army.[2] However, running concurrently with this negative view of the Indian Army was another radically different appreciation of its utility. This opinion held primarily by senior officials at Whitehall began to regard the Indian Army as nothing less than an indispensible partner to the smaller British Army in the defence of the entire British Empire; a view no doubt consolidated by India's considerable contribution in the Great War. These optimists won the debate on military modernization in the inter-war period. They helped initiate events that would not only better integrate the Indian Army into the greater scheme of imperial defence, but also dramatically influence the military doctrines of the two armies. This chapter is an attempt to analyze the doctrinal evolution of the Indian Army in the post 1919 era. It will seek to demonstrate just how changing perceptions of the Indian Army altered its role from that of internal and border security to that of a conventional 'medium-power' army capable of intervening in any theater of combat throughout the world.

115

A Matter of Money

The 1919 appointment of the 'Army in India Committee' led by Lord Reginald Esher signaled the first moves towards integrating the Indian Army with the British Army. The committee considered among other things the impact dominion status would have upon India's contribution to imperial defense. According to the Esher Report

> India has now been admitted into partnership with the Empire, and the Indian Army has fought, alongside troops from other parts of the Empire, in every theatre of war. Its responsibilities have thus been greatly widened, and it can no longer be regarded as a local force, whose sphere of activity is limited to India and the surrounding frontier territories. It must be treated as part of an Imperial Army, ready to serve in any part of the world.[3]

The committee's report, submitted in 1920, put forth the radical recommendation that the Indian Army be made directly responsible to the British Government rather than the Viceroy. The report suggested that the Indian Army could be used to bypass restrictions on the size of the British military as agreed upon in the postwar negotiations. The Esher committee essentially called for the all-important appointment to the post of the Military Secretary of the India office be made by the Chief of Imperial General Staff (C.I.G.S.). Furthermore the committee suggested that the appointment of the Commander-in-Chief India should only be made after taking the 'advise' of the C.I.G.S. The proposals merely served to alarm the Indian Government which had no intention of handing over control of the army to the British Government and the Committee for Imperial Defence (C.I.D.). Fortunately for it, unexpected help came from the nascent Indian Legislative Assembly. One of Esher's ill thought out plans had been to make extensive use of the Indian Army to police the British Empire and the mandated territories. This proposal immediately ran-afoul of the Indian politicians. Sir P. S. Sivaswamy Aiyer introduced fifteen resolutions, basically rejecting the entire Esher Committee report. The resolutions also emphatically rejected any proposal to make the Indian Government relinquish control of the army to Whitehall. The new Legislative Assembly declared

That the Army in India should not, as a rule, be employed for service outside the external frontiers of India except for purely defensive purposes, or with the previous consent of the Governor General-in-Council in very grave emergencies, provided that this resolution does preclude the employment on garrison duties overseas of Indian troops at the expense of His Majesty's Government and with the consent of the Government of India.[4]

Indeed as far back as 1919 when the Esher Committe was formulating its report, Lord Chelmsford had insisted -

So long as India pays, – and I do not suppose the War Office are going to propose to the English Treasury to take over the charges of the Indian Army, – India must control its own Army.[5]

The next year the Secretary of State for India, Edwin Montagu, also declared

.......We must definitely get it out of our heads the vague idea too often entertained that India is an inexhaustable reservoir from which men and money can be drawn towards the support of Imperial resources or in pursuance of Imperial strategy.[6]

The Indian Government led by the Viceroy Lord Chelmsford gratefully accepted the Sivaswamy Resolutions passed by the Legislative Assembly in 1921. Like the Indian politicians the Indian Government had no intention of paying to police the rest of the empire. In regard to this particular issue at least the two traditional rivals could agree upon fully. In fact, relations between the Indian Government and the Indian legislators were so good at this time that the Commander-in-Chief Lord Rawlinson was of the opinion that the Legislative Assembly's attitude was one of 'pleasing moderation'. He noted that the budget which included some extra taxation to fund army spending, passed through 'without much serious difficulty'.[7]

Despite this unlikely cooperation to defeat the Esher proposals, in reality the Indian Government found itself pushed inexorably into the orbit of increasing imperial defence commitments. In 1927 contingency plans were initiated for sending Indian troops to protect the Persian oil-fields, but with the understanding that 'no financial liability whatsoever will fall upon

India.'[8] In 1928 the Indian Army was committed to sending a division to Iraq and two independent brigades to Singapore.[9] By the 1930's the Indian Army had much of its strength scattered in outposts ranging from the Far-East to Africa, just the sort of situation the Indian Government had intended to avoid. Even worse, until 1933 the army received no financial assistance from the British Government. How then did this come about? In order to answer this question we must examine the shift in the strategic perception of the leadership of the Indian Army during the inter-war period.

The lack of funds posed the main stumbling block to any enhanced Indian involvement in Imperial Defence. Indeed in 1922 soon after the Great War a Retrenchment Committee led by Lord Inchappe effectively froze any prospects of the army's expansion or modernization.[10] If, therefore, the army was to modernize for its role as an Imperial Defence Force, the British treasury would have to help. A C.I.D. sub-committee report on Indian Defence Requirements supported this view by noting in June 1922 that it 'recognized that the Indian Army cannot be treated as if were absolutely at the disposal of His Majesty's Government for service outside India'. The committee accepted the Indian Government's view that 'the Indian Army should not be required to permanently provide large overseas garrisons'. The cost of such a garrison, moreover, 'should be borne by His Majesty's Government, or by the dependency or colony requiring their services'.[11] In 1933 the British Cabinet – appointed Garran Tribunal allotted an amount of 1.5 million pounds to India from the British treasury to finance that portion of the Indian Army which would act as an imperial intervention force.[12] With the prospect of British Government financial backing for a modern intervention force, the Indian Government's attitude towards imperial defense softened considerably. As Viceroy Lord Linlithgow noted in 1937, 'You have the money – we have the men'.[13]

In March 1938, amidst a worsening security situation in Europe, at the urging of the Secretary of State for War, Hore-Belisha, the CID set up a committee led by Major General H.R. Pownall to look into the reorganization and modernization of the Indian Army.[14] The committee acknowledged that the system of collective security had failed and that the Empire was seriously threatened by the axis powers. Yet on the other hand, the committee noted that the frontier menace to India from Afghanistan and Russia had decreased. The committee noted that

......there are grounds for the belief that on the present scale of her defence forces India is less under insured than are other parts of the British Empire. Moreover, the degree of readiness of the forces in India is in some respects higher than elsewhere, andshe maintains a large standing army in peace.[15]

The committee noted that the Indian Government felt willing to place one division at Britain's disposal 'contingent upon effect being given to certain measures reorganizing and reequipment of the army in India'. In order to successfully implement the new role of the Indian Army, the committee deemed it essential that those Indian units slated for the imperial reserve must adhere strictly to the standards of British home units. Thus modernization of a portion of the Indian Army became imperative. At the time of the filing of the report, the Indian Army was divided into three categories – Covering Troops, the Field Army, and Internal Security Forces – with the following allotment of forces:-

APPENDIX A
ALLOTMENT OF THE ARMY IN INDIA[16]

Units	Covering Troops	Field Army	Internal Security	Total
Cavalry: British	-	4	-	4
Indian (horse)	3	8	5	16
Indian (armoured car)	1	1	-	2
Artillery: R.H.A. Batterys	1	3	-	3
Field	4	40	-	44(a)
Mountain	16 1/2	8	-	24 1/2(b)
Medium	1/2	5 1/2	-	6
Heavy	-	-	2	2
A.A.	-	1	-	1
Infantry:	7	10	26	43
British Bns				
Indian Bns	46	30	20	96

(a) Includes 'A'(Indian) Brigade (b) Includes 7th Light Battery

For financing this modernization and reorganization, the committee drew attention to the fact that the Government of India had made it clear that no increase could be made in the current (1938) estimates, amounting to Rs. 45 crores (33,750,000 British pounds). The Pownall Committee itself estimated that the British Government would have to provide an additional 2,285,000 pounds annually, and that a further sum of 870,000 Pounds from Imperial funds might be needed each year.[17]

With general agreement on the Pownall proposal, fuelled in part by the deteriorating security situation in Europe, a further committee established in the summer of 1938 under Admiral of the Fleet Lord Chatfield sought to examine just how the modernization scheme would be paid for and implemented. The Chatfield Committee, while agreeing with the general conclusions of the Pownall Report, felt that the whole Indian Army and not just a single imperial reserve division needed modernization. The committee proposed a more elaborate reorganization of the army -

TABLE 5

Detailed Distribution of Units[18]

Unit	Permanent Garrison	Northern Command Reserve	Coast Defence	Internal Defence	General Reserve	Total
British Cavalry: Light Tank Regt	-	-	-	-	2	2
Indian Cavalry Light Tank Regt	-	-	-	-	4	4
Indian Cavalry Armd Regt	4	-	-	-	4	4
Field Arty Regt (British)	2	2	-	-	5	5
Field Arty Regt (India)	-	-	-	-	2	2
Mountain Arty Regt (India)	4	1	-	-	5	5
Medium Arty Regt (British)	1	-	-	-	1	1
Heavy Arty Btty (India- Coastal)	-	-	2	-	2	2
A.A. Btty (India)	-	-	-	-	3	3
A.Tk. Btty(British)	-	-	-	-	1	1

Ind Field Pack Co: Sappers & Miners	1	1	-	-	1	3
British Infantry Bns	5	-	-	-	2	2
British Infantry Bns	5	4	5 1/2	5 1/2	4	34
IndianInfantry Bns	45	10	3	8	9	75

In addition to the reorganization plan, the committee submitted an estimate of the finances needed to modernize and expand certain key defence industries - Metal and Steel factory: for the manufacture of heavy and light bombs (Rs. 80 lacs).

Gun and Shell factory (Rs. 73 lacs).

Rifle factory (Rs. 73 lacs).

Ammunition factory (Rs. 10 lacs).

Gun Carriage factory (Rs. 6 lacs).

Cordite factory (Rs. 24 lacs).

Filing factory (Rs. 32 lacs).

T.N.T. factory (Kirkee) (Rs. 70 lacs).[19]

On the crucial financing estimate the committee calculated that the total cost would be -

Army   – Rs. 36.26 Crores = 27.20 million British pounds.

Air Force – Rs. 6.21   "   = 4.66   "   "   "

Navy   – Rs. 2.62   "   = 1.96   "   "   "

Total: – Rs. 45.09   "   = 33.82   "   "   "

The committee felt that while India should bear some of the burden, the bulk of the 33.82 million pounds for the initial modernization cost must come from Britain over a 5 year period.[20]

India generally welcomed the sweeping proposals by the Chatfield Committee. Generals Muspratt (Military Secretary 1931-33) and Auchinleck (DCGS, India 1936-38) noted that the

> ......conclusions of the Chatfield Committee are far-reaching and the recommendations made in report are likely to influence profoundly the future of the forces in India.[21]

Their only objection was to the committee's proposal to reduce the army size,[22] a long-time goal of British reformers, including the Secretary of State for War. As Muspratt and Auchinleck observed -

Coming at a time when the rest of the world is furiously increasing its armed forces, the proposed reductions of the army in India on the score of then being surplus are certain to prove controversial.[23]

They were correct. With the imminent outbreak of war, the British General Staff refused to approve any troop reductions. In June 1939 the British Cabinet agreed to assuming the added cost in the Chatfield report. The same year the General Staff in India issued its first modernization plan. The plan detailed the peace-time unit strength of the army, and allocated units for deployment in either the External Defence force based in the Deccan or the General Reserve (HQ at Meerut and Lucknow). The plan called for a major expansion and modernization of defence-related production facilities, including gun and shell, metal and steel, ammunition and explosive factories. It also called for an immediate conversion from the obsolete Berthier section machine- gun to the more modern Czech inspired Bren section machine-gun.[24]

The Obstacles

While the various official committees attempted to modernize and reorganize the Indian Army and its supporting British units within the existing framework of the Cardwell System, the radical reformers on the other hand were in complete opposition to it. According to Liddell Hart-

......so long as the Cardwell system is maintained they [British battalions in India] are worse than superflous, since not only are they preserved in a form that does not meet the conditions of modern war, but a similar number of units of the same type have to be maintained at home.[25]

The proposed remedy of the radical reformers was the seperation of the two armies. According to J.F.C. Fuller -

If mechanised arms cannot operate in this [Afghanistan] theatre of war, the reorganization of the army at home will either be seriously delayed, or two armies will have to be maintained, one for European warfare and the other for Oriental.[26]

The most common scheme proposed was the creation of two separate active armies: the first one of long service (20 years) for colonial duty, and the second of shorter service for continental duty in the event of a major war.[27]

The reformers complained vociferously that the Cardwell System forced the British Army at home to maintain similar units to reenforce those in India, thus deflecting it from mechanization. There is, however, no reason to believe that the reformers would have gotten their wishes had the British garrison (45 battalions) in India been drastically cut. After all to begin with the British battalions in India were maintained wholly by Indian taxpayer money. In the event of them being removed from India, they would in all probability have been disbanded, further reducing the emaciated British Army. One British official noted morosely that a reduction in British units would throw those units

> on to the Imperial Budget, or, as the only alternative, force us to disband them and so to weaken the armed strength of the Empire as a whole without any relief to the British taxpayer.[28]

So even without these battalions, no extra money or forces would be made available in Britain to contribute towards the military modernization as the reformers had hoped. The main obstacle to the mechanization of the army was not the Cardwell system, but rather the extreme paucity of funds.

When Lord Rawlinson (1920-25) succeeded Sir Charles Monro (1916-20) as Commander-in-Chief India in the autumn of 1920 he was plunged into 'the old problems of military efficiency and financial stringency'.[29] Although Rawlinson considered that -

> the provision for internal defence is already dangerously small, he had reluctantly suggested a reduction in the British establishment of 6,000 troops to 59,000 in all, but this would not be possible before 1922. As it was the British contingent was under-strength an required an actual increase of 7,000 men even to reach the proposed reduction total.[30]

The Viceroy Lord Chelmsford (1917-21) concurred with the above views noting that recruitment and organization of the British Army always took into account the fact that India maintained a minimum strength of British troops. Hence any reduction of the British garrison in India would raise a vast number of difficult and complex questions.[31] India saved the British taxpayers from supporting no less than a quarter of the British Army. Of the

252,000 British troops in 1921, 65,501 (26 %) were stationed in India (including Aden garrison), and supported wholly by Indian tax money.[32] Not surprisingly, opposition to any massive reduction of the forces in India did not come from India alone, but also from the British General Staff. The Chief of Imperial General Staff General Sir Cyril Deverell (1935-37) staunchly opposed any attempts by the Secretary of State for War Hore-Belisha (1937-40) to reduce the India garrison. In a letter to the Prime Minister in November 1937 Hore-Belisha noted -

> the elimination of the Indian obsession, which refuses to allow objective examination of the proper disposition and organization of our Imperial Forces, and assumes that the Indian commitment is fixed for all time on unchanging traditions and that it must govern the pace and capacity of development of the rest of the army.[33]

In another letter he noted -

> a cardinal feature of readaption of the Army is an impartial examination of whether India's share of our personnel is not disproportionate. Such an examination he [Deverell] is unwilling to undertake......[34]

Having reached an impasse with Deverell, Hore-Belisha decided to replace him with General Gort

> .....who is the most dynamic personality I have met in the Army, and who is bred in an independent school. He could devote most of his time to executive reorganization of the Army.[35]

With Deverell out of the way an exuberant Hore-Belisha delivered his first Army Estimates speech at the House of Commons in March 1938. He outlined a total sum of 108,500,000 pounds; the highest since 1914-18, and repeated his view that

> India must no longer govern Army organization and distribution. For this reason the Prime Minister was prepared to initiate discussions between the War Office and the India Office.[36]

In reality the Indian Army was not as averse to reductions as critics have made it out to be. The military budget was in fact placing a great strain on the economy. In 1920 the Indian Government spent more than 40% of its budget on the military.[37] In May 1921, the new Viceroy Lord Reading appointed a committee under the Commander-in-Chief (India), General Rawlinson to examine 'Indian Military requirements'. Rawlinson, despite the objections of the his General Staff acquiesed to the committee's plan for the removal of 3 British cavalry regiments, and 5 battalions of British infantry.[38] However, as soon as the committee submitted its report, the Muslims of the Madras Presidency began a violent anti-British agitation – 'the Moplah rebellion'- which postponed consideration of it.[39] A similar rejection of the proposal by the British cabinet quickly followed.[40] Although Rawlinson was pleased by the cabinet's decision, with the help of the Inchappe Committee's report he did manage to push through some reductions in both the British and Indian components of the army. 'It is', he argued, 'more important for the internal peace of India that we should balance our budget, than we should keep extra troops'.[41] By 1925 the army in India had been reduced to an establishment of 197,000: 57,000 British soldiers and 140,000 Indian troops – respectively 24,000 and 12,000 fewer than in 1914.[42]

It is also important to note that India was neither the only nor for that matter the most draining region in terms of imperial commitment. Restoring order in Ireland remained the single largest burden which the British Army had to bear in the early 1920's. The 'Irish Ulcer' more than anything else prevented the Cardwell System from functioning effectively and upset traditional patterns of training and deployment. At the height of the conflict in Ireland, on 10 December 1920 when martial law was proclaimed in four Irish counties – Cork, Tipperary, Kerry, and Limerick – no less than 51 British battalions were deployed in Ireland.[43] In August 1921 the British Cabinet actually decided to hold back troops destined for India in order to deploy them in Ireland if necessary.[44] Only after the Anglo-Irish agreement in December 1921 did a gradual removal of the British garrison in the Irish Free State begin.[45]

The Doctrine

While the Indian army lagged behind the British Army in terms of equipment, the same deficiency did not necessarily apply to doctrine. When

Sir Giffard Martel arrived in India in the late 1920's prior to taking a instructors position at the Staff College Quetta, he wrote to Liddell Hart – a fellow military reformer and staunch critic of the Indian Army – that the 'army in India in no way the dud show that people at home suggest – real live show in many ways though short of equipment'.[46] Even though the Indian Army did not take to armoured warfare as enthusiastically as the reformers would have wished, it certainly did not stop its Staff College at Quetta from planning and war-gaming the latest mechanized warfare doctrine.

In fact, ever since the Indian Army established the Staff College at Quetta it had kept abreast of the latest doctrines from Europe. A joint entrance exam for the Staff Colleges at Quetta and Camberly indicates that these two vital operational training centres closely coordinated their educational programmes. Candidates had to be well versed in the latest debates on military modernization. There questions covered British military strategy during the Great War ('Westerners' vs 'Easterners'), the possession of mobility for a fighting force, the role of armoured fighting vehicles and planes in policing empire, the impact of the Cardwell System and ideas to change it.[47]

Significantly the more 'realistic' of the many inter- and postwar British officers who propogated mechanized warfare doctrines spent a significant portion of their formative years at Quetta. Even Martel who often chaffed at what he perceived to be the army's foot-dragging on mechanization conducted numerous mechanized war-games at Quetta. In 1932 he and his students drafted a bold plan for taking Kandahar (in Afghanistan) in 70 days with light tanks and aircraft.[48] General Percy Hobart ('Hobo') the first commander of the permanent tank brigade (1933), also served as instructor at Quetta where he developed many of his radical views on armoured warfare.[49] General Burnett-Stuart, one of the most influential British officers with regard to armoured warfare, also spent a considerable portion of his time in India. His biographer records that

> he received a sound education in small-units tactics during his service with the Rifle Brigade [1897-98] in India.[50]

In 1920 Burnett-Stuart returned to India as General Officer Commanding Madras District, and was instrumental in putting down the Moplah disturbance. During those operations he became one of the few and probably the only inter-war British officer to make large scale use of highly mobile columns of infantry, armoured cars, and pack-artillery in an operational environment.[51]

Quetta contributed to the doctrinal maturation of another British officer – General B.L. Montgomery. In June 1934, freshly promoted to the rank of full colonel, Montgomery assumed the post of Chief Instructor at Quetta. His brother Brian and close friend General Dudley Ward felt that it was in Quetta that Monty's 'tactical concept of war had......fully matured'. General Ward noted -

> People like Liddell Hart I think are vastly overrated. They were obsessed
> with mobility – which is fine if you can have it. But it isn't often so; and
> the only way you can win battles is to defeat the enemy who wants to
> deprive you of that mobility. It was Monty who taught us how to do
> this.[52]

Service in India tended to give many of these reformers (with the exception of Hobart) a more realistic approach to mechanization. As commander of the 3rd division, Burnett-Stuart believed that mechanization was an inevitable but slow process. He recognized the continued existence of the Cardwell System and felt favourable toward partial mobility – 4 armoured divisions with at least one in Egypt and India.[53]

Furthermore, the image of an Indian General Staff obsessed with frontier soldiering as painted by the reformers and critics of the Indian Army is also inaccurate. The majority of the interwar Indian Army commanders, including Rawlinson (1920-25), Chetwode (1930-35), Auchinleck (1941, 1943-47), and Wavell (1941-43) were all dynamic and progressive military leaders. Chetwoode in fact served as the General Officer Commanding, Aldershot Command prior to becoming Commander-in-Chief India. In September 1925 Chetwoode commanded one side in Britain's first large-scale peace-time manoeuvers since 1914. This was the first exercise to test the new concepts of mechanized warfare. It predictably turned into a fiasco, and strengthened Chetwoode's caution against rapidly adopting such a radical new method of fighting without adequate preparation.[54]

As Commander-in-Chief India (1930-33) Chetwoode stood alongside the ranks of cautious modernizers but he had no intention of being a defender of the status-quo. In an address to the cadets at the Staff College Quetta he bitterly criticized the intellectual stagnation of the officer corps in both the British and Indian Armies -

> I do not think that, as a class, they [officers] have improved in general education, or military instinct and leadership, since the war......I have found men all over India who evidently scarcely read the papers, and quite unaware of the larger aspects of what is going on in India around them, and still less of a stupendous events outside this country.....I am rather afraid that quite a number of the average Staff College students aim at being correct, methodical, 'sealed pattern' staff officer, ground out to pattern by the Quetta and Camberley mill. Am I altogether wrong in thinking that, to many Englishmen, to be independent in thought, to have imagination, to go outside the obvious, to be different to others, is to be almost un-English, or even that more frightful 'not sound'.[55]

Even Brian Bond, who labels Chetwoode as one of the conservatives on mechanization, felt compelled to describe Chetwoode's Quetta address as '.....the most devastating indictment of the military profession by a senior-ranking officer in the inter-war period'.[56]

Prior to taking over as Army chief in India, Wavell served as commander of the experimental 6th infantry brigade, during which time he penned an article in the *Journal of the Royal United Services Institute*, noting that while mechanization was inevitable, it would happen gradually. More importantly, Wavell noted that a mixed combined-arms unit of tanks and highly trained infantry would be the way of the future.[57] Wavell's emphasis on infantry support was actually a step ahead of the solely armour-based concepts of his fellow reformers and would play an important role in his efforts to modernize the Indian Army, during his tenure as its Commander-in-Chief from 1941-43.[58]

The caution of these Indian commanders-in-chiefs towards rushing headlong into a new system of warfare has often been seized upon by the reformers and researchers as evidence of their lack of progressive ideas. In reality the Indian General Staff more often than not had a far better idea of the true capability of their army and officers, and of the limitations of resources and finances than did reformers.[59] This came about due to the fact that the Indian Army was almost permanently deployed in operational conditions from the Far-East to the Middle-East. Constantly embroiled in coping with unexpected situations, the Indian General Staff had to make the best possible use of a significantly smaller financial budget than its British counterpart. An excellent example of this commonsense approach is evident on the question of whether tanks should be used in India or not. Tanks as Fuller pointed out may well have been useful on the frontier, but were they necessary? The Indian Army had already secured a firm handle on the tribesmen with a combination infantry, armoured cars, and a few RAF squadrons. In view of the financial situation, would it have been possible or even desirable to establish tank regiments on the frontier with all the tremendous costs it would have entailed? In fact the first twelve production Mk 1 Carden-Loyd light tanks arrived in India in July 1932 they were joined by eighteen more in September. Plagued by mechanical failure in the harsh terrain and high temperature of the subcontinent, the tanks were used primarily as experimental units with two companies being formed – neither of them saw any service on the frontier.[60]

The metamorphosis of the Indian Army's strategic role to that of Imperial Defence off-course necessitated a radical move towards mechanization. But even at this eleventh hour the level heads of the Indian Army led the way in helping to establish the standard doctrine for the British and Commonwealth armies in the forthcoming war. Actual material change in the army was slow; for the need to rearm the British home army first saw to that. But the Indian Army was already moving ahead with its own reorganizational plans.

The Anatomy of Military Modernization

In December 1939, even as the Chatfield Committee worked through its report, the Chief of General Staff's office sent a note to all regional command headquarters in India. The note pointed out that the rapid mechanization of armies in Europe had

> ....appreciably modified the theory and practice warfare developed with the older types of forces and now a tactical technique is rapidly being evolved.[61]

The note called for the closing of the gap between British and Indian armies. However, the note also stated that

> stereotyped higher formations such as corps and divisions which form the basis of organization of European armies are not likely to be needed by a modernized army in India.[62]

The note continued that cavalry and infantry brigades were the best formations in peacetime. The last stipulation is puzzling for it seemed to go against the move to match the Indian Army with the British Army. The Chatfield Committee, which originally put forth the proposal, felt that such peacetime organization was wasteful, and that in time of war these units would be specially created and organized.[63] The note indicated that future modernization plans would enable the cavalry light tank regiments to be equipped with the latest 2pdr gun tanks, the artillery would be fully mechanized with modern guns and tractors, and the infantry battalions would get sufficient transports to carry all weapons and unit equipment bringing it approximately upto the 1938 model for British U.K. based battalions.[64]

All of these plans, coming to fruition as they did on the eve of war, did not transform the Indian Army into a well- equipped modern army overnight. As Brian Bond points out -

> Clearly these decisions came too late for any real progress in the modernization of the army in India to be made before the outbreak of the Second World War. Indeed it was weaker and less prepared for war in 1939 than in 1914 with a total of 205,038 British and Indian troops as compared with 269,954 in 1914. As for up-to- date equipment, as late as February 1939 there was still one anti-aircraft battery in the whole of India. The Indian forces fell far short of being able to fulfill the internal and external roles envisaged for them by the Chatfield Committee.[65]

Bond and other researchers including Martin Wainwright are quite right in their belief that in terms of equipment in 1939 the Indian Army was woefully short of the lofty goals set for it by the Chatfield Committee. But was the Indian Army 'less prepared for war' as Bond alleges above? A detailed examination of the tactical doctrines of the British and Indian armies during the war years will reveal that even if the Indian Army had lacked the material resources to wage a modern war, in terms of doctrine at least it had entered the Second World War with a far more realistic appreciation of its capabilities and limitations than it had for the 1914-19 war. Indeed, the true dynamics of the military modernization in the Indian Army are not to be found in the highly visible 'material' sphere, but rather in the ideology and mind-set of that army, as will be evident in the following chapter.

TABLE 6

PLANNED COMPOSITION OF INDIAN UNITS [66]

British or Indian Light Tank Regt:	3 sqdns (squadrons) + sqdn HQ and Regt HQ – 3 troops of 4 light tanks in each sqdn – 4 tank mortars = 41 tanks and 80 wheeled vehicles.
Indian Cavalry Armoured Regt:	Regt HQ + sqdn HQ – 3 troops of 3 armoured cars – 1 sqdn of 3 troops of 4 light tanks each – 4 tank mortars = 14 light tanks, 24 armoured cars, 68 wheeled vehicles.
Indian Cavalry Motor Regt:	Regt HQ + sqdn HQ – 3 sqdn of 3 troops of 3 sections – each section in one 15 cwt trucks – 1 LMG = 46 LMG's, 2 At-Tk rifles, 9 2in mortars, 108 wheeled vehicles.
British and Indian Field Artillery Regt:	Regt HQ – 4 batteries of 4 guns – 113 vehicles.
Indian Mountain Artillery Regiment:	As at present.
British Medium Artillery Regt:	Regt HQ – 3 batteries of 4 howitzers – 80 vehicles.
Anti-Aircraft Battery:	HQ – 4 sections of 2AA guns – 17 vehicles.
Anti-Tank Battery:	HQ – 3 troops of 2 sections of 2 anti-tank guns – 27 vehicles + supt units.
British and Indian Infantry Battalions:	Bn HQ + Co HQs – 4 companies of 3 platoons of 3 sections each = 49 LMGs, 42 2in mortars, 4 At-Tk rifles, 48 wheeled vehicles.

Notes

1   Major B. C. Denning, *The Future of the British Army*, (London: Witherby, 1928), pp.60-1.

2   Robin Higham, *The Military Intellectuals in Britain, 1918-1939*, (New Brunswick, NJ: Rutgers University Press, 1966); Brian Bond, *British Military Policy Between the Two World Wars*, (Oxford: Clarendon Press, 1980).

3   Report of the Army in India Committee, 1919-1920, [Esher Committee], BL/IOR, L/MIL/5/1762, Pt IV, p.7. In the summer of 1920 the Indian Army maintained ten battalions of infantry in Mesopotamia, nine in Egypt, seven in Palestine, six around the Black Sea and various other smaller garrisons. 13 July 1920, CAB 4/7 252-B.

4   *Legislative Assembly Debates*, Vol. 1, No. 15, pp.1683-1762, in BL/IOR, L/MIL/7/10822.

5   Letter from Chelmsford to Montagu, 12 February 1919, Montagu Collection, BL/IOR, Mss.D.523, Vol. 8., 26. In 1920 the Viceroy stated bluntly to the British Cabinet that the Government of India 'could not accept any obligation to supply permanent overseas garrisons to the mandated territories.' See 'Supply of overseas garrisons from the Indian Army,' 3 September 1920, CAB 24/11 C.P. 1844. In October the Secretary of State for India Edwin Montagu adding his voice to the chorus of demands calling on the British Government to withdraw from Mesopotamia, pointed out to the cabinet that the Dominions had refused help in this matter and that the Government of India including the Commander-in-Chief General Rawlinson were demanding the return of Indian soldiers. 'The Mesopotamian Mandate,' 9 October 1920, CAB 23/112 C.P. 1948.

6   'Indian Military Expenditure,'memorandum by Montagu, 24 December 1920, C.I.D. 118-D, CAB 6/4.

7   Rawlinson to Lord Derby, 30 March 1921, IOR, Derby Collection, BL/IOR, Mss. D.605/5.

8   C.I.D. Minutes, 29 June 1931, CAB 2/5.

9   Memorandum by India Office, 3 May 1928, 318-C, CAB 5/7..

10   Report of the Indian Retrenchment Committee, 1922-1923, London: HMSO, 1923., BL/IOR, L/MIL/17/5/1780.

11   Report of the Indian Military Requirements Sub-committee, 22 June 1922, CAB.16/38 Vol. I, paper 130-D.

12   Tribunal on certain questions in regard to defence expenditure in dispute between the Government of India and the War Office and the Air Ministry, [Garran Tribunal], India Office, November 1932., BL/IOR, L/MIL/17/5/1911.

13   Bond, *British Military Policy between the two World Wars*, p.112.By October of 1936, as it became evident that British industrial resources would be inadequate for her own rearmament program British ministers were initiating 'urgent' enquiries about the possibility of purchasing anti-aircraft munitions and weapons from the Dominions and India. See C.I.D. Minutes, 29 October 1936, CAB 2/6(2).

14   Director General of Ordnance and Intelligence.

15   The Defence Problems of India and the Composition and Organization of the Army and R.A.F. in India, [Pownall Committee], 12 May 1938, BL/IOR, L/MIL/5/886, 331. Earlier that very year it was decided that in the event of a war with Italy, India was slated to provide two brigade groups and four air squadrons for Egypt, one brigade group and two air squadrons for Singapore, a brigade to Persia, a brigade to Aden as well as a force of indefinite size to Iraq. C.I.D. Minutes, 25 March 1938, CAB 2/7.

16   Ibid, L/MIL/5/886, 360.

17   Ibid, 393-395. See also J.O Rawson, 'The role of India in Imperial Defense beyond Indian frontiers and home waters,' unpublished D.Phil, Oxford, (1976), pp.287-97. At the same time the Pownall Committee was making its report, an unofficial Indian Army Committee led by the DCGS Major General Auchinleck was reaching much the same conclusion and urging the Government of India was to set up local munition and weapon manufacturing facilities to modernize the army. Report of the Modernization Committee, Simla: Army HQ, Oct 1938, [Auchinleck Committtee], BL/IOR, L/MIL/17/5/1801.

18   Reorganization Proposal: Detailed Distribution of Units, BL/IOR, L/MIL/5/886, 463.

19   Ibid, 476.

20   Report of the Expert committee on the Defence of India, 1938-1939, [Chatfield Committee], Ibid, pp.451, 459, 463, 477-78; See also 'Cabinet Committee on the defence of India. Report of the Expert Committee on the defence of India,' 23 June 1939, CAB 24/287; and 'Draft Report by Committee on Defence of India,' 7 June 1939, ID (38), CAB 27/65A.

21   Defence Requirements India 1938-39, Chatfield Committee: Notes on Report by Generals Muspratt and Auchinleck, BL/IOR, WS 1934 – L/WS/1/155, 15.

22   1 British cavalry regiment, and 6 British infantry battalions to return to England, and 3 Indian cavalry regiments, 4 companies of Indian Sappers and Miners, and 14 Indian infantry battalions to be disbanded.

23   Ibid, p.7.

24   Plan for Modernization of the army, 1939 (operations), General Staff India, BL/IOR, WS 2099 – L/WS/1/170.

25   B.H. Liddell Hart, *The Defence of Britain*, (London: Faber, 1939), pp.305-6; See also Lidell Hart, *Memoirs*, (London: Cassell, 1959), pp.91-7. Lidell Hart along with Percy Hobart, another radical reformer, felt that the entire British Army in India was little more than a police force, and that it could in fact be replaced by a police force, which could be effectively supported by a single mobile division. Mark Houston Jacobsen, 'The Modernization of the Indian Army 1925-1939,' p.55.

26   This was after his 1927 tour of India. See J.F.C. Fuller, *On Future War*, (London: Sifton Praed & Co, 1928), p.262.

27   Harold R. Winton, *To Change an Army: General Sir Burnett-Stuart and British Armoured Doctrine, 1927-1938*, (Lawrence, Kansas: University Press of Kansas, 1988), p.124; See also Captain J.Kieth Edwards, 'Second (Military) Prize Winning Essay for 1927', *Journal of the Royal United Services Institute*, No. 73 (August 1928), pp.458-473.

28   Future Military Expenditure, August 1921, CAB. 27 – Cabinet Committees, 27/164 G.R.C. (D.D.)8.

29   Rawlinson to Derby, 25 November 1920, BL/IOR, Mss.D.605/1.

30   Secretary of State to Viceroy, 18 January 1921, Chelmsford Collection, BL/IOR, Mss. E.264, Vol. 14., 50.

31   Viceroy of Secretary of State, 22 January 1921, Ibid, p.33.

32   Monthly Returns: distribution of the army, P.R.O., W.O. 73/115.

33   Letter from Secretary of State for War to P.M., 1 November 1937, quoted in R.J. Minney, *The Private Papers of Hore-Belisha*, (London: Collin's, 1960), p. 66.

34   Ibid, p.66.

35   On 1st December 1937 he writes to Deverell asking him to step down. The latter concurs with a comment 'Time will show that your criticisms as far as I am concerned are unjust as they are cruel'. Ibid, pp.69 and 72.

36   Hore-Belisha also called for a 'the new army to be made more flexible'. Among other things he proposed the reduction of personnel by creating a greater number of 'smaller' divisions which would be easier to move and support. Ibid, pp.92-4.

37   Memorandum by Finance Department, India Office, circulated by Montagu, 7 December 1920, CAB 6/4.

38   CAB. 16 – Ad-hoc Sub-committees of the Committee for Imperial Defence. CAB.16/38 Vol. II, I.M.R./14.

39   Viceroy (Army Dept) to Secretary of State, 21 July 1921, BL/IOR, L/MIL/3/2513, 1631.

40   Since November 1921 a C.I.D. sub-committee had been examining the Rawlinson proposals at a leisurely pace. 'The Proceedings of the Indian Military Requirements Sub-Committee', CAB.16/38. Vol. I. In explaining the

British Cabinets rejection of the proposal the Secretary of State Montagu stated that the cabinet felt that further reduction of British troops in India was not possible in view of the political condition in India and the frontier situation. Secretary of State to Viceroy, 14 February 1922, BL/IOR, L/MIL/3/2534 M.1348/1922, No. 1.

41   Sir Frederick Maurice, *The Life of General Lord Rawlinson of Trent*, (London: Cassell, 1928), p.313.

42   Ibid, p.109. The Viceroy Lord Reading himself was firmly of the opinion that the budget could not be balanced without substantial reductions in military expenditure. Reading to Peel, 3 August 1922, Reading Mss. BL/IOR, E.238, Vol. 5, p.112.

43   Keith Jeffery, *The British Army and the Crisis of Empire 1918-1922*, (Manchester: Manchester University Press, 1984), p.88.

44   CAB. 23 – Minutes and conclusions of Cabinet meetings and conferences of ministers, Cabinet Meeting, 25 August 1921, CAB. 23/26/72(21).

45   The withdrawal began in December 1922. Ibid, CAB. 23/32/68(22), appdx II.

46   Bond, *British Military Policy between the Two World Wars*, p.106.

47   Examination for Admission to the Staff Colleges at Camberly and Quetta, 1936, 1937 (February-March), War Office: London, HMSO, BL/IOR, L/MIL/17/5/2281, 2-4.

48   Bond, *British Military Policy*, p.106.

49   Kenneth Macksey, *Armoured Crusader: Major General Percy Hobart*, (London: Hutchinson, 1967), pp.82-3.

50   Winton, *To Change an Army*, p.65.

51   Although mopping-up operations continued until the second half of 1922, the back of the rebellion had been broken by November, 1921, thanks to Burnett-Stuart's mobile columns. A.C.B. Mackinnon, 'The Moplah Rebelion 1921-1922', *Army Quarterly*, No. viii (1924), pp.260-77. In 1926 he became commander of the 3rd division at Salisbury Plains, and oversaw the development of the Experimental Armoured Force from 1927 onwards. Bond, *British Military Policy*, pp.62, 65.

52   While at Quetta Montgomery met Auchinleck and Alexander both brigade commanders. He is reported to have remarked that 'the best man, was a chap called Auchinleck'. Auchinleck had also served as Chief Instructor at Quetta from 1930-32 and was 3 years older than Montgomery. Nigel Hamilton, *Monty: The Making of a General (1887-1942)*, (New York: McGraw-Hill, 1981), pp.248-49, 258.

53   Winton, *To Change an Army*, p.85.

54   Ibid, pp.33-4.

55   Bond, *British Military Policy*, pp.67-68.

56 Ibid, p.67.

57 A.P. Wavell, 'The Army and the Prophets', *Journal of the Royal Services Institute*, No. 75, (November, 1930), p.671.

58 Wavell also served as commander of the 2nd Aldershot Division from 1935-37.

59 Recent research indicates that senior British Home Army Generals (including Haig) who were also bitterly criticized and later sidelined by the reformers were actually enthusiastic supporters of mechanization. However, like their counterparts in India they had a more realistic understanding of Britain's ability to finance and implement such complex reforms. See J.P. Harris, *Men, Ideas and Tanks: British Military Thought and Armoured Forces, 1903-1939*, (New York: St Martin's Press, 1996).

60 Review of important military events in India, 1932, W.O. 32/1285.

61 C.G.S. Army HQ to all commands, 13 December 1938, BL/IOR, WS 2047 – L/WS/1/164, 94.

62 Ibid, 95.

63 Ibid, Letter from Army HQ to Southern Command 15 July 1039, 56.

64 Ibid, C.G.S. Army HQ to all commands, 96-7.

65 Bond, *British Military Policy*, pp.123-24.

66 C.G.S. Army HQ to all commands, 13 December 1938, BL/IOR, WS 2047 – L/WS/1/164, 98.

Chapter 6
The Crucible of War:
The Second world War and the Emergence
of the Indian General Staff

The very same day Prime Minister Winston Churchill announced to Parliament that Britain was at war with Germany, the Viceroy, Lord Linlithgow, informed India over the radio of the circumstances in which 'we find ourselves at war with Germany today.'[1] The Viceroy's declaration set off a political firestorm. The Indian National Congress, angered by the Viceroy's lack of consultation with them, rejected his declaration and Congress party ministers of all seven provinces where the Congress held a majority resigned.[2] Although non-cooperation and political agitation by the Congress represented a potential problem for the Indian Army, Linlithgow was more concerned about preventing Hindu – Muslim conflict among the soldiers.[3]

The war itself came as no surprise to the Indian Government. Feverish planning (if not action) had been underway for some time to transform the Indian Army into a capable modern intervention force. The first real test for the Indian Army came in the desert of North Africa. Here two armies – the British Commonwealth and the German – pitted their imperfect doctrines of warfare against each other. At the end of an immense struggle the Afrika Korps was all but wiped-out and the British Commonwealth forces emerged with a radically different appreciation of how to wage 'modern' war. In the East, in Burma and Malaya this scenario too repeated itself between the British Commonwealth forces and the armies of Imperial Japan, with the same end result.

By the conclusion of the Second World War, India had become the single largest colonial[4] contributor to the British war effort. During the war India raised a military force of 2,500,000 professional soldiers, sailors and airmen, the largest force of its kind in the world. This force suffered casualties including 24,338 killed, 64,354 wounded, 11,754 missing and 79,489 POW's, for a total of 179,935.[5] It fought in Malaya, Burma, East Africa, North Africa, Tunisia, Middle East, Sicily, Italy and in a number of smaller wars ranging from Greece to Indo-China. It won 4,028 awards for gallantry, including 31 Victoria Crosses (27 in Burma – including 20 by members of the Indian Army). The British 14th Army in Burma became the largest single army in the world with 1,000,000 men, 700,000 of whom were Indian. It fought along a 700 mile front, almost the equivalent of the Eastern Front. The Japanese incurred half their total casualties of the entire war in Burma alone![6]

Within this global crucible of war the army of independent India was born. During the course of this conflict the future leaders and architects of the army of independent India developed and honed their skills of war-making. This chapter is primarily an analysis of how the Commonwealth armies emerged with a winning tactical doctrine in the war. It is also an examination of how the rapidly growing Indian officer corps matured as a professional organization during this period.

The War in the West

The historiography of the war in North Africa has generally tended to dismiss the early campaigns against the Italians. Most of the research on this period has dwelled upon General O'Connor's highly mobile campaigns against the Italians with his 'Jock' columns. These small motorized units of infantry, artillery, and armour wrought havoc on disorganized and retreating Italian forces. What has passed almost without notice is the excellent use of Indian artillery during these campaigns in both the infantry and tank support roles. In the December 1940 battles against the fortified Italian camps at Nibeiwa and East Tumar the division CRA (Chief of Royal Artillery) of 4th Indian Division[7] used his entire divisional artillery – 56 18pdrs (pounders) and 25pdrs, 8 6in howitzer, and 8 60pdrs – as a single group to support each Brigade's (3 per division) attack in an excellent fire-plan.[8]

The same coordination with artillery is evident in the East African campaign when the 4th and 5th[9] Indian divisions took on the Italians at their best – defending well-prepared defensive positions with their best troops. Throughout the campaign and especially during the decisive battle to seize the key stronghold of Keren, the artillery worked in close conjunction with the Indian infantry. At the fall of Keren, the British commander General Platt praised '....the continuous support given to the infantry by the Royal Artillery....'[10] The performance of the artillery was all the more creditable because the Commonwealth forces had a limited force of only 124 guns.[11] Indeed, the entire Eritrean campaign ranks as one of the most effective displays of the optimum use of limited firepower resources. The Indian Army displayed its traditional flair for making the most of extremely limited resources.

The arrival of Rommel and his Afrika Korps changed the complexion of the desert war in more ways than one. Not only were the Germans a qualitatatively superior opponent compared to the Italians, the Indian Army no longer constituted the bulk of the 8th Army. The 'new' British-dominated 8th Army immediately revealed serious deficiencies in functioning as a cohesive combined-arms force, something at which the Germans were much more successful. Furthermore, mobility – that long sought after goal and the core of many a staff-college war-game at Quetta and Camberly – proved as elusive as a mirage in the desert. Successive 8th Army commanders from Generals Cunningham to Ritichie failed miserably to concentrate their forces at the decisive point. Even when they achieved such a rare concentration, British armour proved unable to work in concert with the artillery and infantry and was repeatedly mauled by German anti-tank defences.[12]

In his authoritative three-part study of British Field Artillery tactics in the *Journal of Royal Artillery*, Brigadier Bidwell comments extensively on the misuse of artillery by the British Army in the early period of the North African campaign against the Germans. Yet he notes with some puzzlement that

> This, however, does not explain why it was from India, the most starved and backward of commands, that two divisions [the 4th and the 5th] came who at Keren and in the early desert operations showed how artillery should be handled. It was later that the decline began.[13]

The obsession with mobility deflected the 8th Army from appreciating the need for 'true' combined-arms operations with infantry and artillery. Under the influence of the radical reformers the British Army entered the war with a gross over-appreciation of the capabilities of armor only formations.

The British 7th Armoured Division – a division trained by General Percy Hobart – a great believer of armoured-only formations – entered the war in June 1940 with a ratio of about 330 tanks (2 armoured brigades) to only two infantry battalions and two artillery regiments. At the Sidi Rezegh battle there were no less than 500 tanks (3 armoured brigades) backed by a support group of only 3 infantry battalions.[14] After Sidi Rezegh General Auchinleck (an Indian Army officer), Commander-in-Chief Middle East, proposed measures to create a parity between armour and infantry. He specifically wanted to reduce the number of armoured brigades in a division to one and replace the ad-hoc support group with a full infantry brigade.[15] In addition Auchinleck felt that

> We must, therefore, while retaining the divisional HQ organization, ensure that it is capable of handling a collection of brigades of varying numbers and types. That is to say, the real basic tactical unit must be the brigade group, whether armoured, motorized or lorried, and that each brigade group must be capable of being transferred from one divisional command to another as a matter of course and habit, and without having to resort to a last minute improvisation which must occur with our present divisional organizational whether it be armoured corps or infantry.[16]

Auchinleck also proposed mobile field divisions of mixed armour and infantry for the army of manoeuver to regain the initiative from the Germans.[17] The main problem he faced was that Ritchie (his 8th Army commander) was unable to carry out his directives. Auchinleck finally sacked Ritchie and took personal command of the army on 25 June 1942. With an Indian Army officer in command of the desert campaign, the effect was immediate. At the first battle of Alamein the German commander Rommel noted -

> General Auchinleck, who had meanwhile taken over command himself at El Alamein, was handling his forces with considerable skill and tactically better than Ritchie had done. He seemed to view the situation with decided coolness, for he was not allowing himself to be rushed into accepting a 'second best' solution by any move we made.[18]

Indeed by June 1942 Auchinleck had stabilized a defensive line at Alamein. Here he reverted to the positional warfare tactics utilized so successfully in the East African campaign against the Italians. For possibly the first time in the campaign against the Afrika Korps, the 8th Army was successful in concentrating its artillery resources for a major defensive battle. At the battle of First Alamein in July 1942, the 8th Army concentrated the fire of nine artillery regiments on more than one occasion. In the midst of the raging battle on 15 July, the 8th Army, Chief of General Staff, T.W. Corbett, declared, 'the artillery is being restored to its rightful place in the battlefield'.[19] Unfortunately for Auchinleck, Churchill and the Chief of Imperial General Staff General Alanbrooke failed to see the true measure of his achievement and sacked him! The immediate reason given was his failure to punch through German lines in the subsequent counterattacks. However, these counterattacks launched under tremendous pressure from Whitehall collapsed as a result of the demoralized state of the British armour, which simply refused to advance in support of the infantry! Alanbrooke, who was well aware of the tremendous difficulties confronting Auchinleck, was not prepared to take on Churchill on his behalf as he would on many later occasions for Montgomery.

Nevertheless, Auchinleck's brief stint as commander of the 8th Army marks a sea change in British military operations during the war.[20] Henceforth all British operations would centre on positional warfare tactics, the centrepiece of which was the battle of attrition. Massed artillery, air-power and infantry would dominate henceforth. The armor would operate as a supporting arm of the infantry. This 'change' represented a return to the operational style favoured by the Indian Army. A style which was dictated not out of any orthodoxy, but by a realization that British and Indian armies quite simply lacked the training and equipment to carry out complex combined-arms mobile operations.[21]

Historians are only now beginning to appreciate the fact that Montgomery's assumption of the leadership of the 8th Army was not a revolution in British military leadership or tactics, but rather an evolution of the system introduced (reintroduced to be precise) by Auchinleck when he was army commander. The Second Alamein battle was predominantly an artillery and infantry offensive by the British. The armour came into play much later in the battle after the infantry had broken through the German defences. Even with Rommel on the run, Montgomery dared not send his armour in pursuit – so complete was the British disillusionment in their own ability to conduct even basic manoeuver operations with armour.[22] It is not surprising that the artillery which played such a vital role in Second Alamein was literally a continuation of Auchinleck's organization. As General Tuker recalls -

> On the night of 23 October, 30th Corps attacked under a barrage on a four division front, the barrage co-ordinated by the good gunner, Brigadier Meade Dennis, the same officer who had well served Auchinleck as artillery commander on the northern sector of the Alamein front. He was now used to handling hundreds of guns.[23]

The Second battle of Alamein proved significant for the artillery as it saw the introduction of complex artillery fire-control.

> Fire-plans could be arranged quickly, and what is more important, modified in mid-career to match the ebb and flow of battle.[24]

According to Colonel G.R. Stevens, the official historian of the 4th Indian Division, the new system of fire planning was in all probability originated by the divisional CRA (Chief of Royal Artillery) Brigadier Dimoline, who by

> constant training and experiment evolved a technique for crash saturation shoots well in advance of current practice. Gun surveys and the artillery communications grid were elaborated until the C.R.A. could sit in his battle headquarters with trace sheets which blended like a musical score, from which he could play his weapons singly, in unison or in harmony.[25]

The effect on the battlefield was startling, as General Tuker notes:Lacking an efficient armoured force, Eighth Army was now using much of its field artillery in a mobile role to halt the Axis advance, a role which was properly that of self-propelled artillery but nonetheless most effective in country where a few heights afforded such wide observation for the gunners and where mechanical traction enabled them to concentrate at speed. The records of the 9th Light and other [German] formations bespeak the punishment they received from South African and British guns, field – and medium. The method showed a reading of circumstances, of ground, resources and enemy which was refreshing after so many months of neglect. Throughout July the application of artillery in the sector from Ruweisat northwards was about as good as it could be.[26]

The techniques used by Dimoline continued to evolve throughout the desert campaign. In fact, they represent the early manifestation of TOT (Time on Target) synchronized shoots and 70 gun battery (div artillery) 'stonks' which became very common in the European theatre.[27]

The 8th Army Montgomery inherited from Auchinleck was by no means a 'lame-duck'. General Sir Francis Tuker, who commanded the 4th Indian Division at the time of Montgomery's assumption of command, agreed with Montgomery's assertion that the 8th Army was ill-trained, but wondered to what he was comparing them, as troops from the U.K. were even less competent. Tuker felt that the best trained allied infantry came from Australia, New Zealand, India and South Africa.[28] British units entering the North African theatre showed considerable inexperience and doctrinal rigidity. Tuker noted that during the battle of Medjerda, Tunis in May 1943, the British units refused to execute a night attack, a standard procedure for Indian units. During the same battle the British 1st Army, who were strangers to Brigadier Dimoline's new artillery fire-plans, hesitated before allowing him to take charge of a 400+ artillery concentration.[29]

When the war moved from Africa to Italy so too did the Indian Army – with the 4th, 8th, and 10th infantry divisions. Here also it became obvious that the Indian Army's emphasis upon infantry was not misplaced. The campaign in Italy proved that '....even in modern combat infantrymen were often more relevant than either tanks or planes.'[30] General Alphonse Juin, commander of the Free French forces, even went so far as to remark

> .....that the widespread mechanization of the British and American forces constituted a serious obstacle to any swift progress up the Italian peninsula.[31]

Under the circumstances it was not surprising that the Indian infantry divisions representing some of the most experienced infantry divisions in the theatre, saw almost continuous action right up to the German surrender in Italy in September 1945.[32]

The War in the East

The campaign in South East Asia witnessed the largest use of Indian troops during the war. No less than nine Indian Infantry Divisions and a large number of Independent brigades (armor and infantry) plus support groups became involved in that theater of conflict. Included in this force were the only Indian tank units to see extensive action during the war, the 50th, 254th, and the 255th Indian tank brigades.[33]

Early in the conflict, the excellent mobility of the veteran Japanese forces and their total disregard for flanking security took the British/Indian forces completely by surprise. Hong-Kong, Singapore and Malaya fell in quick succession. In Singapore alone 85,000 Commonwealth troops surrendered to the Japanese! Only in Burma did the British manage to slow the Japanese momentarily and to stage a fighting retreat. Outmanouvered and outfought by a remarkably lightly armed, albiet experienced, Japanese Army, the Commonwealth and Chinese forces fell back into India. Here at last the indomitable Imperial Japanese forces paused to regroup and consolidate their over-extended supply lines.

In India the battered Commonwealth forces built up their strength and planned for the next phase of the war under the guidance of (an Indian Army Officer) Lieutenant General Sir William Slim. The significance of Slim's assumption of command of the 14th Army is comparable to Auchinleck's take-over of the 8th Army in North Africa. The effect in terms of both the course of the war and allied military doctrine proved to be the same. However, Slim, unlike Auchinleck, was under less pressure from Churchill to produce instant victories, and had the luxury of being able to mold his forces into the best possible condition before going on the offensive. One of his first acts was to issue an eight point training directive to all of his units to '....get used to having Japanese parties in their rear, and when that happens, regard not themselves but the Japanese as "surrounded".' Point five of the directive cautioned infantry on Japanese style tactics -

> There should rarely be frontal attacks and never frontal attacks on narrow fronts. Attacks should follow hooks and come in from flank or rear, while pressure holds the enemy in the front.

On the issue of armour, Slim sought to change the prevalent view that tanks were useless in the jungle. He argued -

> Tanks can be used in most country except. In close country they must always have infantry with them to defend and reconnoitre for them They should always be used in the maximum numbers available and capable of being deployed.[34]

Slim was in fact laying the framework for allied tactics in the coming campaign whereby superior allied firepower and logistics would deflect Japanese mobility and ultimately destroy their light-weight infantry-based army.

In the allied counter-offensive against the Japanese in Burma, infantry bore the main responsibility of assaulting the enemy, closely supported by tanks when available, and always heavily backed by artillery and air-strikes. Although artillery and air-support never reached the numbers employed in North Africa and Europe, divisional artillery concentrations like those used to support the 37th brigade's (of the 23rd Indian Division) assault on Tamu in July 1944 became commonplace.[35] The Japanese, by contrast, rarely managed to concentrate more than a battalion worth of artillery. At Kangaw, for instance, the heaviest reported Japanese artillery concentration of the war comprised of only one battalion firing 600 rounds per day.[36] 'Cab-Ranks' provided close air-support whereby forward observers (F.O.'s) called down fire from fighters circling over the advancing troops.[37]

The campaign in Burma witnessed some of the best all-arms coordination of British and Commonwealth forces in the entire war. This was particularly true in the case of armour and infantry whose cooperation exceeded the level reached in Africa and Europe. Undoubtedly this was partly due to the weakness of the Japanese who could deploy only a fraction of the tanks and artillery the Germans had in Africa and Europe. This has led some observers to conclude that due to the Commonwealth's overwhelming superiority in material and men '....tactics were not so important as the logistics of manoeuvering such a force into position....'[38] This, however, is inaccurate for the mere sustaining of logistics and the concentration of forces would not have been enough to defeat the extremely mobile Japanese forces. This was accomplished through relentless pursuit of the enemy by all Commonwealth forces operating as a well-oiled combined-arms team of air, artillery, tanks and infantry. Mobility – that much sought after quality in the pre-Auchinleck 8th Army and a concept that found little place in Monty's set-piece battles – became a vital element in Slim's Burma campaign.

Apprentices of War

The small group of Indian officers were caught in the midst of this catastrophic struggle; for them the Second World War proved a defining moment in their military careers. While peace-time training and education had given them a largely theoretical grasp of warfare, actual combat enabled them to mature considerably as military leaders. The lessons learned by the young Indian officers during the war years formed the core of Indian military doctrine in the post-independence period and continues to play a major role in the evolution of the Indian Army today.

Individual Indian officers who later rose in their careers to assume senior positions in the independent Indian Army participated in the often painful learning process that the Indian and other allied armies endured during the war. In the deserts of North Africa Indian officers took part in the well orchestrated campaign against the Italians. Early during the campaign in East Africa the advancing 4th Indian division encountered large well-situated mine-fields left behind by the retreating Italians. Second Lieutenant Premindrah Singh Bhagat (later Major General), of the 21st Field Company, Royal Bombay Sappers and Miners spearheaded the advance through the mine-fields relying solely on his eyesight and a bayonet. Despite an ambush and two mine explosions which destroyed his vehicles, Bhagat stuck to his task for five days enabling the pursuit to flow smoothly. For his actions, Bhagat became the first Indian Commissioned Officer to be awarded the Victoria Cross.[39]

Indian officers also participated in the chaotic early campaigns against the German Afrika Korps. Many learned first hand the disastrous consequences of being unable to concentrate forces and the artillery. Quite early in the campaign against the Germans in 1942, Major (later General) P.P. Kumaramangalam's 7th Field Battery put up a tremendous defence against the attacking Germans at Bir Hachiem, and he received a D.S.O.

146   **The Army Officer Corps and Military Modernisation in Later Colonial India**

(Distinguished Service Order) in the process.[40] In the confused retreat following this battle the Germans took four Indian artillery officers including Kumaramangalam prisoner.[41] Other Indian officers also became embroiled in the chronic indecision that infected the 8th Army during this period. In June 1942 Major S.D. Verma (later Lieutenant General) of the 10th Indian division held a position along the tenous defensive line on the coast road at Mersa Matruh, and recalled -

> We kept getting conflicting reports and orders. One day it would be that we were to stay and 'fight to the last man last round'. The next day's rumours would announce that we would have to make a breakout.[42]

The division eventually broke out of the German encirclement with heavy casualties. Verma himself became separated from his convoy, but managed to find his way back to British-held territory (El Daba). Amidst defeat he learned a lasting lesson on military leadership -

> .....the memory of the dishevelled and dirty uniforms the men were wearing and the vacant looks in their eyes is still fresh. The fact that some of their officers were slowly locating them and trying to cheer them up must have been a great morale booster for them, because soon they were showing their normal spirit.[43]

The few Indian armoured units that took part in this campaign became part of the debacle. Many learned of the urgent need for artillery support in the face of German armoured superiority. In April 1941 Major (later Army Chief) Rajendrasinhji organized a 2 squadron rearguard of the 2nd Lancers to cover the retreat of the remnants of 3rd Indian Motor Brigade Group after its gallant defence against the Germans at El Mekili. The rearguard action ended quickly and relied mainly on artillery to keep the German tanks at bay. In the retreat to El Adem, Rajendrasinhji's column surprised and captured a German encampment. For his actions he became the first Indian officer to be awarded the DSO.[44]

For most of the Indian officers who fought on the Western front, and the North African desert in particular, their primary wartime memory involved defeat by the Germans. These officers learnt first-hand the disastrous consequences of a British led Commonwealth Army engaging the

Germans without a coherent military doctrine. These experiences no doubt molded their attitudes towards warfare in the post-independent Indian Army. Rajendrasinhji and Kumaramangalam both became Army Chiefs of the independent Indian Army. Verma and Bhagat also rose in the hierarchy to become senior General officers. The underlying theme in all of the actions and writings of these officers in the post-independent Indian Army rested on a firm belief in the infantry-artillery, defensive-offensive doctrine originated by Auchinleck in North Africa.

The main theatre of war where most Indian officers saw action during the war lay in the East, with the 14th Army. In this conflict with the cream of the Japanese Imperial Army the seeds of the independent Indian Army's tactical doctrine emerged. The majority of the senior commanders of the post-independence army also gained their war experience on this front. In the early part of the campaign against the Japanese many Indian officers became Japanese POW's with disastrous consequences for their military careers. In Chapter Four we examined in some detail the wartime career of Captain Mohan Singh who joined with the Japanese to establish the INA. In all 400 Indian officers joined the I.N.A., about 250 of them came from the medical corps.[45] The independent Indian Army had no use for these deserters despite the 'nationalistic' motives for their desertion and cooperation with the enemy. There were, however, many Indian officers who as prisoners of the Japanese refused to join the INA. The treatment of these officers was often much worse than those of other British and Commonwealth officers.

The Japanese tortured many officers including Captains Dhargalkar and Badhwar for weeks on end.[46] Their unit, the 3rd Indian Cavalry, had been operating in support of the 11th Indian division in Malaya during the Japanese invasion of November 1942. The unit's armoured cars could put up little resistance against the fast moving Japanese infantry and armor. Its remnants retreated into Singapore on 31 January 1942, where it along with the rest of the garrison surrendered on 14 February. Two Indian officers of the unit, Captains Dhargalkar (later Lieutenant General) and Badhwar (later Major General) became Japanese POW's.[47] The trauma of prolonged detention in Japanese POW camps no doubt sapped the morale and resilience of these and other officers. It also deprived them of valuable combat experience. Few of these officers, including Dhargalkar and Badhwar, rose to high command positions in the independent Indian Army.

Not all Indian officers, however, fell prey to the early Japanese offensives. Captain S.H.F.J. Manekshaw (later Field Marshall) launched one of the few successful British counterattacks in the early part of the war to retake a hill (Pagoda Hill) during the battle of Sittang river.[48] Manekshaw became one of the few Indian officers to see extensive action against the Japanese throughout the war to the very end. His tremendous drive and energy eventually resulted in the award of an MC (Military Cross) in June 1942.[49] Manekshaw rose in the Indian Army to become not only Army Chief, but also India's first Field Marshall. He commanded the Indian Army during its very successful campaign in East Pakistan in 1971. The tactics of that campaign bore remarkable similarities to Slim's successful campaign against the Japanese in Burma and Malaya.

Additionally Indian officers had the opportunity to command Battalion and Brigade level units in combat in the Eastern theatre. These officers became very involved in implementing General Slim's radical eight point plan to carry the war to the Japanese. The most visible example is of course that of Brigadier Thimayya. His first action as Battalion commander (Colonel) in which he seized a heavily defended Japanese hill in a night attack with a brief artillery shoot would have undoubtedly earned high marks from his instructors at the Staff College Quetta.[50]

Colonels L.P. Sen and S.P.P. Thorat also commanded Battalion level formations in the field during the war. Like Thimayya before him Thorat's entry into the war was preceded by a stint at Quetta (1941). After a brief posting to Army HQ, Thorat joined the 4/14th Punjab which as part of 114th Brigade of 7th Indian division, played a role in clearing Japanese forces from the Naga hills. After a short stay which involved taking part in many 'small but savage' actions he moved to 9/14th Punjab part of 20th Indian division engaged in fighting in the Imphal plains.[51] Here Thorat took over temporary command of the battalion replacing his commanding officer who had been struck down with dysentary. Unused to his new found rank Thorat accompanied his troops on a lengthy reconnaissance mission. The brigade commander, while happy with Thorat's initiative, did not approve of his involvement in patrol actions. In November 1944 Thorat received his first official Battalion command – the 2/2nd Punjab part of 51st Indian Infantry Brigade. This particular brigade became known as the 'Indian Brigade' for unlike other Indian army brigades it had three Indian Battalions instead of one British and two Indian. More significantly, all three battalions had Indian commanders – Thimayya, Thorat and Sen.

In January of 1945 the battalion took part in the bloody battle of Kangaw. The 51st Brigade had the assigned the task of clearing the strongly fortified Japanese rearguard positions. In this action Thorat had to coordinate his battalion attack with artillery and air support. Despite such firepower, his battalion suffered heavy casualties as it advanced through the rice paddies to close with the Japanese. At one point Thorat flung himself into the intense hand-to-hand combat to bolster his men. (During this action Thorat killed a young Japanese officer and seized his sword.) The battle only ended when Thorat called in air strikes to smash a Japanese counterattack. Thorat appears to have been fully aware of the Japanese tactic of evacuating a position under attack and then swiftly counterattacking to retake it thus inflicting maximum casualties on the enemy. After his initial attack had succeeded, Thorat limited any extension of his advance and consolidated his position on half of the hill feature. The inevitable Japanese counterattack followed and was thrown back by the well-prepared battalion defences. Thorat's battalion played a key role in the bloodiest battle of the Arrakan campaign and emerged from it as battle-hardened veterans.[52]

Along with Sen and Thimmaya, Thorat was one of the few Indian officers above the rank of Major to see such intense action during the war. His maturation as a professional and veteran officer is clearly evident from the first limited action he saw at Kohima to the culminating brutal battle at Kangaw. His firm grasp of his soldiers, mentality, his easy ability to inspire them to Herculean efforts by his sheer presence, and his cool, calculating appreciation of the tactical solution and the enemy's likely moves are all hallmarks of a budding commander, a role he fulfilled as Chief of the Army in independent India. Thimayya too became army chief and Sen a senior General officer.

It was in the Eastern theatre rather than the Western front that the Indian Armored Corps came of age. The Burma/Malaya campaign involved the only extensive combat use of large brigade and regiment-sized Indian tank formations in the entire war. Large tank divisions so popular in Africa and Europe were not useful in the East. A staff report in 1945 outlines the Indian Army's approach towards armoured corps formations -

> As a result of the outstanding success of the German Panzer divisions in France in 1940, military opinion swung strongly in favour of the creation of numerous armoured formations. Under pressure from the prevailing military thought, it was decided in India to embark on a program of mechanization and expansion which included the formation of a I.A.C [Indian Armoured Corps] of 3 armoured divisions........it was [then] decided in 1944, to abolishthe remaining Indian armoured division in the India Command, and to concentrate on the production of Indian tank brigades to suit conditions of possible operations against the Japanese.[53]

The senior-most Indian cavalry officer of the war was Lieutenant Colonel J.N. Chaudhuri who became the first and only Indian to command a Cavalry Regiment, the 16th Cavalry (armoured cars).[54] Chaudhuri's greatest challenge came when the G.O.C. 17th division established a special mobile column including Stuart light tanks and Sherman medium tanks of 7th Light Cavalry and Probyn's Horse under his command. The aim was to take Rangoon before the 26th Indian division got there. Although the column failed to beat the 26th Indian division to the punch, it showed a remarkable degree of tank-infantry cooperation in sweeping aside Japanese bunkers and roadblocks.[55] In addition to providing reconnaissance and fire-support to the 17th Indian division, the 16th cavalry saw extensive action after the war fighting communist nationalists in Indo-China.[56] Several Indian officers including Captain Sheodatt Singh of the Deccan Horse (part of 255th Indian Tank brigade) saw extensive action with tank units in the East. These officers and their units performed invaluable fire-support tasks for attacking Indian infantry, gaining invaluable experience in combined-arms operations as a result.

More so than that in North Africa, the fighting in Burma and Malaya laid the foundation of the future tactical doctrine of the Indian Army. It was in Burma that the combined-arms battle concept reached its zenith for the British Commonwealth forces. Artillery, although fewer in number than in the European or North African theatre, played an equally crucial role in the conflict.[57] Many future senior Indian artillery officers learned their trade in the jungles and mountains of Burma. Captain J.K. Khanna won the MC while serving with the 3rd Indian Field Regiment at Palel. His sixth Indian Field Battery moved a troop of guns over steep mountains so that Japanese positions on the reverse slopes could be engaged. This initiative operation involved the partial dismantling of heavy 25pdr guns, as well as literally carrying them by hand over the mountains amidst torrential monsoon rains.[58]

The Second World War resulted in the lifting of most of the time constraints on the Indianization programme and dramatically altered its careful progress. Thousands of Emergency Commissioned Indian Officers (henceforth IECO's) now flooded into the Indian Army. For many of them service in the war provided an ideal opportunity to consolidate and enhance their career prospects in the post-independence period. One such officer, S.K. Sinha, became the 11,555th IECO during the war. He joined the 4/12 Frontier Force Rifles – part of 17th Indian division in Burma – and took part in 'low key' operations until war's end. At the close of the war most of the IECO's were not given permanent commissions. Out of a grand total of about 13,000 IECO's only 450 were selected for permanent commission in 1945 and 1946. Sinha and Captain B.N. Sarkar were the only two selected from their batch of 40.[59]

More often than not, it was only after the war that many of the now permanantly commissioned IECO's began to see extensive action as 'peace-keepers'. Sinha was posted as General Staff Officer Grade III (Operations) to HQ 15th Indian Corps at Batavia (Jakarta) Indonesia. This Corps HQ was redesignated HQ Allied Forces Netherlands East Indies (AFNEI). It had three Indian divisions, two Dutch divisions, an independent armored brigade, and an independent parachute brigade. The original purpose was to take over from the Japanese forces and release the thousands of allied POW's and civilian European captives. However, the mission soon turned into a war against Indonesian nationalist forces led by Sukarno, who had no desire to see a Dutch re-occupation of the Islands.

Since the Dutch divisions were still being raised and trained, it was the veteran Indian 5th, 23rd and 26th infantry divisions which bore the brunt of the fighting and secured the port towns of Batavia, Semarang, and

Surabaya in Java; Medan, Pedang, and Pallembang in Sumatra and Macasser in the Celebes. Here the Indian officers were exposed to intense guerilla warfare, and several Indian officers including Lieutenant Colonel Sarvajeet Singh Kalha – who had won the DSO in Burma – were killed. Sinha recalled feeling awkward about the role Indian troops were playing in subduing Indonesian nationalist while India herself was on the threshold of independence.[60] But most Indian officers, well aware of the fact that independence for India was imminent, were more interested in maintaining high professional standards.The British in India were not complacent about the use of Indian troops in such situations. In the first of a series of letters to the Secretary of State for India Pethick-Lawrence, Wavell urged him to make it clear to the British Government the serious repercussions likely to arise from using Indian troops to suppress the Indonesian nationalists.[61]

Major T.N. Raina with the Kumaon Battalion at Macassar in the Celebes and a close friend of Sinha told him -

> Indian officers must maintain the highest standard of discipline and ensure that their troops did the same. We should not allow ourselves to get swayed by emotion or by the contradiction inherent in the role we are asked to perform in Indonesia. This was necessary not only in our individual interest but also in the interest of our country.[62]

It is doubtful if the British policy makers who had despatched the Indian troops to Indonesia could have come out with a better statement to highlight the long-term goal of establishing a professional and obedient Indian officer corps. Raina's commitment to his professional ethos seems to have worked, for he retired as Chief of Army Staff, and Sinha himself retired as a senior General officer. Indeed in Vietnam, when the 20th Indian Division moved in to accept the Japanese surrender and to keep the peace until the arrival of the French, the Viet Minh issued propaganda leaflets urging the 'heroic sons of Gandhi' not to wage war against the Viet Minh. This appeal however fell on deaf ears since all the Indian soldiers were well aware that the British were preparing to leave India.[63] In September 1946, even after the withdrawal of 20th Indian Division from Vietnam in March, there were 44,800 Indian troops in Burma, 59,000 in Malaya, 16,000 in Iraq, 12,500 in the Middle East, 11,400 in Japan, 5,800 in Hong Kong, 1,500 in Ceylon,

1,000 in Borneo, and 400 in Italy. All told the total number of Indian troops deployed overseas in September amounted to 274,900.[64] On the eve of independence the Indian Army was one of the few armies in the world which emerged with extensive experience in guerilla warfare as a result of its extensive deployments from Vietnam to Indonesia. This experience proved invaluable in enabling the post-independence Indian Army to wage a successful if protracted campaign against communist separatist movements in North East India.

Not all Indian officers participated in combat operations during the war. Indeed many of them sat out the war behind a desk or as an aide-de-camp to a British General. One such officer was Gul Hasan Khan who spent most of the war as an ADC to various British Generals culminating with General Slim. His most challenging task seems to have been the organization of an improptu meal for the Army Commander and his staff at Monywa (Burma).[65] Despite this fact, a substantial number did indeed gain considerable experience in the field.[66] In the process they imbibed many of the tactical and strategic doctrines that the Indian Army helped evolve during the course of the war. On the eve of Indian and Pakistani independence, all that remained to be answered was whether these officers were mature enough to take over the reigns of command in the Indian Army from their departing British mentors.

Notes

1   *Gazette of India*, 3 September 1939.

2   B.R. Tomlinson, *The Indian National Congress and the Raj, 1929-1942: The Penultimate Phase*, (London: Macmillan, 1976), p.144. Although most India political parties including the Congress were eager to see the end of British rule in India, they were decidedly anti-Nazi and roundly denounced fascism and racism. See Sir Albion Bonerji, 'The Indian attitude towards the war aims of the Allies', *Asiatic Review*, (1940), XXXVI, 312.

3   The Congress had decided not to give any support for the war effort unless the British promised to grant independence immediately. The Muslim League responded with a call for the partition of India, to enable Muslims to have an independent state of their own. Linlithgow to Zetland, 8 March 1940, Linlithgow Papers, BL/IOR, Mss.Eur.F.125/28, 141.

4   Dominions included.

5   A very coservative 'official' estimate.

6   India and the War 1939-1945: The Facts, Information Department, India Office, 1 January 1946, BL/IOR, L/MIL/17/5/4263.

7   The famous 'Red Eagles'.

8   Major P.C. Bharucha, *The North African Campaign 1940-1943*, part of Bisheswar Prasad ed., *Official History of the Indian Armed Forces in the Second World War 1939-1945*, (New Delhi: Combined Inter-Services Historical Section India and Pakistan, 1956), pp.91-3; Lt. Col G.R. Stevens, *Fourth Indian Division*, (Toronto: Mclaren & Son, n.d.), p.16.

9   The HQ of Deccan district which had proceeded to Egypt to form HQ 4th Indian division, was reconstituted, and these new brigades plus Poona Horse were formed into the 5th Indian division. India's Part in the War 1940, General Staff India: Government of India Press, Simla, 1940, BL/IOR, L/MIL/5/4261, 5.

10 Individual battalion attacks like those by 4/16 Rajputana Rifles during the first battle of Keren received the support of the entire divisional artillery – 44 25pdrs, 8 6in howitzers, and 4 3.7in howitzers. Bisheswar Prasad ed., *Official History of the Indian Armed Forces in the Second World War; East African Campaign 1940-1941*, (New Delhi, Combined Inter-Services Historical Section India and Pakistan: Orient Longmans, 1956), pp.68, 121.

11 Stevens, *Fourth Indian Division*, p.46.

12 An Indian Army circular issued in 1942 acknowledged that minefields and German 88mm high-velocity anti-tank guns posed a serious obstacle to tank/infantry cooperation. War Information Circular No. 26A, General Staff, New Delhi: Government of India Press, 1942, BL/IOR, L/MIL/17/5/4265.

13   Brigadier R.G.S. Bidwell, 'The development of British Field Artillery Tactics 1940-1942', *Journal of Royal Artillery*, Vol. XCIV., No. 2., (September 1967), p.92.

14   I.S.O. Playfair, *The Mediterranean and the Middle East*, Vol I, p.103; J.A.I. Agar-Hamilton and L.C.F. Turner, *The Sidi Rezegh Battles*, (Cape Town, South Africa: Oxford University Press, 1957) Apdx I, pp.474-75.

15   These proposals were accepted by the War Office, and a circular was sent to all commands specifying the folowing composition for armoured and infantry divisions -

> Infantry division – 2 infantry brigades, 1 tank brigade,
> plus supporting arms.(armoured brigade
> later replaced by infantry brigade).
> Armoured division – 1 armoured brigade, 1 lorried infantry
> brigade, plus supporting arms.

W.O. letter to various commands and theatres, 20 May 1942, BL/IOR, WS 12048 – L/WS/1/616, 264.

16   Proposals from C-in-C Middle East – extensive reorganization of armoured division in that theatre, BL/IOR, WS 6385 – L/WS/1/448, 281. Auchinleck also proposed to give brigades more supporting arms to make tham a self-sufficient tactical unit – the so-called 'Brigade Group' – capable of fighting independent of a division; This proposal was in part influenced by similar independent formations frequently utilized by the Afrika Korps. I.S.O. Playfair, *The Mediterranean and the Middle East*, Vol III, (London: HMSO, 1954-56), pp.213-215, 254, 286-7; This proposal, however, was not well received. The Secretary to the India Office, Military Department felt that independent brigade groups would not be an economic use of force, and that if supporting arms were permanently decentralized to brigade groups they would be difficult to withdraw. Major General R.M.M. Lockhart to General S.W. Kirby, G.H.Q. New Delhi, 9 April 1942, BL/IOR, WS 6385 – L/WS/448, 218-9.

17   John Connell, *Auchinleck*, p.684.

18   *The Rommel Papers*, p.248.

19   'Agenda and minutes of Commanders Conference, Meeting at GHQ BTE, 15 July 1942', WO 201/2050.

20   There is a considerable debate amongst 'pro-Auchinleck' and 'pro-Montgomery' historians about just which of these commanders played a pivotal role in determining the emergence of a 'winning' British tactical doctrine for the rest of the war. Recent work reveals that both sides are beginning to take compromise positions, which would seem to suggest that the evolution of British military doctrine in North Africa was an evolutionary process, with both Auchinleck and Montgomery making

important contributions. However, even Michael Carver a 'pro-Monty' scholar (and former 8th Army officer) has acknowledged that unlike Montgomery, Auchinleck was never given the luxury of time to prepare adequately for battle. Michael Carver, *Dilemmas of the Desert War: A New Look at the Libyan Campaign, 1940-1942*, (Bloomington: Indiana University Press, 1986), pp.132, 145.

21   Indeed, with the exception of the U.S. Army, none of the combatants in the Second World War had the necessary material to conduct large scale mechanized operations.

22   Carver notes that when Montgomery arrived in Egypt, he had an overly optimistic plan as far as the role of the armour was concerned. He subsequently changed his plans to a less ambitious one. As a result of which, his pursuit of the Germans was 'over-insured'. Ibid, pp.138-9.

23   Stevens, *Fourth Indian Division*, p.191.

24   Bidwell, 'The Development of British Field Artillery Tactics, 1940-42', p.90.

25   Stevens, *Fourth Indian Division*, p.191.

26   Tuker, *Approach to Battle*, p.153.

27   J.B.A. Bailey, *Field Artillery and Firepower*, (Oxford: The Military Press, 1989), pp.185-6, fn.44. It must be noted here that 8th Army's artillery tactics were in turn derived largely from artillery techniques evolved towards the end of the First World War. See Ibid, p.184.

28   Lieutenant General Sir Francis Tuker, *Approach to Battle*, (London: Cassell, 1963), p.224.

29   Ibid, pp.361-4.

30   John A. English, *A Perspective on Infantry*, (New York: Praeger, 1981), p.175.

31   Alphonse Juin, *Memoires*, Vol. I, (Paris: Fayard, 1959), p.232.

32   The Indian Army experience considerable difficulty in trying to pry its divisions away from the Italian theatre. In a letter to the Allied HQ in Algiers, the C-inC's office in New Delhi pointed out that the 4th Indian division was needed in Burma, and that the Indian Government had never contracted 'to keep three or any other number of Indian divisions in the Mediterranean theatre – the fact that five Indian divisions are there is purely fortuitous'. Telegram C-in-C India to W.O. and Armed Forces HQ Algiers, 13 June 1944, BL/IOR, WS 5725 – L/WS/1/431 3-4. The 4th Indian division never went to Burma, it was transferred to Greece in September 1944 to try and put a damper on the budding civil war.

33   See Annexure 9. *Report to the Combined Chiefs of Staff: by the Supreme Commander South East Asia 1943-1945*, (London: HMSO, 1951), pp.265-72.

34   Field Marshall the Viscount Slim, *Defeat into Victory*, (New York: David

McKay C0, 1961), pp.116-7.

35 Prasad ed., *Reconquest of Burma*, Vol. 2., p.48.

36 A.L. Pemberton, *The Development of Artillery Tactics and Equipment*, (London: The War Office, 1950), pp.308-9.

37 F.O.'s were then called V.C.P. or Visual Command Post. Ibid, p.341, fn.67.

38 Brigadier Michael Calvert, 'Victory in Burma', in E.Bauer, *The History of World War II*, (London: Orbis, 1979), p.631.

39 Charles Chevenix Trench, *The Indian Army and the King's Enemies*, (London: Thames & Hudson, 1988), pp.143-44.

40 *The Statesman*, 30 August 1942. 2nd Field Battery was part of the 2nd Indian Field Regiment, which was in turn part of the 3rd Indian Motor Brigade Group.

41 Y.B. Gulati, *History of the Regiment of Artillery: Indian Army*, [Published under the authority of the Director of Artillery, Army HQ, New Delhi], (London: Leo Cooper, 1972), p.71.

42 Lieutenant General S.D. Verma, *To Serve With Honour: My Memoirs*, (Kasauli, India: by author, 1988), p.33.

43 Ibid, p.36.

44 The delay imposed by the 3rd Indian Motor Brigade upon the Afrika Korps between 6th and 8th April allowed the Australian forces enough time to reach and fortify Tobruk. Major General Gurcharan Singh Sandhu, *The Indian Armour: History of the Indian Armoured Corps 1941-1971*, (New Delhi: Vision Books, 1987), pp.77-8.

45 Cohen interview with Lieutenant General K.P. Dhagalkar, London, 9 December 1963.

46 Chapter 4. fn. 51.

47 Sandhu, *The Indian Armour 1941-1971*, pp.118-23.

48 Bishesar Prasad ed., *Campaign in the Eastern Theatre: The Retreat From Burma 1941-1942*, (New Delhi: Combined Inter-Services Historical Section, India and Pakistan, Orient Longmans, 1959), p.167.

49 Sinha and Chandra, *Valour and Wisdom*, p.150.

50 Chapter 4. fns. 19, 20.

51 S.P.P. Thorat, *From Revielle to Retreat*, p.54.

52 Ibid, chapter 6.

53 GHQ India to BGS, I.O., 8 February 1945, BL/IOR, WS 12048 – L/WS/1/616, 3.

54 Sandhu, *The Indian Armour 1941-1971*, p.212.

55 The 26th Indian division preempted Chaudhuri's move into Rangoon with a sea-borne landing. Ibid, p.233.

56 Ibid, p.241.

57 An Army circular, however, noted that the Japanese were even weaker in

artillery, relying primarily on mortars for fire-support. 'War Information Circular, Foreign Armies', GHQ INida, New Delhi: Government of India Press, 1943, BL/IOR, L/MIL/17/5/4266.

58 Y.B. Gulati for the Director of Artillery, Army HQ, New Delhi, *History of the Regiment of Artillery*, p.78.

59 S.K. Sinha, *A Soldier Recalls*, (New Delhi: Spantech and Lancer, 1992), p.67.

60 Ibid, p.68.

61 Wavell to Pethick-Lawrence 1 October 1945, *Transfer of Power, India*, Vol VI, pp.46, 306 (para9), 323-4, 337.

62 Sinha, *A Soldier Recalls*, p.75.

63 Peter M. Dunn, *The First Vietnam War*, (London: C.Hurst & Co., 1985), p.168.

64 The Indian Government was placed in a predicament by this deployment, because 250,000 Indian soldiers were due to be released by 31 March 1947. See 'Note on a wholesale and urgent withdrawal of all Indian troops serving outside India,' Wavell to London 8 September 1946, *Transfer of Power, India*, Vol VIII, (1979), pp.464-5.

65 Gul Hasan Khan, *Memoirs*, pp.39-41.

66 A fact readily acknowledged by the Secretary of State Leo Amery who in a triumphant letter to Churchill on 27 April 1945 declared that Indianization was a success with most Indian officers performing 'extraordinarily well in the war'. See Amery to Churchill 27 April 1945, L/WS/1/924, in *Transfer of Power, India*, Vol V, p.427.

Staff College, Quetta
© Pradeep Barua

Chapter 7
The Indian Army and the Colonial Legacy

In addition to its considerable combat role, India served as a major allied assault base during the Second World War. India accommodated 1,320,000 men (British and American) and built 42,000,000 square feet of covered storage area. The Indian Government established 70 new training establishments to take up to 470,000 men at a time. Over 200 fully-equipped airfields were built, as were 7 major air-bases with one mile long runways for the American Air-Force to fly supplies to China. The total value of the supplies given to the U.S. forces in India totalled 129,180,000 British Pounds or $516,720,000. India also supplied vast quantities of food and material to Commonwealth forces all over the world. In many cases it was the sole supplier of certain equipment; for example – India produced all the jungle green uniforms and battle-dress worn in Burma.[1] It is hardly surprising then that at the end of the war India's debt to Britain had been eliminated, and India had built up a credit for $1240 million.[2]

India emerged from the war as a regional military power. Its contribution to the British war effort and the resultant size of its military forces and defence infrastructure left it in an ideal position to fulfill the goals the Chatfield Committee had set for it in the inter-war period – i.e. becoming the bulwark of British Imperial Defence. The subsequent onset of the 'Cold War' only served to further enhance India's strategic potential in the eyes of British defence analysts in both New Delhi and Whitehall.

The volatile political situation in India, however, remained the main stumbling block to this rosy future. Political events in India were fast outstripping the understanding of the governments in India and Britain. That the British would ultimately leave India no longer remained doubtful. The Labour Government elected in August 1945 had already publicly declared its intention of giving India independence. The problem looming was how to implement the transfer of power. Would there be one undivided India or two independent states of India and Pakistan? While the politicians attempted to thrash out this intractable issue, the soldiers, led by the Commander-in-Chief General Auchinleck (re-appointed C-in-C India in June 1943) worked feverishly to prepare the Indian Army for independence. Initially Auchinleck and his staff had felt that the Indian Army would not be partitioned. A unified Indian Army was, after-all, the core of the Commonwealth's future defence strategy. The British even at this eleventh hour had hoped that although India and Pakistan may well be partitioned, the two dominions would continue to maintain a undivided military establishment. This, however, proved to be wishful thinking and on 3 June 1947 Auchinleck and his staff had to confront the fact (after Mountbatten's speech) that they had only 72 days within which to 'reconstitute' (Auchinleck preferred this to 'partition') the Indian Army.

Where are the Generals?

One fact remained constant regardless of whether the army would be divided or not: the Indian Army was desperately short of senior Indian officers. Even the most favourable of pre-war estimates on the schedule for Indianization had projected the mid 1950's as the period when senior Indian officers would assume high rank in the army. Independence had preempted this goal by almost a decade. An official memo from the British Chiefs of Staff highlighted the dilemma.

> If the present standard is to be maintained, complete nationalization should be spread over at least ten years, which for political reasons is considered to be too long.[3]

Initially Auchinleck resisted efforts to accelerate the process. In response to a resolution that a time limit be set down for the nationalization of the entire officer corps, moved in the Council of State by Pandit Kunzru, Auchinleck reiterated that while complete Indianization remained his final goal, he did not want to accomplish this by lowering the very high standards of efficiency attained by the Indian Army. He pointed out that there was no automatic correlation between an officer proving himself to be a good junior leader in war, and then becoming a good senior officer in peace. He further opined that the Indian Army

> needed the best regular officers to maintain the essential minimum of efficiency in peace, officers with the ability to judge men and events soberly and with a deep knowledge of men and things, which can only come from long experience.

Auchinleck presented statistics proving that of 9,000 regular officers needed, only 5,100 could be found within the next years without recourse to some unpalatable temporary expedients. These included – the secondment of British officers from the British Army to fill the gap, the retention of ECOs, British and Indian, who might have been willing to extend their services for a year or two, and the conferment of a number of short-service commissions on Indians already serving in the army.[4]

The political pressure, however, proved too much and in November 1946 Auchinleck decided to give Indian regular officers, none of whom had progressed beyond the rank of Brigadier, accelerated promotion over the heads of British officers.[5] However, he continued to express doubts about promoting Indian officers to senior positions while they had less than 9 years of service. He pointed out that in regular European armies candidates for such senior appointments would have had no less than 20 years of service. Furthermore, most of the 8,000 or so junior officers who made up the bulk of the officer corps had less than 8 years service instead of the usual 12 to 14 years.[6] To ensure that newly commissioned Indian officers received the best possible training, Auchinleck gave the IMA top priority for people insuring that its staff could be 'filled with the best officers who could be spared.'[7]

Auchinleck's task was further complicated by the fact that the quality of Indian candidates coming up before the selection board was very poor, and the percentage of rejections very high, resulting in the filling of only half the new vacancies at the first regular course of the I.M.A.[8] Auchinleck, determined not to lower the standards of admission, called for a drastic overhaul of the selection process, including the establishment of a pre-selection training school. Indeed as early as April 1945 at a session of the National Defence Council in New Delhi Auchinleck had made it clear that while all efforts were being made to increase the number of Indians in command positions, only the best man available would be selected.[9] Brigadier Nathu Singh, the newly appointed Director of officer selection was given the express task of publicizing the IMA to capable candidates. He also had the onerous task of convincing Indian cabinet members that this was the best possible course.[10]

To further implement the goal of preparing Indian officers for senior command positions and to consolidate the links with Commonwealth defence, the British decided to send Indian officers to the Imperial Defence College (IDC). The IDC had been established to train

> selected members of the armed forces and civil services of the United Kingdom, the Dominions, and British overseas territories in the broadest aspects of strategy; and the study of the organization and direction of the whole resources of the Commonwealth and Empire for war....[11]

Two Indian officers, Brigadier K.M. Cariappa (OBE) and Brigadier J.N. Chaudhuri (OBE), completed the second post-war course at the academy from January 1947 to December 1947.[12] They were fortunate to have General Slim as their commandant during the course. Chaudhuri, who was greatly impressed by Slim, recalled his opening lecture

> You have been sent on this course as you are good workers. There are no examinations and tests on this course. We only present you the material.[13]

Meanwhile, back in India, the Staff College at Quetta prepared to train Indian officers for mid-level command positions. The first post-war course placed a heavy emphasis on preparing officers for the function of command. In addition to providing a thorough grounding in staff duties, all officers were to have frequent opportunities of acting as the appropriate commander in 'syndicate exercises and schemes, so that they may gain an insight into the responsibilities and functions of command.'[14] At a tactical level, too, Indian officers were introduced to various aspects of handling and maintaining all types of Division-sized formations. The instructors placed particular emphasis upon

> 'detailed staff planning of all phases of the battle, and will incorporate all arms of the service and such elements of the Navy and Air Force which are capable of cooperation or supporting the division.'[15]

The last requirement would enhance and reinforce the considerable experience gained in combined-arms operations during the Second World War.

Concurrent with the desire to shore up the Indian officer corps, the British had an additional and urgent need to further modernize the Indian

Army. This requirement would ensure that the army of independent India could continue to play an important role in the defence of the British Commonwealth. Right up to the very eve of independence the British Cabinet in London and the British authorities in India remained convinced that military ties between Britain and India would remain basically unchanged. At one point the Attlee Government considered having the Congress sign a defence treaty as a condition for granting independence.[16] This has led at least one researcher to allege a conspiracy theory – that India's right to secede from the Commonwealth was only theoretical.[17] However, the fact that this directive was never carried out leads one researcher to suggest that the British were confident that India's military inferiority with regard to equipment and officers would ensure Indian dependence on Whitehall.[18]

Indeed there is some evidence to support this view. Auchinleck himself seems to have been convinced of this. Writing to the C.I.G.S. Lord Alanbrooke in January 1946, Auchinleck stated that it was unlikely that the autonomous Indian Government would decline the invitation to maintain British troops in India.[19] In August in a speech to the students of the Staff College Quetta, he continued to assume that India would remain in the Commonwealth as a fully autonomous Dominion. He pointed out severe shortages in the Army, Navy and Air-Forces, and suggested that if the British and Indian Governments were mutually agreeable, British troops could be retained in India and organized in Independent Brigade Groups. Auchinleck obviously anticipated little change taking place in the military relationship between India and Britain after Indian independence. The emphasis continued to be placed upon training Indian officers and creating a 'smaller, highly protected, extremely mobile, very hard hitting and self-contained' Indian Army. It would be just the sort of intervention force the military planners in the inter-war period had envisioned.[20]

Not all British policy-makers, however, were entirely confident of India's continued cooperation in Commonwealth defence after independence. The British Chiefs of Staff, including the new C.I.G.S., Field Marshal Viscount Montgomery, were extremely worried about sharing secret defence-related material with Indian officers attending the Imperial Defence College. The British Chiefs of Staff including the Director of

Military Intelligence felt that Indian officers should be excluded from courses at the I.D.C. for security reasons. At the '11th hour' the Chiefs of Staff decided not to ban the Indians from the course. Instead General Slim the commandant of the college was told to arrange things so that 'super-secret information was not divulged.'[21]

An enraged Auchinleck declared –

> The D.M.I. and all his clan are of course merely running true to their usual form of never running any risk at all! They are just the same everywhere!! They can't help themselves.....My ideas have not changed. So long as India is part of the Commonwealth, Indian officers must be accepted [to the I.D.C.] on an equality with any other regular officers.[22]

Montgomery was unmoved, and in a letter to Auchinleck he reaffirmed the ban on releasing top-secret information, noting that there was concern in London about Nehru's recent resolution in favour of an Indian Republic and the fact that this had been passed in the Indian Assembly. Not only did Montgomery reinforce the ban on Indian officers at the I.D.C. from attending 'certain highly secret lectures,' he also declared his intention not to send 'top-secret' papers in connection with recent Camberly exercises to India, as requested by Auchinleck.[23] By March of 1947, Auchinleck himself was forced to come round to this point of view, noting that it would be logical to ban Indian officers from the I.D.C. until the future constitutional status of India became more clearly defined.[24]

In early 1947 the Armed Forces Nationalization Committee had set 1 July 1949 as the goal for the complete nationalization of the Indian Army. This program based upon 'plan 287' called for an officer cadre of 9,000 Indian officers (excluding medical and veterinary). A February 1947 meeting of the Chief of Staff Committee including Lieutenant General Sir Arthur Smith the COS deliberated this plan. The committee concluded that

> It is our considered opinion that, by 1 January 1949, there will NOT be enough Indian officers fit by experience to be given all the higher command and senior staff appointments without accepting a very big drop in the present high standard. This applies in even greater force, to the technical posts in both lower and higher grades. Officers qualified for these posts will NOT exist.[25]

According to the Chief of Staff's own figures, there were 34,100 British officers to 7,800 Indian officers on 1 October 1945. This ratio changed dramatically by 1 April 1947 to 11,500 British officers to 8,400 Indian officers (it must be noted that the Indian Army had substantially reduced its strength during the same period). This would seem to suggest that the goal of 9,000 Indian officers by 1949 could have easily been met. However, a considerable number of these officers were IECOS with little experience, most of whom would not obtain permanent commissions.[26]

On 5 July 1946 the Chief of Staff Committee issued a final report addressing the strategic advantages and disadvantages should India become a sovereign state outside the Commonwealth. The committee noted that the only advantage to be seen in the existence of independent India was that it would relieve Britain of considerable manpower commitments. The disadvantages on the other hand were numerous. The committee noted that an independent and unfriendly India influenced by powers hostile to the Commonwealth, such as Russia, China or Japan, would make it impossible to move freely by sea and air in the northern part of the Indian Ocean area, which is of supreme importance to the Commonwealth.[27] The committee urged that in order to plan for such a contingency the Andaman Islands should be retained as an outpost to Burma and Malaya.[28]

TABLE 7

RATIO OF BRITISH AND INDIAN OFFICERS FROM 1926-1947[29]

Date	British Officers	Indian Officers	Total
1926	-	74	-
1931	3033	108	3141
1 Oct 1939	4028	396	4424
1 Jan 1940	4028	415	4443
1 Jan 1941	7194	596	7790
1 Jan 1942	13833	1667	15500
1 Jan 1943	25565	3676	29241
1 Jan 1944	29740	6566	36306
1 Jan 1945	32344	7546	39890
1 Sept 1945	34590	8340	42930
1 Oct 1945	34100	7800	42000
1 Apr 1947	11500	8400	19900

Partition

On 3 June 1947, Lord Mountbatten the last Viceroy announced that power would be transferred to the two independent Dominions of India and Pakistan on 15 August 1947. In May Nehru rejected a last attempt to maintain an undivided defence establishment, giving Auchinleck little more than ten weeks in which to divide the Armed Forces between the two emerging nations. The Indian Government established a Joint Defence Council (JDC) to facilitate this task. According to Martin Wainwright, this was yet another last-ditch attempt by Mountbatten 'to retain the unity of and British influence over the command structure of the two dominions.'[30] The same month Mountbatten made this historic announcement he set up the Armed Forces Reconstruction Committee (AFRC) to suggest just how defence resources could be divided between the two dominions.[31] The JDC chaired by Lord Mountbatten supplanted this role by the 15th August. It controlled all the military assets and manpower until they were divided between the two dominions.

On 30th June the interim Cabinet accepted the Chief of Staff's proposal that the armed forces and defence assets be divided along a 70:30 ratio in favour of India. However, this clean mathematical divide proved difficult to implement. To begin, many of the army Regiments were ethnically diverse (there were no Muslim only units). So it was decided that while units would in fact be divided along the 70:30 ratio, the personnel of these units would have the option of transferring to the other dominion's armed forces. A different problem arose over the division of military establishments. For various, but primarily strategic reasons, most of the defence establishments were located in the interior of the sub-continent. It would obviously be impractical to physically uproot these facilities to transfer them to Pakistan, so it was decided that only movable assets would be divided. Consequently, India walked away from the partition with one of the largest defence-production establishments in the world.[32]

Once the division of political power had taken place, it became increasingly difficult for the JDC to coordinate the division of military resources. One of the problems was India's reluctance and slowness in complying with the redistribution of military stores. Auchinleck, however, considered this a minor point and felt most of the JDC's task had been completed. Yet it was increasingly becoming apparent that the JDC was becoming a defunct body. The two dominions simply could not agree on anything substantial. Any high hopes Mountbatten might have had for continued cooperation were finally dashed when on 22 October 1947 Pakistan launched 'Operation Gibraltar', its covert guerrilla war to wrest control of the princely state of Kashmir. In November amidst escalating conflict in the Kashmir valley, the Supreme Commanders HQ was dissolved and Auchinleck left India.

Independence

Although in strict legal terms Britain's control of the armies of India and Pakistan ended on 15 August 1947, she continued to exercise considerable influence over these armies well into 1950, and even beyond that in the case of Pakistan. This was a direct result of the severe shortage of senior officers in both of these armies. Both India and Pakistan embarked towards their independent future with British Army commanders – General Douglas Gracey for Pakistan and General Roy Bucher for India. Furthermore, for several years after independence in India's case and a half decade in Pakistan's case, both the armies utilized several senior British officers at various command/advisory level positions in their armies; this was particularly so in the case of technical arms (the same was the case with the Navies and the Air Force). These deficiencies meant that actual colonial military disengagement from in the sub-continent came about only in the mid 1950's.

Soon after independence the British found themselves in a unique position with regard to the two armies. They were no longer saddled with the heavy responsibilities of managing these armies, while coping with the accompanying thankless political consequences. However, they were in a situation where they could watch most closely the evolution of these armies, and, if the situation demanded, exercise subtle yet significant influence on them. The presence of a number of senior British officers who continued to be employed by these armies made this situation possible. These officers, although nominally under the control of either the Indian or the Pakistan governments, would in the final analysis be answerable only to the British government.

The undeclared war over Kashmir posed the main post-independence crisis for the emerging nations. This war provided the British with an opportunity – unwelcome though it might have been – to witness firsthand the military performance of their erstwhile proteges. The main focus of their attention not surprisingly was the nascent officer corps and in particular the senior commanders of the two armies. The war in Kashmir quickly highlighted the deficiencies in the officer corps of the two armies. The British were determined to ensure that no serving British officer in either of these armies would become involved in the fighting. To guarantee this the British Government was prepared to withdraw all its officers by issuing a 'stand-down' order if either army sought to utilize its British officers in combat.[33] Such an order would have had a disastrous effect upon the Pakistani Army and, just as the British had intended, this threat did considerably restrain Pakistani activity in Kashmir for some time.[34]

During the early stages of the Kashmir conflict (26 October 1947), the Pakistani leader Jinnah ordered the British Commander-in-Chief of the Pakistan Army General Gracey to seize the strategic Kashmiri locations of Baramulla, Srinagar and Banihal Pass. Gracey refused to comply and informed the Supreme Commander, Auchinleck (27 October 1947). The next day Auchinleck flew to Lahore and informed Jinnah of the 'incalculable consequences' of the military violation of 'what is now territory of the Indian Union.' General Gracey emphasized Pakistani weaknesses, including no doubt its lack of officers. Jinnah although 'angry and disturbed' withdrew his order which Gracey had in any case refused to obey. According to a British intelligence report, the Pakistani Army had a

> clear 36 hours between the time Mr. Jinnah issued orders for their move to Srinagar and Banihal and the arrival of Indian troops by air in Srinagar.

The report suggested that the presence of even a few Pakistani troops at Srinagar would have dissuaded the Indians from landing there. As the report concluded -

> We know that the air move of Indian Army to Srinagar was completely unpremeditated and carried out on a non-tactical basis.[35]

Indeed the shortage of officers in the Pakistani Army was so serious that in the process of raising four new divisions, it became necessary to reduce the number of regular officers in the Battalions from twelve to eight, and to greatly increase the responsibility of the J.C.O.s.[36] The shortage of officers in the Pakistani Air Force was even more urgent, forcing the latter to engage Polish flying officers from Britain in order to avoid using British officers in the conflict.[37] The main problem Pakistan faced with its officer corps was that most Pakistani officers, unlike their Indian counterparts, had little combat experience and lacked the 'necessary background'.[38]

According to Auchinleck, at partition there were few good Muslim officers, most of them had been sidetracked to support units, while at the same time there were a great number of able Hindu officers in fighting units.[39] In General Gracey's view, the reason for this was that Muslims did not do well in competitive exams with Hindus. Gracey, who became the first Commander-in-Chief of the Pakistan Army, pointed out that at partition Pakistan had only 4 Lieutenant Colonels – Ayub Khan, Akbar Khan, M. Hayyauddin, and N.M. Sher Ali Khan.[40] Another British officer, Brigadier Stephenson, also noted that Hindus on the whole were were better staff officers than Muslims.[41]

The British opinion of the Pakistani Army's senior leadership was equally gloomy. Mr. A.H. Reed a British junior councilor reporting on the issue of the future Pakistani Army Commander noted that Major General Raza 'a born intriguer, had been lobbying hard for the Commander-in-Chief position.' Reed felt that Raza had neither the ability nor the personality for the job. He was feared by his juniors and disliked by the majority of the British and other senior Pakistani officers. Reed's own 'two favorite bets' were the respective commanders of the 10th and 9th Divisions, Iftikhar-Ud Din and Nazir Ahmed Khan.[42]

The British did not enjoy a similar leverage over India. As Brigadier J.F. Walker the Military Adviser to the U.K. High Commissioner in Pakistan drew attention to the fact that there were no British officers serving in the fighting forces of India, and that most of the British officers in the Indian Army were only employed in an advisory capacity.[43] Once the replacement of British junior and mid-level officers with Indian officers had begun proceeding fairly smoothly, the British became almost entirely obsessed with the senior Indian Army officers. In 1948 the main question occupying the minds of the British was who would succeed General Bucher as the Commander-in-Chief. Brigadier Walker, the Military Adviser to the British High Commissioner in Pakistan, quoted General Gracey as saying that the post would go to General Rajendra-Sinjhi who commanded the successful police action to incorporate the princely state of Hyderabad into the Indian Union. In his conversation with Gracey, Walker noted that Rajendra-Sinjhi was not considered to be 'too able', to which Gracey replied 'Yes but Reggie is a Gentleman.'[44]

Apparently professional qualification alone was not enough for some senior British officers in order for them to approve the appointments of senior Indian officers. Personality traits, in fact, played a major role in British opinions of the Indian General Staff in the post-independence period. In a secret telegram to the Commonwealth Relations Office almost a year after General Cariappa had been appointed as the first Indian Commander-in-Chief of the Indian Army, Sir Terence Shone, the British High Commissioner to India, complained that the departing British commander General Bucher had not been consulted about Cariappa's appointment. In Shone's view

> .....there is no officer in the Indian Army fit to be Commander-in-Chief but there are some probably better qualified than Cariappa. He is vain, superficial, impetuous, lacking in stability, moral courage and above all military judgement.[45]

This scathing vilification of India's senior-most military officer by Sir Shone is somewhat puzzling, for although Cariappa is not thought of as a great field commander, he is considered by many qualified observers within and outside of the Indian Army to have done a commendable job as its first Indian Commander-in-Chief. Shone's attacks on Cariappa are all the more remarkable when one considers the fact that his own Military Adviser Brigadier Loring held a most favourable opinion on Cariappa's appointment. In his first report as Military Adviser, Brigadier Loring noted with 'pride and pleasure' that an Indian Commander-in-Chief had at last been appointed. He noted that there were no anti-British feelings in the Indian High Command; in fact, there was a desire to keep liaison with British officers. Loring felt that-the Government of India have behaved extremely generously towards General Bucher in making him a full General in the Indian Army.[46]

Loring also noted that Cariappa was the officer with more staff experience and senior to Rajendra-Sinjhi, and had the Government of India not chosen him, the army could have been split into Cariappa and Sinjhi factions. As for Cariappa as Commander-in-Chief Loring was very impressed by his 'firm' assumption of command.[47]

This strong assumption of command is very much in evidence in Cariappa's first set of Indian Army Orders. He had declared -

> It has been noted that the military bearing of personnel in certain units is below the required standard. This is mainly due to the insufficient time being devoted to drill, with and without arms, and to insufficient attention being paid to precision in drill movements. In order to bring military-bearing to the standard requirement throughout the Army, a period of not less than ten minutes will be spent during each days parade hours on close order drill, by every unit in the Army. The term unit will be taken to include detachments of Army or Corps, wherever they may be employed. When practical to do so, this drill will be carried out with arms. Alertness and precision will be insisted upon.

Cariappa went on to note that many junior officers in Kashmir lacked experience. He recommended a 'period' of guidance by senior officers and also suggested that whenever possible plans be 'vetted' by seniors. Cariappa also noted that many senior officers were not conversant with their duties in the new appointments. He called for senior General officers to initiate training of their immediate subordinates, eg: Brigadiers who in turn would train Colonels.[48] The press reaction to Cariappa was equally favourable. Reuters news service of India and Pakistan Service described him as a

> lithe 6 footer.....like Monty [Montgomery] he rates the 'human factor' a top priority in any campaign.....speaks in clipped, effective sentences.....[49]

Sir Shone's virulent, albeit behind the scene, attack on Cariappa stemmed partly from his belief that -

> Although my relations with Cariappa, whom I have known for many years is friendly. I think it unlikely he will seek my advice, and, I would naturally be very cautious of offering it gratuitously. Our influence in military circles will therefore diminish a disappear altogether....[50]

Sir Shone's views, however, flew straight in the face of his own Military Adviser Brigadier Loring. He stated that Lieutenant General Dudley Russell, the senior British Adviser to the Indian Army, had been constantly sought for his advice, and that he – Russell – enjoyed an influential position in the Army.[51]

Loring's endorsement of Cariappa notwithstanding, he did note several problems in the Indian General Staff. In fact his Report No. 1 of 1949 is a comprehensive and qualified review of the performance of the Indian Army's senior leadership in the two years since independence. Commenting on Lieutenant General Shrinagesh who left 5th Corps in Kashmir to take over from Cariappa as General Officer Commander-in-Chief (GOC-in-C) Western Command, Loring noted that, 'He is an extremely nice little man with a good deal of common sense but has very little experience as a senior commander.' On Major General Hira Lal Atal the new Adjutant General -

> Atal is a curious officer who for many years was suspected of being extremely anti-British......British officers wrong in thinking he was anti-British – probably pro-nationalism.......However, as Commander of 18th Cavalry he seemed to mistrust all the British officers serving under him, the regiment was an extremely unhappy one and I, as Brigade Commander, had to ask for him to be transferred elsewhere. This fact will make my dealings with him somewhat delicate.

On Major General Lakhinder Singh the Master General of Ordinance – a newly created position – Loring expressed his doubts as to whether the General would be able to cope with his new job. Loring also noted that Brigadier Dillon had been appointed as Director of Movements and Quartering because Brigadier Verma the incumbent had not been up to the task. On the other hand, Loring felt that Brigadier N.D. Bilimoria, the Director of Personnel Selection, was an extremely capable officer. With regard to General Chaudhuri, Loring noted that he was extremely ambitious with the backing of an equally ambitious wife. He foresaw a diplomatic appointment for him after his posting as Military Governor of Hyderabad.

Commenting on the Army HQ, Loring pointed out that very little proper planning about the final set-up of the Army (then 372,000) existed at their level. At least one serving British officer, Brigadier N.J.B. Stuart told Loring that he was

> extremely depressed because there appeared to be no planning whatsoever and that everything was done on an ad-hoc basis.

Summing up his report, Loring stated -

> Taking into consideration the partition of the army in August 1947 and what has happened since, the extremely rapid promotion of most of the officers in the army, I think the army has put up an extremely creditable performance. I have seen no deterioration in discipline, turn out or saluting. General Cariappa himself is extremely keen on maintaining a very high standard.[52]

Endgames

The Indian Army marched into independence a creature quite different from what the British had intended. Not only was this army no longer the bastion of a greater Commonwealth defensive alliance, it was no longer a single entity. In many ways the partition of the Indian Army, and not Nehru's decision to make India a Republic, came as the greater shock to the British. The division itself, without a doubt, weakened the Sub-Continent's military potential. Did this unforeseen calamity then destroy decades of painstaking effort by the British to modernize the Indian Army? The answer has to be no, for the Indian Army emerged relatively unscathed from the partition. In regards to the most important asset of any emerging army – the officer corps – the Indian Army easily emerged in a superior position compared to Pakistan (see Appendix A). Not only did the new Indian Army have many more officers than Pakistan, but it had the most capable and experienced officers. Indeed it is in the Indian Officer Corps that we see the true measure of success of the British efforts.

Although most Indian officers were not prepared for senior command positions in 1947, they did, however, after an initial process of trial and error, settle down to do a fairly competent job. Their professional competence combined with the maturity of the Indian political system ensured that the they would continue to remain one of the few officer-corps in the developing world to be untainted by involvement in politics. The military action in Kashmir (1947-50) also indicated that these senior officers had fully absorbed the cautious defensive-offensive military doctrine of their British mentors. This is a doctrine to which the Indian military continues to adhere to even to this day with reasonable success. Furthermore, with the exception of the conflict with Pakistan, recent Indian military involvement in Sri Lanka and the Maldives does seem to indicate that India is at last fulfilling the stabilizing role in the Indian Ocean region envisioned by the British in the years leading to independence.

Pakistan, on the other hand, followed a different road. Not only did it end up obtaining a fraction of the defence material and establishments of undivided India, but more crucially its officer corps was woefully inadequate in both numbers and seniority (See Appendix A). The reports of the British Military Advisers in Pakistan in the early years after independence bemoaned the fact that promotions were coming fast and furious at the cost of professionalism and quality. Pakistan's senior most Army Chiefs and Generals found themselves catapulted virtually overnight into positions of tremendous responsibility and authority with little or no training for the job. An immature military leadership along with a relatively weak political system resulted in the Pakistani Army's involvement in politics. In terms of military doctrine, too, the Pakistani Army diverged from the Indian Army. In the place of the defensive-offensive military doctrine, the Pakistanis adopted an offensive-defensive military doctrine. Evidence of such a doctrine is revealed in the planning for 'Operation Gibraltar' (plan to seize Kashmir in 1947). Pakistan's adherence to such a doctrine without having the necessary resources and skills resulted in repeated failure, culminating with the disastrous 1971 war against India. Although this doctrine was in part necessitated by India's superiority in resources and manpower, it was mainly engendered by a Pakistan Army leadership which had few – if any – doctrinal links to its British past. The Pakistani military leadership, seduced by the high-tech military technology and doctrines of the United States, became convinced that a technologically advanced Pakistani Army could easily defeat a numerically superior Indian Army with speed and surprise. The Pakistani military was also a firm believer in the 'martial races' theory, and felt that their numerical inferiority was more than offset by a decided 'martial' dominance over the Hindu masses.

In vain, the Pakistan military tried to fulfill its ambition of becoming a bastion of 'freedom' against communism in South Asia by joining the U.S. inspired anti-communist military alliances – SEATO and CENTO. The politicization of its officer corps, its adherence to a military doctrine beyond its capabilities, and its long-standing obsession with India ensured such failure. Although the legacy of the old British-Indian Army with regard to its professional officer corps and an operationally sound military doctrine continue to live on and evolve primarily in the Indian Army today; the Pakistani Army and even the Bangladeshi Army do maintain a high degree of professional competence, especially in comparison to most other developing world armies.

TABLE 8
LIST OF OFFICERS OF THE RANK OF COLONEL AND ABOVE
IN THE PAKISTAN ARMY (1948)[53]

G.H.Q.
Commander-in-Chief: General Sir Douglas Gracey
Chief of Staff: Lieutenant General R.C. McCay
Offg.Dy.COS: Major General W.J. Cawthorne

M.S. Branch
Military Secretary: Brigadier Rahman Kallno
Deputy Secretary: Colonel K.C. Campbell-Meiklojohn

G.S. Branch
Chief of General Staff: Major General R.A. Hutton
D.M.O. : Brigadier M. Sher Khan
D.M.I. : Colonel M.A. Latif Khan
D.S.D. : Brigadier S.W. Packwood

D.W.E. : Colonel M.H. Hussain
D.M.T. : Brigadier C.J. Jerrard
Dir.Arty. : Brigadier R. Morley
Dir.Sigs. : Brigadier H.L. Lewis

A.G.s Branch

Adjutant General: Major General N.A.M. Raza
D of O : Brigadier C.P. Murray
D.P.S. : Brigadier H.L. Hill
D.G.M.S. : Major General S.M.A. Faruki
D.D.G.M.S. : Colonel W.A. Burki
J.A.G. : Colonel S. Sherjan

Q.M.G.s Branch

Quarter Master General: Major General S.Greeves
Brig `Q" : Brigadier Nasir Ali Khan
D.S.T. : Brigadier M.J.A. Sheehan
D.D.S.T. : Colonel Jamal Dar
D.R.V.&E. : Brigadier Malik Gulsher Khan

M.G.O. Branch

Master General Ordinance: Major General A. Whiteside
C.T.D. : Colonel J. Browne
D.O.S : Brigadier E.C.O. Morphy
Dy D.O.S. : Colonel N.L. Crumby
D Dos (Stores) : Colonel M.A. Khanzada
D.E.M.E. : Brigadier W.P.B. Ashton
Offg.D.D.E.M.E. (Tech) : Colonel D.F. Bartlett

E-in-C's Branch

Engineer-in-Chief: Major General Sir Willis R. Jeffries
Dy.E-in-C. & Dir Works: Brigadier W.L.B. Veitch
Col. Eng. Staff: Colonel D.R. Martin

7th Division

Commander: Major Genral F.J. Loftus-Tottenham

2 i/c : Brigadier M. Hayauddin MC

C.R.A. : Brigadier J.M.L. Crawford

10th Bde Cmdr : Brigadier H.I. Ahmad

25th Bde Cmdr : Brigadier Mohammed Azam Khan

2 i/c : Colonel F.W. Gibb

101 Bde Cmnd : Brigadier Akbar Khan DSO (transferred to 9th Div)

8th Division

Commander: Major General Mohammed Akbar Khan MBE

2 i/c : Brigadier P.W. Parker

C.R.A. : Brigadier P.H.L. Findlay

51st Bde Cmdr : Brigadier H.I. Majid

9th Division

Commander: Major General Nazir Ahmed

110th Bde Cmdr : Brigadier K.M. Sheik

101st Bde Cmdr : Brigadier Akbar Khan DSO (Trg and Admin)

102nd Bde Cmdr : Brigadier Mohammed Yousuf Khan

10th Division

Commander: Major Genral Mohammed Iftikhar Khan

2 i/c : Brigadier F.H. Stevens

14th Bde Cmdr : Brigadier Nawalzada Mohammed Sher Ali Khan

103rd Bde Cmdr : Brigadier Mohammed Musa

2 i/c : Colonel K. Ata Mohammed Khan

114th Bde Cmdr : Brigadier C.H.B. Rodham

2 i/c : Colonel S.M. Afzal

Instructional Establishments, Etc.

Commandant Staff College: Brigadier I.C.A. Lauder

Assistant Comdnt & Comdnt-

Staff Wing Staff College: Local/Colonel R.T. Prince

Comdnt T&A Wing-

Staff College: Local/Colonel J.E.G. Malsey
Commandant Pak Infantry School: Colonel N.J.G. Jones
Commandant Pak Military Academy: Colonel F.H.B. Ingall
Comdnt Pak Signal
Corps Centre & School: Colonel P.H. Smitherman
Comdnt Pak Training Centre/School: Colonel G.M. Stroud
Comdnt PEME Regtl Trg Centre: Colonel A.L. Ellison
Comdnt PAOCC Centre: Colonel G. Murphy
Comdnt RPASC Centre & Records: Colonel A.B.M. Way
Admin Comdnt Karachi: Colonel C.F. Featherstone
President 52SS Board: Colonel Malik Mohammed Khan
President 53SS Board: Colonel Faiz Mohammed Khan
Comdnt Baluch RC: Colonel R.E. Fellows
MS to Quaid-i-Azam [Jinnah]: Local/Colonel G. Knowles
I.G. Frontier Corps: Brigadier D.H.J. Williams
Dy. I.G. Frontier Corps: Colonel W.H. Fitzmaurice
Commandant RPA Centre: Colonel W.G.P. Stirling
CRE Quetta: Colonel E.J. Palairet
DCE Quetta: Colonel N. Boddington
Comdnt RPE Centre: Colonel J.R. Connor

LIST OF OFFICERS OF THE RANK OF COLONEL AND ABOVE IN THE INDIAN ARMY (1948)[54]

Army H.Q. India

Commander-in-Chief: General F.F.R. Bucher
M.S. : Major General P.N. Thapar
C.G.S. : Major General J.N. Chaudhuri (being replaced by Major General Kalwant Singh)
D.M.O. : Brigadier S.H.J.F. Manekshaw
D.M.I. : Brigadier Chand Das
D.S.P. : Brigadier Som Dutt
D.M.T. : Brigadier J.H. Wilkinson
Dir.Sigs. : Brigadier C.H.I. Akehurst
Dir.Arty. : Brigadier P.S. Gyani

D.C.G.S. (W&E) : Brigadier H.D. Billimoria
D.M.E. : Brigadier R.F. Worthington
D.T.D. : Brigadier H.C. Parcell
Military Adviser-
in Chief State Forces: Major General Himatsinjhi

A.G.s Branch

Adjutant General: Major General S.M. Shrinagesh
D.P.S. : Brigadier P.C. Banerji
D.of O. : Brigadier C.D.L. Turner
J.A.G. : Brigadier W.G.H. Wells
D.M.S. : Major General K.S. Master

Q.M.G.s Branch

Quarter Master General: Major General B.S. Chimni
D.S.T. : Major General G.S. Dhillon
Dir. Movt & Qrtrng: Brigadier K.K. Verma
D.O.S. : Brigadier F.A. Rodrigues
Dir. Remount, Vets & Farms: Brigadier Gurbachan Singh

E-in-C's Branch

Engineer-in-Chief: Major General H. Williams
C.E.S. : Colonel R.E. Aserappa
Dir. Tpt. : Brigadier Arjan Singh
Dir. Works: Brigadier F.B. Pigott

Western Command

Commander: Lieutenant General Cariappa
B.G.S. : Brigadier M.S. Wadalia

H.Q. J&K Force

Commander: Major General Kalwant Singh (in Jammu – being replaced by
Major General Thimayya)
Colonel G.S. : Colonel J.T. Satarawalla
Brig. Admin : Brigadier Umrao Singh

C.R.A. : Brigadier S.J. Sathe
HQ 19th Inf Bde : Brigadier Usman Khan (Jhangar)
HQ 80th Bde Grp : Brigadier V.D. Jayal DSO (Akhnur)
HQ 161st Bde Grp : Brigadier L.P. Sen (Uri)
HQ 268th Bde : Brigadier Bikram Singh (Jammu – Miran Sahib)
Poonch Bde : Brigadier Pritam Singh (Poonch)
HQ 50th Para Bde : Brigadier Yadunath Singh? (Rajauri)
HQ 77th Para Bde : Brigadier Sankaran Nair (Jasmigarh)
HQ L of C Sub Area : Brigadier Jai Singh (Pathankot)

H.Q. East Punjab Area

Commander: Major General Thimayya (Jullunder – being replaced by
Major General Thorat)
HQ Ambala Sub Area : Brigadier Roy (Ambala)
HQ Jullunder Sub Area : Brigadier Lakhinder Singh (Jullunder)

4th Infantry Division

Commander: Major General Sant Singh (Ambala)
HQ 5th Bde :
HQ 11th Bde : Brigadier Henderson Brooks (Anglo-Indian) – (Gurdaspur)
HQ 123rd Bde : Brigadier M.S. Chopra (Amritsar)
HQ 43rd Lorried Bde : Brigadier Dhargalkar (Ferozepore – moving to Poona)

H.Q. Delhi Area

Commander: Major General Tara Singh Bal (Delhi Cantonment)
1/5 Gurkhas (Delhi Fort), 6/5 Gurkhas (New Delhi), 2 Mahar Regt (Delhi
Cantonment).

Eastern Command

Commander: Major General Nathu Singh (Ranchi – Panagar Base)

1st Armoured Division

Commander: Major General Hira Lal Atal (Jhansi – being replaced by
Major General J.N. Chaudhuri)
HQ 1st Armd Bde : Brigadier S.D. Verma (Babina)

HQ 2nd (Indep) Armd Bde : Brigadier Daulat Singh (Meerut)
HQ 9th Inf Bde : Brigadier Atma Singh (Bangalore)
B.G.S. : Brigadier N.J.B. Stuart

H.Q. Bengal, Bihar and Orissa
Commander: Major General F.R.L. Goodby (Calcutta)
HQ Bihar & Orissa Sub Area : Brigadier Paranjpe (Dinapore)
HQ Shillong (Indep) Sub Area : Brigadier Habibullah (Shillong)

H.Q. U.P. Area
Commander: To be commanded by Major General Hira Lal Atal (Lucknow)
HQ Meerut Sub Area :
HQ Lucknow Sub Area : Brigadier K. Sherif (Lucknow)
HQ Allahabad Sub Area : Brigadier C.H. Ponappa (Allahabad)

Southern Command
Commander: Lieutenant General E.N.Goddard (Poona – being replaced by
Lieutenant General Rajendra Sinjhi 1.5.48)
Brig. B.G.S. : Brigadier H.M. Mohite (being replaced by Brigadier Dillon
12.5.48)
HQ 7th Inf Bde :
HQ Bombay Area : Major General D.R. Bateman (Bombay – being
replaced by Brigadier Brar)
HQ Bombay Sub Area : Brigadier D.S. Brar
HQ Poona Sub Area : Brigadier J.D.S. Keenan (Poona – being replaced by
Brigadier Mohite 12.5.48)

H.Q. Madras Area
Commander: Major General A.A. Rudra (Madras)
HQ Madras Sub Area : Brigadier Madhur Sinjhi (Madras)
HQ Bangalore Sub Area : Brigadier G. Creffield (Bangalore)
HQ Jubbulpore Sub Area (Indep) : Brigadier Sheodatt Singh (Jubbulpore)

5th Infantry Division
Officiating Commander: Brigadier Kripal (Ranchi)

9th Inf.Bde. : Brigadier Atma Singh (Bangalore)
Other Units forming

Instructional Establishments, Etc.

Staff College Wellington: Major General W.D.A. Lentaigne
I.M.A. Dehra Dun : Brigadier Mahadeo Singh DSO
Infantry School Mhow : Brigadier N. MacDonald DSO
Tac & Admin Mhow : Brigadier J.C. Hudson
Armoured Corps School : Colonel Aspinall
Artillery School Deolali : Brigadier A.W. Littlefield
School of Military-
Engineering Kirkee : Colonel J.S. Forbes
RIASC School Baraeilly : Colonel J.S. Grewal
RIASC Trg Centre (North) : Colonel P.R. Broadway
RIASC Trg School (South) : Colonel G.S.Gill
IEME School Kirkee : Colonel I.H. Reeves
IEME Trg Centre Katni : Colonel Newton King
IAOC School Jubbulpore : Colonel J.M. Blyth
Army Medical Trg College Poona : Colonel P.P.Choudry

Notes

1   India and the War 1939-1945: The Facts, Information Department, India Office, 1 January 1946, BL/IOR, L/MIL/17/5/4263.

2   T.W. Wallbank, *A Short History of India and Pakistan*, (New York: Scott, Foresman & Co, 1958), A Mentor Book, pp.208, 214-5, 219.

3   Nationalization of the Armed Forces of India, Memo by General Sir Geoffrey Scoones, 5 March 1947, BL/IOR, WS 17089 – L/WS/1/1096, 134.

4   Speech made by Auchinleck, 8 April 1946 in Margaret M. Wright, *The Military Papers, 1940-1948, of Field-Marshal Sir Claude Auchinleck*, Bulletin of the John Rylands University Library of Manchester, Vol. 70, No. 2., Summer 1988, Doc.No. 1147. pp.312-3.

5   T.A. Heathcote, *The Military in British India: The Development of British Land Forces in South Asia, 1600-1947*, (Manchester and New York: Manchester University Press, 1995), p.252.

6   Auchinleck to Mountbatten, 8 March 1947, Correspondence and Memoranda on the Indian Armed Forces, Mountbatten collection, BL/IOR, Mss Eur F/200/6.

7   The last I.M.A. wartime course passed out on 2nd February 1946, and the regular courses began on 25th of the same month. Sinha and Chandra, *Valour and Wisdom*, pp.169, 174.

8   During the war the standards for entry into the officer-corps were greatly relaxed. This opened the door for a large number of less well-educated and motivated Indian candidates, who continued to flood the selection board after the war. After the war, however, the selection process was tightened up to the pre-war standards resulting in the rejection of many of these candidates.

9   Colville to Amery. L/PO/10/22 Secret. 16 April 1945, *The Transfer of Power, India*, Vol V, p.393.

10   Army Commanders Conference at G.H.Q. October 1946: C-in-C's Opening Address, BL/IOR, WS 13023 – L/WS/1/1523, 30.

11   Schools: Imperial Defence College, Annex VII Charter of the Imperial Defence College (revised) 23 June 11948, BL/IOR, WS 14044 – L/WS/1/806, 7.

12   Ibid, p.10.

13   Narayan, *General J.N. Chaudhuri: An Autobiography*, p.137.

14   Training: Staff College Quetta, BL/IOR, WS 14066 – L/WS/1/824, 17.

15   Ibid.

16   Anita Inder Singh. 'Imperial Defence and the Transfer of Power in India, 1946-1947,' *International History Review*, Vol. 4, No. 4, (1982), pp.568-588; 'Keeping India in the Commonwealth: British Political and Military

Aims, 1947-1949,' *Journal of Contemporary History*, Vol. 20, No. 3, (1985), pp.469-81; 'Post Imperial British Attitudes to India: The Military Aspect, 1947-1951,' *Round Table*, No. 296 (1985), pp.360-75; Ayesha Jalal, 'India's Partition and the Defence of Pakistan: An Historical Perspective,' *Journal of Imperial and Commonwealth History*, Vol. 15, No. 3, (1987), pp.290-310.

17 Inder Singh, 'Imperial Defence,' pp.574-6.

18 A. Martin Wainwright, *Inheritance of Empire Britain, India and the Balance of Power in Asia*, (New York: Praeger, 1994), p.62.

19 Auchinleck suggested that British troops might be put into independent Brigades to make their stay more acceptable. Wright, *Military Papers of Field Marshal Auchinleck*, No. 1136, p.308.

20 Address by Auchinleck to Students of the Staff College at Quetta, 2 August 1946, Ibid, No. 1191, pp.320-1.

21 Schools: Imperial Defence College, Attendance of Indian Officers at Imperial Defence College, 11/12/46, BL/IOR, WS 14044 – L/WS/1/806, 41.

22 'Extract from Letter from H.E. Field Marshal Sir Claude Auchinleck C-in-C India, 3 December 1946,' Ibid, p.43.

23 Montgomery to Auchinleck, 30 January 1947, Wright, *Military Papers of Field Marshal Auchinleck*, No. 1213, p.328.

24 Auchinleck to Sir Geoffrey Scoones, Principal Staff Officer to Under Secretary of State for India, 2 March 1947, Ibid, No.1215, pp.328-9.

25 C.O.S. India Papers, C.O.S. Committee's 207th meeting, 13 February 1947, BL/IOR, WS 17089 – L/WS/1/1096, 216-19, 221-31.

26 C.G.S. Monthly Liaison Letters, Vol. II., Lieutenant General Arthur Smith to Lieutenant General Frank Simpson, 9 June 1947, BL/IOR, WS 17096 – L/WS/1/1107, 74-6.

27 Chiefs of Staff Committee: appreciation on the strategic value of India to the British Commonwealth of Nations, in Wright, *Military Papers of Field-Marshal Auchinleck*, No. 1188, p.319.

28 Chiefs of Staff (India)Committee, 'Appreciation of the Strategic Value of India', n.d. July 1946, *Transfer of Power, India*, Vol VIII, (1979), pp.53-7. These views were echoed at a meeting of the Defence Committee of the British cabinet on 20th October, when the CIGS Montgomery noted that if India did not remain in the Commonwealth then the U.K. should maintain a prime interest in the Andaman and Nicobar Islands. Cabinet Defence Committee, D.O. (46) 26th Meeting, Ibid, p.646.

29 This data has been gathered from a variety of sources: BL/IOR, WS 17096 – L/WS/1/1107, p.75; *Report of the Indian Sandhurst Committee, 14 November 1926*, [Skeen Committee], p.56, Apdx II; Bisheshwar Prasad (ed.), *Expansion of the Armed Forces and Defence Organisation*, (New Delhi:

Combined Inter-Services Historical Section India & Pakistan, Orient Longmans, 1956), pp.170, 180-2; 'Report of Sub-Committee VII, Indian Round Table Conference (Defence)' quoted in Sinha and Chandra, *Valour and Wisdom*, p.29. The fall in the number of Indian officers between September and October 1945 may be explained by the fact that the Army was getting rid of a number of the IECO's between 1945-6.

30 Wainwright, *Inheritance of Empire*, p.68.

31 It was one of 10 expert committees set up to cover every aspect of government.

32 Wainwright, *Inheritance of Empire*, p.77.

33 Cabinet, Commonwealth Affairs Committee, C.A. (47) 2nd meeting, No. 4, STAND DOWN in India and Pakistan. CAB 134/54.

34 Report of the Military Advisers to the High Commissioners [Britain] in India and Pakistan, 12 April 1948, BL/IOR, WS 17169 – L/WS/1/1187, 13.

35 A brief examination of the results, which the intervention of the Pakistani Army in the initial stages of the Kashmir dispute, might have achieved. Ibid, 106.

36 Brigadier Walker [Military Adviser to the U.K. High Commissioner of Pakistan] to Major General Redman [DMO, War Office], Ibid, 37-8.

37 Reports from the Air Advisers to U.K. High Commissioners India and Pakistan, Ibid, 84.

38 First periodical report – Military Adviser to U.K. High Commissioner Pakistan to Under Secretary of State, War Office, 2 April 1948, Ibid, pp.168-72.

39 Cohen interview with Field Marshall Sir Claude Auchinleck, London, 7 December 1963.

40 Cohen interview with General Gracey, London, 25 November 1963.

41 Cohen interview with Brigadier John Stephenson, Director R.U.S.I., London, 3 December 1963.

42 Letter from Mr A.H. Reed – office of the U.K. High Commission – Flashman's Hotel, Rawalpindi to S.J.L. Oliver -office of the U.K. High Commission – Karachi, 14 June 1949, BL/IOR, WS 17169/II – L/WS/1/1188, 30-1.

43 Second periodical report – Military Adviser to U.K. High Commissioner Pakistan to Under Secretary of State, War Office, No. 1000/MA., 24 April 1948, Ibid, 153-65.

44 Brigadier Walker of Major General Redman, DMO, War Office 24 September 1948, Ibid, 42.

45 Secret Telegram from the U.K. High Commissioner in India to Commonwealth Relations Office, 6 December 1948, No.4183, BL/IOR, WS 17196 – L/WS/1/1217, 8b.

46   Report No.1, of 1949, 5 April 1949, to Brigadier Barker Commonwealth
     Relations Office, BL/IOR, WS 17215 – L/WS/1/1234, 39.
47   Ibid.
48   Reports from the Military Adviser to the U.K. High Commissioner in India
     to Commonwealth Relations Office, 6 December 1948, No.4193, BL/IOR,
     WS 17215 – L/WS/1/1234, 14-7.
49   Press Clippings, Reuters India and Pakistan Service 5/12/48, BL/IOR, WS
     17195 – L/WS/1/1217, 8a.
50   Sir Shone even suggested that Cariappa may regard his new appointment as
     an opportunity for achieving personal military glory. Secret Telegram from
     the U.K. High Commissioner in India to the Commonwealth Relations
     Office, 6 December 1948, No.4193, BL/IOR, WS 17195 – L/WS/1/1217, 8b.
51   Periodical Report No. 1., of 1949 from Military Adviser to the U.K. High
     Commissioner in India to Brigadier Barker, Commonwealth Relations
     Office, 5 April 1949, Ibid, 40.
52   Reports from the Military Adviser to the U.K. High Commissioner India,
     Periodical Report No. 1, of 1949 by Brigadier W.W. Loring, 5 April 1949,
     BL/IOR, WS 17215 – L/WS/1/1234, pp.38-42.
53   Brigadier Walker to Under Secretary of State, War Office, 17 May 1948, WS
     17169 – L/WS/1/1187, 120-3.
54   I have excluded officers below the rank of Colonel who are mentioned in
     the original report. See Report of Brigadier W.W. Loring Military Adviser to
     the U.K. High Commissioner India, 6 May 1948, Ibid, 145-51.

189

Armed Forces HQ with Prime Minister Nehru
© Pradeep Barua

Conclusion

The previous chapters have told the story of remarkable metamorphosis – the dramatic transformation of a small British-led colonial force into a large modern national army. It is a unique event, without parallel anywhere in the world. Indeed, the modernization of the Indian Army flies straight in the face of many current theories on the nature of British colonial rule in India. The fact that it actually occurred forces us to re-examine aspects of the British 'Raj' from a different perspective.

We now know that from 1919 – onwards and quite possibly before that – a substantial element of the British civilian and military leadership in India had begun to envision a highly professional and nationalized Indian Army, an army that would be one of the primary assets of India when it emerged as a 'responsible' dominion of the greater British Commonwealth of nations. Indian nationalist politicians who railed against alleged British stalling tactics on Indianization were in reality almost irrelevant to this process, and may even have hampered its progress. Their main concern was not so much the welfare of the budding Indian officer corps, but rather the realization that they could do little to influence British military policy in India. In the midst of this highly visible if ineffective political maelstrom surrounding Indianization, the Indian Army continued to evolve and adapt. It established its own military academy in 1932, and eventually consolidated its own military doctrine independent of that of the British Army. Herein lay another problem, for opposition to modernization also came from radical military reformers in Britain. These reformers mis-identified India as the main cause for the stifling of their own efforts to mechanize the British Army, a view no doubt fueled by the knowledge that the Indian Army was becoming an independent entity of its own.

Beginning around 1919 the Indian Army did in fact work and evolve separately from the British home army. Although its senior officers were British, they often acted in the best interests of the Indian and not the British Army. These officers and the British civil servants who worked with them had a specific vision of a professional Indian Army, and they determined to see it through regardless of the opposition from either the British Army and

Government or the Indian politicians. It is thanks mainly to the determination of these individuals that the Indian Army officer corps emerged in 1947 with at least the bare minimum strength and experience necessary to assume the mantle of command. Another positive side-effect of the Indian Army's intellectual independence from the British 'Camberley' school of thought is manifest in the emergence of a military leadership core around Auchinleck and Slim which helped guide Britain and India to a winning and sustainable military doctrine in the Second World War. As a result, independent India inherited not only a professional officer corps but also a proven military doctrine well adapted to its limited defensive needs.

The Officer Corps Post-Independence

In the post-independence period the Indian officer corps has undergone a startling evolution, reflecting both continuity and discontinuity with its colonial past. In the former category, the most visible and crucial example has been the evolution of Indian military doctrine. In all the three major campaigns fought by the Indian Army since independence – 1947-8, 1965 and 1971 – the army has relied almost exclusively on the positional warfare or defensive-offensive tactics perfected during the Second World War. In all three conflicts the army achieved a fair degree of success in attaining the limited military-political objectives set out for it by the Indian Government, namely the defence of Indian territorial integrity. The army did in fact undertake limited offensive actions in all of these three wars, especially in 1971 when several corps seized East Pakistan in a swift fourteen-day campaign. On the whole, however, the army's operations have been essentially reactive in nature – counter-offensives to be precise. Even the campaign to liberate Bangladesh was a painstakingly planned operation executed in a 'controlled military environment' extremely favourable to the attacking Indian forces.

The reasons for this continued adherence to what is seen by many to be an obsolete infantry-based fighting doctrine are quite complex. First, the army's main opponent in these wars has been the Pakistani Army which, of course, evolved from the partition of the British-Indian Army in 1947. From the early 1960's onwards, however, the Pakistani Army shifted its doctrinal sights from positional warfare to an offensive warfare doctrine based on highly mobile mechanized forces. Consequently, prior to the 1965 War the

Pakistanis amassed a reasonably powerful armoured strike force with U.S. M-47 *Patton* tanks and M-113 APC's. The reasoning behind this was that the more mobile Pakistani forces could outmanoeuver the larger infantry-based Indian forces. The tactic failed. The Indian forces operating behind a screen of anti-tank defences which included dig-in tanks and recoilless guns backed by artillery devastated the attacking Pakistani armour in much the same way the British 8th Army's guns and tanks had destroyed attacking German armour in the latter half of the Desert War. This scenario was essentially repeated in 1971 on the Western Front (Punjab). The Pakistani failure to successfully integrate and put into effective use the complex mechanisms of a highly mobile mechanized doctrine no doubt strengthened the Indian General Staff's cautionary approach to such doctrine. On the other hand the Indian Army has taken an evolutionary approach to mechanized warfare. Successive seminars conducted at the United Services Institute, Delhi in 1973 and 1976 reveal a general satisfaction with the infantry-based structure of the Indian infantry divisions.[1] At the same time, the Indian infantry formations have continued to evolve to meet changing conditions. An expert independent research team noted that -

> There are a number of variations in the organization of India's infantry divisions, based on their roles. Weapons and equipment have kept up with modern technology and modern war fighting skills been assimilated as they emerged.[2]

Rather than transform many of its infantry divisions into mechanized formations the Indian Army has gone in for 'Reorganized Army Plains Infantry Divisions' or RAPIDS. These divisions have a single mechanized brigade and two infantry brigades, thus retaining a strong link to the infantry-dominated armies and doctrines of the past. In fact, the Mechanized Infantry Regiment is one of the newest arms of the Indian Army, having been established as recently as 1979.[3] Most of the Indian armoured forces continue to be deployed in a defensive role to the infantry divisions and in independent brigades.[4]

This cautious approach (some would refer to it as stagnation) to mobile warfare is very much in character with the mind-set of the army's General Staff during the inter-war period (1919-38), and like the latter, the independent Indian Army's doctrine, too, has critics both within and without the army.[5] Regardless, there is no denying the fact that the Indian Army has had its greatest operational successes when it has carried out carefully planned defensive-offensive movements. In 1962 when the ill-prepared Indian Army sought to take on the veteran PLA along the Himalayas in a dangerous borderline confrontation, the result was a humiliating defeat. Similarly, in 1988 when the army initiated a hurried offensive against the Tamil Tiger rebel army in northern Sri Lanka, it found itself embroiled in a bloody and indecisive three-year guerilla campaign. Offensive-defensive military operations of the type described above, especially against an opponent of unknown quantity, have not been one of the Indian Army's strengths.

The doctrinal conservatism of the Indian Army's General Staff must, however, be placed within the context of a frequent paucity of funds to carry out the sweeping re-equipment, and more importantly, the constant military exercises needed to transform units into effective mechanized fighting forces. Thus, in many ways the budgetary problems confronting the post-independence Indian Army are once again similar to those faced by its inter-war colonial predecessor. Military innovation and modernization, even when attempted on a very modest scale, has often been dependent upon the availability of funds rather than on the will of the General Staff to accept change.

To make matters worse for the army, in many cases its doctrinal and operational evolution is often held hostage to conflicts in the political arena. In this respect the post-independence army differs radically from its colonial predecessor. The latter had the luxury of being able to alter and even reject civilian policies which affected it adversely. The post-independence army, on the other hand, has all too frequently had to surrender even its tactical decision making processes to the civilian leadership. The most startling example of course is the Nehru Cabinet's insistence that the army initiate an ambitious tactical push to establish new border posts along the disputed Himalayan border with Chinese-controlled Tibet (1961) despite strong opposition from many of the commanders in the ground. In the late 1980's a rather naive (and some would even say willing) Indian High Command was once again thrust into a so-called 'peace-keeping' role in northern Sri Lanka by the ruling Congress Party led Government. With the Indian Army's tactical/operational plans once again being overwhelmingly controlled by dictates from the civilian leadership in Delhi and Columbo the army jetti-soned all its hard-learned lessons from decades of counter-insurgency in north-east India, and suffered heavy casualties as a result.

Civilian interference has not been restricted to tactics and operations. Frequently Indian governments have dictated what the army could and could not acquire in terms of big-budget military hardware. By itself, government control of the military's finances is not surprising, and indeed is to be expect-ed.[6] What stands out in the Indian Army's case is that even when financial considerations have not been in dispute, the civilian leadership has forced the army to acquire weapon-systems it considered to be inferior and often too expensive and unnecessary. A case in point is the tank acquisition debacle in the 1960's. The Indian Army was in the market to acquire a main battle tank to re-equip its obsolete armoured fleet. The new tank would also be license produced by the thousands in India, making this one of the most lucrative military contracts in the world. The army's expert committee recommended that the West German *Leopard-I* tank was by far the most superior tank available in the market. However, the Indian Government led by defence minister Krishna Menon, rejected the committee's recommendation and acquired instead the new and unproven British Vickers medium tank.[7] This tank has proved to be a disaster in Indian Army service. Its chronic mechan-ical unreliability and inadequate armour protection eventually led to it being side-lined by massive acquisitions of Soviet designed T-54/55 medium tanks. In the mid and late 1980's the army's long awaited acquisition of 155mm medium artillery guns was almost scuttled when a major scandal erupted over the payment of dubious commissions by the Swedish firm Bofors (who manufactured the guns) to middlemen and to unnamed Congress-I party chiefs from the government.[8]

To a large extent, the dislocation of the army's interests with that of the civilian authorities has in a large part been due a vast communication gulf between the Indian General Staff and the important civilian policy mak-ing bodies. The Indian Army is unique amongst former colonial armies in that it has had a virtually non-existent role in the security policy-making process in the state. The civilian leadership has a tight reign on the military resulting in the micro-management of all security policy within and without the army as outlined above.[9] At least one retired General has taken this to mean that the civilian leadership and the Gandhi family in particular have had a low opinion of the westernized and elitist officer corp, considering it to be at best an anti-nationalist remnant of the British empire, and at worst a potential threat to continued democracy in India.[10] While there is considerable evidence to support this view in the era of Nehru's administration, no real basis currently exists for such a claim any more. Especially so, because as I shall explain later on, the Indian Army is no longer the socially elite institution it was prior to independence, but rather a more heterogenous body broadly representative of middle to lower-middle class strata of Indian society. It seems that the debacle in 1962 and the many scandals surrounding equipment procurement have only strengthened the resolve of the civilian leadership to even further micro-manage all aspects of defence policy making. Within the past decade the post of defence minister in the Indian Cabinet has all but become defunct with the Prime Minister often reserving for himself the defense portfolio. Similarly, all attempts to establish a National Security Council (NSC) to evolve Indian security doctrine with substantial input from the three defense chiefs has come to naught.[11] The secretive Cabinet Committee on Political Affairs (CCPA) first established in 1971 remains the only institutional establishment for defence/security related decision making in the country. And even in this case the most important decisions are made exclusively by the Prime Ministers Officer (PMO), at the expense of the cabinet.

The most radical difference between the pre and post-independence officer corps, however, comes from within the corps itself. Today the social composition of the Indian officer corps is very different from its colonial past. In 1937, for example, the Indian officer corps was comprised of no less than 22.5% recruits who came from either princely or landed aristocracy. By 1985 this figure had declined to 0%.[12] Indeed, there is some evidence to suggest that the declining pay scale of the army and the corresponding rise in private sector jobs has drained the upper-middle class and middle class recruiting base of the army. In fact, the government contributed to this situation in 1947 when it arbitrarily cut absolute pay by 40%. Further erosion of the military's status developed in 1955 when the Government abolished the office of Commander-in-Chief. The Warrant of Precedence places the Army Chief of Staff in twenty-fifth place behind a host of relatively minor civilian officers such as the Comptroller and Auditor General, chief justices of the state courts, members of the planning commission and state cabinet ministers.[13] The subsequent inability or reluctance of the government to maintain army pay scales to the level of not only the private sector but also the Indian Administrative Services has further stymied middle-class interest in army careers. Some studies have indicated that many of the officers joining the army from the late 1960's are in fact sons of the former OR's (other ranks) and JCO's.[14] Data also indicates that the number of candidates who are sons of gazetted officers (senior civil servants) has dropped from 30% in 1932 to 14.94% in 1987, while the number of candidates who were sons of non-gazetted officers (junior level civil servants) rose from 0% in 1932 to 25.4% in 1987.[15] Further evidence of the decline in the social standing of the Indian officer from this period comes from studies which have indicated that the demand for Indian officers in the marriage market had declined considerably![16] Yet another study has indicated that in 1985 students graduating from many of the top-ranked Indian high schools rated the military 11th out of 15 listed professions.[17] In 1987 the government attempted to rectify the worsening situation by nearly doubling the pay for officers and giving the enlisted men free food allowances.[18] But this move seems to have been too little too late. In any case the floating of the Rupee in the International currency market in the early 1990's has meant that inflation has shot up and there is an even greater disparity between the pay for officers and that for professionals in the private sector.

This transformation of the social origins of the Indian officer corps, however, has not prevented critics from accusing the army and the government of continuing to perpetuate recruitment of 'martial races' cadets into the Indian Army. According to data from Sandhurst and IMA, the overwhelming number of Indian cadets admitted into Sandhurst between 1919-25 and into the IMA between 1932-36 came from northwestern India. This region contributed no less than 68% of the cadets to IMA in the 1932-36 period. This figure fell to 57% in the 1978-82 period, but so did the northwest's share of the Indian population which meant that the region was still over-represented by a factor of 2.5-1 in 1978-82 compared to 2.6-1 in 1932-36. In other words, traditional colonial recruitment patterns have remained the same.[19] The critics assume that various Indian Military Academies continue to maintain the same preference quotas that the British initially (and unsuccessfully) had for 'martial races' cadets. While the numbers certainly support this supposition, there is no evidence to suggest that this is in fact government policy or for that matter desired by the government. The government has in fact admitted to a policy of actively trying to diversify the officer recruiting base by appealing to the 'non-martial' lower castes and tribal communities of India.[20] In 1961 the government established the first of many Sainik or military schools throughout the country. With the establishment of these schools the Indian Government hoped to bring 'public school education of a high standard within the reach of the common man.'[21] The Sainik schools (18 of them in 1985) are located mainly in remote and economically backward regions of the country. The Government's policy set aside 22.5% of their seats for scheduled caste (15%) and scheduled tribe (7.5 %) students, 25% of the seats for children of defence personnel including ex-servicemen. Finally 67% of all seats in a school were reserved for students from the home state. Very few middle-class parents chose to send their children to these schools and most of the students enrolled came from 'poor socio-economic' sections of Indian society. After completing their high school equivalency at the Sainik Schools, the students continued their academic studies for three years at the National Defence Academy (NDA) at Khadakvasla. This education culminated in a degree from Jawaharlal Nehru University. The students, now cadets, then undergo selection to be trained as officers in the army, navy and air-force military academies. By 1985 the Sainik Schools provided 40% of the cadet intake into the NDA. Nevertheless, despite these vigorous attempts by the government to introduce the underprivileged classes into the officer corps, only 9% of the output of the Sainik Schools actually enter the army.[22] So even though the majority of officer candidates still continue to come from traditional recruiting areas, this is probably due to the socio-economic conditions relating to the officer corps as described above. Since a substantial number of Indian officer candidates are sons of other-ranks and JCO's, or the sons of officers who were themselves sons of other ranks and JCO's, it is not surprising that most of the officers do indeed come from the traditional 'martial races' recruiting area of the northwest.[23]

The change in the social composition of the Indian officer corps has been accompanied by a general perception – both within and without the army – that the officer corps, in addition to losing its appeal to the 'best and the brightest' of India's youth, is also falling prey to careerism and corruption.[24] As early as the early 1970's senior Indian officers criticized the 'intellectually mediocre' calibre of officer candidates.[25] These problems have been particularly worrying for the General Staff and in 1986 the new Army Chief of Staff General Sundarji sent out a letter to all officers condemning their 'increasingly careerist, opportunistic, and sycophantic' behaviour. He went on to note that 'standards of integrity have fallen and honor and patriotism are becoming unfashionable'. His criticism also targeted the senior officers, whom he accused of failing to set a 'right example'.[26] Sundarji's complaint about the officer corps is not without precedent; in many respects it has amazing similarities with a biting attack on the intellectual and professional apathy of the largely British-dominated Indian officer corps during the inter-war period by the Army Commander Sir Philip Chetwoode.

Despite the many problems undermining the Indian officer corps, professional integrity, it has on the whole remained a professional institution. While low and mid-level nepotism is frequent, the selection process for senior officers – barring a few scandals – has remained impartial and based purely on merit and seniority.[27] It is this senior leadership core which seems to be guiding the corps through these turbulent evolutionary changes. Even the much criticized junior officer cadres have performed rather well in prolonged and brutal campaigns in Sri Lanka (late 1980's) and on the Siachen glacier (ongoing). It does appear that highly motivated and capable young men in the mold of Thimmaya and Chaudhuri continue to join the army and sustain the viability of the corps.

TABLE 9

Intake of Indian candidates into RMC, Sandhurst (1919-1925) by region.[28]

Province or State Agency	Number of Candidates	Percentage of total number of Candidates
Punjab	35	41.8
Bombay	12	14.12
United Provinces	9	10.59

Bengal	9	10.59
NWFP	5	5.88
Hyderabad State	3	3.53
Rajputana Agency	3	3.53
Burma	2	2.35
Coorg	2	2.35
Bihar	1	1.18
Assam	1	1.18
Central India Agency	1	1.18
Other/Unknown	2	2.35
Total:	85	100.01

TABLE 10

Intake of officers into the IMA, Dehra Dun (1932-36) by region.[29]

Province or State Agency	Number of Candidates	Percentage of total number of Candidates
Punjab	165	41.67
NWFP	50	12.63
United Provinces	41	10.35
Delhi	13	3.28
Bombay	19	2.27
Central Provinces	6	1.52
Madras	6	1.52
Bengal	4	1.01
Gujarat	4	1.01
Kerala	3	0.76
Burma	3	0.76
Bihar	2	0.51
Orissa	1	0.25
Other	1	0.25
Princely States	88	22.22
Total:	396	100.01

TABLE 11

Intake of officers into the IMA, Dehra Dun (1978-82) by region.[30]

Province or State Agency	Number of Candidates	Percentage of total number of Candidates
Uttar Pradesh	721	19.11
Delhi	416	11.03
Punjab	375	9.94
Harayana	321	8.51
Maharashtra	237	6.28
Kerala	207	5.49
Bihar	196	5.20
Andhra Pradesh	138	3.66
Rajasthan	137	3.63
Himachal Pradesh	127	3.37
Madhya Pradesh	115	3.05
West Bengal	105	2.78
Tamil Nadu	103	2.73
Karnataka	100	2.65
Jammu & Kashmir	93	2.47
Orissa	92	2.44
Chandigarh	87	2.31
Gujarat	26	0.69
Assam	24	0.64
Meghalaya	6	0.16
Manipur	5	0.13
Goa, Daman&Diu	4	0.11
Sikkim	3	0.08
Arunachal Pradesh	3	0.08
Tripura	2	0.05
Nagaland	1	0.03
Podicherry	1	0.03
Nepal	9	0.24
Not settled, Not Known	11	83.13
Total:	3772	100.02

TABLE 12

Intake of officers into IMA, Dehra Dun (1983-1987) by region.[31]

Province or State Agency	Number of Candidates	Percentage of total number of Candidates
Andhra Pradesh	240	3.78
Arunachal Pradesh	2	0.03
Assam	35	0.55
Bihar	339	5.34
Bengal	157	2.47
Chandigarh	94	1.48
Delhi	585	9.21
Gujarat	33	0.52
Goa	4	0.06
Himachal Pradesh	237	3.73
Harayana	598	9.42
Jammu&Kashmir	189	2.97
Kerala	334	5.26
Karnataka	192	3.02
Manipur	11	0.17
Meghalaya	8	0.12
Maharashtra	268	4.22
Madhya Pradesh	247	3.89
Nagaland	5	0.07
Orissa	84	1.32
Punjab	782	12.32
Pondicherry	5	0.07
Rajasthan	275	4.33
Sikkim	-	-
Tamil Nadu	146	2.30
Tripura	1	0.01
Uttar Pradesh	1475	23.24
Total:	6346	100

Conclusion

One of the greatest imbalances between the militaries of the developed and the developing worlds is not a technical one, but rather an intellectual one. Most developing-world armies simply lack the necessary leadership and training required to conduct modern conventional warfare. This is not all that surprising when one considers the fact that most developing-world armies are in essence glorified police forces. The mere acquisition of the latest jet-fighters, missile boats, battle tanks, and self-propelled artillery will not automatically transform a developing world army into an effective modern fighting force. This process is almost solely dependent upon the officer corps, and it is here that many developing-world countries have stumbled. In the post-colonial era, it can be argued that with the exception of India no other army in the developing world emerged with a viable officer corps. Many of these officer corps that sprang up in the 1950's and the 1960's (much earlier in the case of Latin America), did so lacking the foundation India had. True, they had all the ritual and symbolic trappings of their colonial predecessors, but there were no intellectual links between the two. Worse, most if not all of these armies continued to be organized as internal security forces rather than conventional armies geared to combat external threats. As a result most of these officers corps continue to search for the necessary skills and doctrine that will make them true 'professional' soldiers, and not just policemen.

An officer corps cannot imbibe a professional ethos and a military doctrine overnight. No amount of equipment and foreign military advisers can offer a short cut to these goals. They can only be arrived at after decades of evolution and adaption. In India this process began in the late 19th century with Curzon's experiments with the I.C.C. and culminated in the late 1940's with the departure of the last of the British officers from the Indian Army. Even then, a half century would have proven inadequate. It took the all-encompassing intensity of the Second World War to finally produce the seeds of a professional Indian officer corps. In the final analysis the greatest impact of the colonial reform is yet to be seen and is still being created as the Indian Army continues to evolve, becoming in the process an enduring legacy of long forgotten generations of Indian officers, British generals and bureaucrats.

Notes

1   Major General Som Dutt (retd.), *Re-organization of the Infantry Division,* (New Delhi: United Services Institute of India, 1973), [seminar no. 1]; Lieutenant General M.L. Thapan (retd.), *Review of the Organizational Pattern of the Indian Army,* (New Delhi: United Services Institute of India, 1976), [seminar no. 7].

2   IDR Research Team, 'Some thoughts on the evolution of infantry organization and tactics,' *Indian Defence Review,* (July 1991), pp.47-56.

3   At Ahmednagar next to the Armoured Regimental Centre, *The Times of India,* (7 February 1988).

4   Lieutenant Colonel J.K. Dutt, 'Wanted: A Doctrine for Armour,' *Journal of the United Services Institute of India,* (henceforth JUSII), (October-December 1977), pp.45-52.

5   Brigadier R.D. Law, 'The Gulf War – the last hundred hours: lessons for the Indian mechanized forces,' *JUSII,* (July-September 1991); Major Gautam Das, 'Turk-Sowar: an Indian mechanized force for the 21st century,'*Combat Journal,* (August 1987); Lieutenant Colonel Mahesh Chahda, 'Mechanized infantry: where have we gone wrong?' *Combat Journal,* (April 1989); Pradeep Barua, 'The evolution of the mechanized infantry,' *Strategic Analysis,* Vol XII, No 9, (December 1988).

6   The Indian civil bureaucracy in fact a maintains a very tight reign on the military particularly in regard to financial matters. See Stephen P. Cohen, 'Civilian control of the military in India,' in Claude E. Welch (ed.), *Civilian Control of the Military: Theory and Cases from Developing Countries,* (Albany, New York: State University of New York Press, 1976), pp.53-5.

7   Major General Pratap Narain, *Indian Arms Bazaar,* (Delhi: Shipra Publications, 1994), pp.73-6.

8   Dilip Bobb, 'The Bofors Blast,' *India Today,* (15 May 1987), p.18.

9   Raju C. Thomas, *India's Security Policy,* (Princeton, NJ: Princeton University Press, 1986), 125-32,160; also Stephen P. Cohen, 'The Military and Indian Democracy,' in Atul Kohli (ed.), *India's Democracy,* (Princeton, NJ: Princeton University Press, 1988), p.119.

10   Major General D.K. Palit, *War in the High Himalaya: The Indian Army in Crisis, 1962,* (New York: St. Martin's Press, 1991), pp.2-3, 21. Prior to independence many Indian nationalists had often considered the army to be an instrument of British cultural and political imperialism. See Lloyd Rudolph and Suzanne Hoeber Rudolph, 'Generals and Politicians in India,' in Wilson C. McWilliams (ed.), *Garrisons and Governments: Politics and the Military in New States,* (San Francisco: Chandler Publishing Co, 1964), p.140.

11 Manoj K. Joshi, 'Directions in India's Defence and Security Policies,' in Ross Babbage and Sandy Gordon (eds.) *India's Strategic Future: Regional State or Global Power?* (London: MacMillan, 1992), pp.88-9.

12 Sinha and Chandra, *Valour and Wisdom*, p.256.

13 Lloyd and Suzanne Rudolph, 'Generals and Politicians,' p.136.

14 See Brigadier B.K. Sinha, "Career Prospects for Officers in the Armed Forces," *JUSII*, (July-September 1968); Lieutenant General M.L. Thapan, "The Army as a Career," *JUSII*, (July-September 1977); Captain Rajiv Kumar, "Man Management: The Present Environ," *JUSII*, (January-March 1983).

15 Sinha and Chandra, *Valour and Wisdom*, pp.256-7.

16 Lloyd and Suzanne Rudolph, 'Generals and Politicians in India,' p.140.

17 R.P. Gautam, 'Status of Services vis-a-vis Other Services,' *JUSII*, (April-June 1985), p.164; also by the same author, 'Causes of Higher Secondary Students' Preference for Military Career,' *JUSII Journal*, (October-December 1979), pp.380-90.

18 Cohen, *The Indian Army*, p.217.

19 Apurba Kundu, 'Over dependence on "Martial Race" Officers,'*Indian Defence Review*, (July 1991), pp.69-84; Sinha and Chandra, *Valour and Wisdom*, pp.254-5; Daljit Singh, 'Military Education in India: Changes from the British Tradition,' *JUSII*, (July-September 1974), pp.227-37.

20 As a student the author recalls several times when recruiting officials made pointed efforts to interest graduating high school students – belonging to the underprivileged 'scheduled caste/tribe' communities – in an army officer's career. This includes high schools in the northeast and western India.

21 The purpose for establishing these schools is not far removed from the Prince of Wales Royal Indian Academy established in the colonial era. Both sought to give prospective officer cadets for the military academies a firm academic and physical grounding for their new careers. Something they would otherwise be unable to receive in the standard civilian schools. However, while the PWRIM was established mainly to cater to students from a princely and educated Indian middle class, the Sainik Schools were created to aid students from the economically and socially underprivileged classes.

22 Lieutenant General M.L. Chibber, *Military Leadership to Prevent Military Coup*, (New Delhi: Lancer International, 1986), pp.39-44, tables 1.1-1.3.

23 See Sinha and Chandra, *Valour and Wisdom*, Table 9. p.256.

24 Cohen, *The Indian Army*, [Epilogue to 1990 edition], pp.214-5.

25 Ibid; and Major General K.S. Bajwa, 'Military Leadership and changing Social Ethos,' *JUSII*, (July – September 1978).

26 Cohen, Ibid, p.218.

27   The exceptions and 'scandals' occurred in 1975 and 1983 respectively when junior commanders superseded senior and arguably more capable General officers to the Army Chief's post. Both incidents took place under Mrs. Indira Gandhi's tenure as Prime Minister, which leads Stephen Cohen to suggest that these actions fit into the 'broader patten of her manipulative style of governance.' Ibid, pp.221-2. See also Lieutenant General S.K. Sinha (retd.), 'Preserving the Army Ethos,' *Indian Defence Review*, (July 1992). Sinha was the senior General superseded in 1983 for the chiefs position. In this remarkable article he analyzes the sorry state of relations between the Army chief and the government. He notes that in 1992 there were no less than 800 cases pending in the Delhi High Court in which army personnel have sought redress.

28   Figures from Longer, *Red Coats to Olive Green*, (New Delhi: Allied Publishers, 1974), p.196; and Kundu, 'Indian Army's Overdependence on Martial Races' Officers', p.71.

29   Chibber, *Military Leadership to Prevent Military Coup*, p.40.

30   Ibid, p.41.

31   Numbers from Sinha and Chandra, *Valour and Wisdom*, pp.254-5, Table 8.

Bibliography

Unpublished Sources

Private Records:
British Library, India Office Records, London.

Barrow Collection	Mss.Eur.E.420/9.
Birdwood Collection	Mss.Eur.D.686/31.
Curzon Collection	Mss.Eur.F.111/253,442,159.
Derby Collection	Mss.Eur.D.605/1,5.
Hoare Collection	
(Templewood Papers)	Mss.Eur.E.240/57.
Irwin Collection	Mss.Eur.C.151/21.
Kirke Collection	Mss.Eur.E.396/11,13,18.
Linlithgow Collection	Mss.Eur.F.125/28.
Montagu Collection	Mss.Eur.D.523/8.
Mountbatten Collection	Mss.Eur.F.200/6.
Reading Collection	Mss.Eur.E.238.
Rudra Collection	Mss.Eur.C.478.
S.K. Brown Collection	Mss.Eur.D.712/14.
	Mss.Eur.D.808/1.
Simon Collection	Mss.Eur.F.77/54.
Interviews	
by Gillian Wright	Mss.Eur.R.193/9.

University of Chicago Library, Chicago:
Diary of Amar Singh
Typescript   DS485.R26R36.

Government Records:
British Library, India Office Records, London.
Military Department:
L/MIL/1/10/39
L/MIl/3/2513
L/MIL/3/2534
L/MIL/5/844
L/MIL/5/857

L/MIL/5/886
L/MIL/5/1762
L/MIL/5/4261
L/MIL/7/10822
L/MIL/7/19006
L/MIL/8/849
L/MIL/8/885
L/MIL/9/319
L/MIL/9/357
L/MIL/17/5/1687
L/MIL/17/5/1721
L/MIL/17/5/1741
L/MIL/17/5/1742
L/MIL/17/5/1745
L/MIL/17/5/1773
L/MIL/17/5/1774
L/MIL/17/5/1778
L/MIL/17/5/1779
L/MIL/17/5/1780
L/MIL/17/5/1800
L/MIL/17/5/1801
L/MIL/17/5/1911
L/MIL/17/5/2225
L/MIL/17/5/2330
L/MIL/17/5/2281
L/MIL/17/5/2282
L/MIL/17/5/2284
L/MIL/17/5/2285
L/MIL/17/5/4263
L/MIL/17/5/4265
L/MIL/17/5/4266
L/MIL/17/5/2290

War Staff:
WS 1934 - L/WS/1/155
WS 2047 - L/WS/1/164
WS 2099 - L/WS/1/170
WS 5725 - L/WS/1/431

WS 6385 - L/WS/1/448
WS 12048 - L/WS/1/616
WS 13023 - L/WS/1/1523
WS 14044 - L/WS/1/806
WS 14066 - L/WS/1/824
WS 17089 - L/WS/1/1096
WS 17195 - L/WS/1/1217
WS 17096 - L/WS/1/1107
WS 17169 - L/WS/1/1187
WS 17169/II - L/WS/1/1188
WS 17196 - L/WS/1/1217
WS 17215 - L/WS/1/1234

Public Records Office, London.
Cabinet Office:
CAB 2/5,6,7
CAB 4/7
CAB 5/7
CAB 6/4
CAB 23/26,72,112
CAB 24/70,111,287
CAB 27/65,164
CAB 27/163
CAB 134/54

War Office:
WO 32/1285
WO 33/173
WO 73/115
WO 95/3911
WO 106/148
WO 161/82
WO 163/11
WO 201/2050

Miscellaneous:

Stephen P. Cohen interview with - Lieutenant General (retd) S.D.Verma, Midhurst, Sussex, 28 November 1963.

Lieutenant General (cashiered) B.M. Kaul, New Delhi, 19 December 1964.

De Witt C. Ellinwood, 'The Special Experiences of Amar Singh,' paper presented at the Conference on South Asia, November 1994, University of Wisconsin at Madison, p.8.

Lloyd I. Rudolf, 'A Soldier of the Raj? Amar Singhs military career,' Ibid, p.21.

J.O Rawson, 'The Role of India in Imperial Defence Beyond Indian Waters, 1919-1939,' unpublished D.Phil dissertation (Oxford, 1976).

Mark Houston Jacobsen, 'The Modernization of the Indian Army 1925-1939,' unpublished Ph.D. dissertation (University of California, Irvine, 1979).

Published Sources

Government Documents:

Cmnd. (1859), Peel Commission.

Constitution Relations Between Britain and India: The Transfer of Power 1942-7, (London: HMSO, 1970-79).

India: Legislative Assembly Debates, 2 September 1938, 1525.

Statistics of the British Military Effort in the Great War, (London: HMSO, 1922).

India's Contribution to the Great War, (Calcutta: Government of India Press, 1923).

Report of the Indian Military College Committee, July 15,1931, (London: HMSO, 1931).

Report of the Indian Sandhurst Committee, November 14, 1926, (London: HMSO, 1927).

Indian Sandhurst Committee: Report of the Sub-Committee which visited the various military education institutions in England and other countries, (Simla: Government of India Press, 1926).

Books:

Agar-Hamilton, J.A.I and Turner, L.C.F., *The Sidi Rezegh Battles*, (Cape Town, South Africa: Oxford University Press, 1957).

Alavi, Seema, *The Sepoys and the Company: Tradition and Transition in Northern India, 1770-1830*, (New York: Oxford University Press, 1995).

Baig, M.R.A., *In Different Saddles*, (Bombay and Calcutta: Asia Publishing House, 1967).

Bailey, J.B.A., *Field Artillery and Firepower*, (Oxford: The Military Press, 1989).

Barnett, Corelli., *The Desert Generals*, (Bloomington: Indiana University Press, 1960).

Besant, Annie, *Speeches and Writings*, (Madras, 1921).

Bienen, Henry (ed.), *The Military and Modernization*, (Chicago: Aldine.Atherton, Inc, 1971).

Bond, Brian, *British Military Policy between the Two World Wars*, (Oxford: Clarendon Press, 1980).

Campbell-Johnson, Allan, *Mission with Mountbatten*, (London, New York: Robert Hale, 1951).

Charteris, Brig.Gen. John, *At GHQ*, (London: Cassell & Co, 1931).

Chibber, Lieutenant General M.L., *Military Leadership to Prevent Military Coup*, (New Delhi: Lancer International, 1986).

Cohen, Stephen P, *The Indian Army: Its Contribution to the Development of a Nation*, (Berkeley: University of California Press, 1971).

Das, M.N., *India under Morley and Minto: Politics behind Revolution, Repression and Reforms*, (London: George Allen & Unwin).

Denning, Major B.C., *The Future of the British Army*, (London: Witherby, 1928).

Dunn, Peter M., *The First Vietnam War*, (London: C. Hurst & Co., 1985).

Dutt, Major Som (retd), *Re-organization of the Infantry Division*, (New Delhi: United Services Institute of India, 1973), [seminar no. 1].

Elliot, T.S. (ed.), *A Choice of Kipling's Verse*, (London: Faber & Faber, 1951).

English, John A., *A Perspective on Infantry*, (New York: Praeger, 1981).

Evans, Humphrey., *Thimmaya of India: A Soldiers Life*, (New York: Harcourt Brace & Co, 1960).

Fuller, J.F.C., *On Future War*, (London: Sifton Praed & Co, 1928).

Gent, John B (ed.), *Croydon Old and New*, (South Croydon, Surrey: Southern Publishing, Brighton, 1975).

Gerth, H.H. and Mills, C., *From Max Weber: Essays in Sociology*, (New York: Oxford University Press, 1946).

Gulati, Y.B., *History of the Regiment of Artillery*, [Published under the authority of the Director of Artillery, Army HQ, New Delhi], (London: Leo Cooper, 1971).

Hamilton, Nigel, *Monty: the Making of a General (1887-1942)*, (New York: McGraw-Hill, 1981).

Hardie, Kier J., *India, Impressions and Suggestions*, (London: Independent Labour Party, 1909).

Hart, B.H. Lidell., *The Defence of Britain*, (London: Faber, 1939).

Memoirs, (London: Cassell, 1959).

Heathcote, T.A., *The Military in British India: The Development of British Land Forces in South Asia, 1600-1947*, (Manchester: Manchester University Press, 1995).

Jeffrey, Keith, *The British Army and the Crisis of Empire 1918-1922*, (Manchester: Manchester University Press, 1984).

Juin, Alphonse, *Memoires*, Vol. 1., (Paris: Fayard, 1959).

Khan, Gul Hassan, *Memoirs*, (Karachi, Oxford: Oxford University Press, 1993).

Khan, Mohhamed Ayub, *Friends not Masters: A Political Autobiography*, (London: Oxford University Press, 1967).

Koss, Stephen E., *John Morley and the India Office 1905-1910*, (New Haven and London: Yale University Press, 1969).

Longer, V., *Red Coats to Olive Green: A History of the Indian Army, 1600-1974*, (New Delhi: Allied Publishers, 1974).

Macksey, Kenneth, *Armoured Crusader: Major General Percy Hobart*, (London: Hutchinson & Co, 1967).

Masani, Zareer, *Indian Tales from the Raj*, (Berkeley, Los Angeles: University of California Press, 1987).

Mason, Phillip, *A Matter of Honor: An Account of the Indian Army and its Officers and Men*, (New York: Holt, Reinhart and Winston, 1974).

Masters, John, *Bugles and a Tiger: A Volume of Autobiography*, (New York: The Viking Press, 1956).

Mehrotra, S.R., *India and the Commonwealth 1885-1929*, (New York: Frederick R. Praeger, 1965).

Minney, R.J., *The Private Papers of Hore-Belisha*, (London: Collins, 1960).

Muthanna, I.M., *General Cariappa*, (Mysore: Usha Press, 1964).

Narian, Major General Pratap, *Indian Arms Bazaar*, (Delhi: Shipra Publications, 1994).

Narayan, B.K., *General J.N. Chaudhuri: An Autobiography*, as narrated to B.K. Narayan, (New Delhi: The Viking Press, 1956).

Omissi, David, *The Sepoy and the Raj: The Indian Army, 1860-1940*, (London: MacMillan, 1994).

Palit, Major General D.K., *War in the High Himalayas: the Indian Army in Crisis in 1962*, (New York: St Martin's Press, 1991).

Parker, Geoffrey, *The Military Revolution: Military Innovation and the Rise of the West, 1500-1800*, (Cambridge: Cambridge University Press, 1988).

Peers, Douglas M., *Between Mars and Mammon: Colonial Armies and the Garrison State in Early Nineteenth-century India*, (New York: Tauris Academic Press, 1995).

Pemberton, A.L., *The Development of Artillery Tactics and Equipment*, (London: The War Office, 1950).

Petrie, Sir Charles, *The Life and Letters of the Right Honourable Sir Austen Chamberlain*, (London: Cassell, 1940).

Ponappa, Brigadier C.B., *Soldier and Citizen: and other writings*, (Bangalore, India: Hosali Press, 1971).

Prasad, Bisheshwar (ed.), *Expansion of the Armed forces and Defence Organisation 1939-45*, (Combined Inter-Services Historical Section India & Pakistan, New Delhi: Orient Longmans, 1956).

–   *Official History of the India Armed Forces in the Second*

World War: East African Campaign 1940-1941, (New Delhi: Combined Inter-Services Historical Section India & Pakistan, Orient Longmans, 1956).

– *Official History of the Indian Armed Forces in the Second World War: The North African Campaign 1940-1945*, (New Delhi: Combined Inter-Services Historical Section India & Pakistan, Orient Longmans, 1956).

– *Official History of the Indian Armed Forces in the Second World War: Campaign in the Eastern Theatre, the Retreat from Burma 1941-1942*, (New Delhi: Combined Inter-Services Historical Section for India & Pakistan, Orient Longmans, 1959).

Robb, P.G., *The Government of India and Reform: Policies towards Politics and the Constitution 1916-1921*, (London: Oxford University Press, 1976).

Sandhu, Gurcharan Singh, *The Indian Armour: History of the Indian Armoured Corps 1941-1971*, (New Delhi: Vision Books, 1987).

Saxena, K.M.L., *The British Military System in India 1800-1900*, (New Delhi: Sterling Publishers, 1974).

Singh, Mohan, *Soldier's Contribution to Indian Independence*, (New Delhi: Radiant Publishers, 1974?).

Sinha, B.P.N. and Chandra, Sunil, *Valour and Wisdom: Genesis and Growth of the Indian Military Academy*, (New Delhi: Oxford and IBH Publishing, 1992).

Sinha, S.K., *A Soldier Recalls*, (New Delhi: Lancer International, 1992).

Stevens, G.R., *Fourth Indian division*, (Toronto: McLaren & Son, n.d.).

Thapan, Lieutenant General M.L. (Retd), *Review of the Organization Pattern of the Indian Army*, (New Delhi: United Services Institute of India, 1976), [seminar no. 7].

Thomas, Raju C., *India's Security Policy*, (Princeton, NJ: Princeton University Press, 1986).

Tomlinson, B.R., *The Indian National Congress and the Raj: The Penultimate Phase*, (London: Macmillan, 1976).

Tuker, General Sir Francis, *Approach to Battle*, (London: Cassell, 1963).

Stokes, Eric, *The English Utilitarians in India*, (London: Oxford University Press, 1959).

Strachan, Hew, *From Waterloo to Balaclava: Tactics Technology and the British Army, 1815-1854*, (Cambridge: Cambridge University Press, 1985).

Thorat S.P.P., *From Revielle to Retreat*, (New Delhi: Allied Publishers, 1986).

Trench, Charles Chevenix., *The Indian Army and the King's Enemys*, (London: Thames & Hudson, 1988).

Verma, S.D., *To Serve with Honour: My Memoirs*, (Kasauli, India: by the author, 1988).

Wainwright, Martin M., *Inheritance of Empire Britiain, India and the Balance of Power in Asia*, (Westport, Connecticut: Praeger, 1994).

Wallbank, T.W., *A Short Histoy of India and Pakistan*, (New York: Scott, Foresman & Co, 1958).

Wallerstein, Immanuel, *The Modern World System*, (New York: Academic Press, 1974).

Winton, Harold R., *To Change an Army: General Sir John Burnett-Stuart and British Armoured Doctrine, 1927-1938*, (Larence, Kansas: University Press of Kansas, 1988).

Wright, Margaret M., *The Military papers, 1940-1948, of Field- Marshal Sir Claude Auchinleck*, [Bulletin of the John Rhylands University Library of Manchester], Vol. 70, No. 2, Summer 1988.

Newspapers:

India
Evening News
Statesman
The Times of India

Articles:

Bajwa, Major General K.S., 'Military Leadership and Changing Social Ethos,' *Journal of the United Services Institute of India*, (July-September 1978).

Barua, Pradeep., 'The Evolution of the Mechanized Infantry,' *Strategic Analysis*, Vol XII, No 9., (December 1988).

Barua, Pradeep., 'Military Developments in India, 1750-1850,' *The Journal of Military History*, Vo. 58, No. 4, (October 1994).

— 'Inventing Race: the British Raj and the Martial Races of India,' *Historian*, Vol. 58, No 1, (1995).

Bobb, Dilip., 'The Bofors Blast,' *India Today*, (15 May 1987).

Bond, Brian, 'The Effect of the Cardwell Reforms,' *Royal United Services Institute Journal*, (November 1960).

Bonerji, Sir Albion, 'The Indian attitude towards the war aims of the Allies,' *Asiatic Review*, XXXVI, (1940).

Bidwell, Brigadier R.G.S., 'The Development of British Field Artillery Tactics 1940-1942,' *Journal of Royal Artillery*, Vol. XCIV, No. 2., (September 1967).

Calvert, Brigadier Michael, 'Victory in Burma,' in E. Bauer, *The History of World War II*, (London: Orbis, 1979).

— 'Cardwells' Army Reforms,' *Army*, (April 1962).

Chahda, Lieutenant Colonel Mahesh, 'Mechanized Infantry: where have we gone wrong?' *Combat Journal*, (April 1989).

Chaudhuri, 'Muchu', 'Sandhurst Revisited,' *Blackwood's Magazine*, Vol. 306, No. 1847., (September 1969).

Cohen, Stephen P., 'Civilian Control of the Military in India,' in Claude E. Welch (ed.), *Civilian Control of the Military: Theory and Cases from Developing Countries*, (Albany, New York: State University of New York Press, 1976).

Cohen, Stephen P., 'The Military and Indian Democracy,' in Atul Kohli (ed.), *India's Democracy*, (Princeton, NJ: Princeton University Press, 1988).

Cooper, R.G.S., 'Wellington and the Marathas in 1803,' *International History Review*, 11 (February 1989).

Das, Major Gautam., 'Turk-Sowar: an Indian Mechanized Force for the 21st Century,' *Combat Journal*, (August 1987).

Dutt, Lieutenant Colonel J.K., 'Wanted a Doctrine for Armour,' *Journal of the United Services Institute of India*, (October-December 1977).

Gautam, R.P, 'Status of Services vis-a-vis other Services,' *Journal of the United Services Institute of India*, (April-June 1985).

__ 'Causes of Higher Secondary Students' Preference for Military Career,' *Journal of the United Services Institute of India*, (October-December 1979).

Garnier, Maurice G., 'Changing Recruitment Patterns and Organizational Ideology: The Case of a British Military Academy,' *Administtrative Science Quarterly*, Vol. 17, No. 4., (December 1872).

Greenhut, Jeffery, 'Sahib and Sepoy: An Inquiry into the Relationship between the British officers and Native Soldiers of the British Indian Army,' *Military Affairs*, (January 1984).

Huntington, Samuel P., "Will more Countries become Democratic," *Political Science Quarterly*, Vol 99, (1984).

Gutteridge, William, 'The Indianization of the Indian Army 1918-1945,' *Race*, Vol. 4, (May 1963).

IDR Research Team, 'Some thoughts on the Evolution of Infantry Organization and Tactics,' *Indian Defence Review*, (July 1991).

Jalal, Ayesha, 'India's Partition and the Defence of Pakistan: An Historical Perspective,' *Journal of Imperial and Commonwealth History*, Vol. 15, No. 3., (1987).

Joshi, Manoj K., 'Directions in India's Defence and Security Policies,' in Ross Babbage and Sandy Gordon (eds.), *India's Strategic Future: Regional State or Global Power?* (London: MacMillan, 1992).

Kumar, Captain Rajiv Kumar, 'Man Management: the Present Environ,' *Journal of the United Services Institute of India*, (January-March 1983).

Kundu, Apurba, 'Over Dependence and "Martial Race" Officers,' *Indian Defence Review*, (July 1991).

Law, Brigadier R.D., 'The Gulf War - the last hundred hours: lessons for the Indian Mechanized Forces,' *Journal of the United Services Institute of India*, (July-September 1991).

Lenman, Bruce P., 'The Transition to European Military Ascendency in India, 1600-1800,"\' in John Lynn (ed), *Tools of War: Instruments, Ideas and Institutions of Warfare, 1445-1871*, (Urbana: University of Illinois Press, 1990).

Otley , C.B., 'The Social Origins of British Army Officers,' *The Sociological Review*, Vol. 18, No. 2, (July 1970).

Lloyd I. Rudolph, 'Self as Other: Amar Singh's Diary as Reflexive 'Native' Ethnography,' *Modern Asian Studies*, Vol 31, No 1, (1997), pp.143-75.

Rudolph, Lloyd and Suzanne, 'Generals and Politicians in India,' in Wilson C. McWilliams (ed.), *Garrisons and Governments: Politics and the Military in New States*, (San Francisco: Chandler Publishing Co, 1964).

Santos, Theotonio Dos, 'The Structure of Dependency,' *American Economic Review*, Vol. 60, (May 1970).

Sharpe, Andrew, 'The Indianization of the Indian Army,' *History Today*, March 1986.

Singh, Anita Inder, 'Imperial Defence and the Transfer of Power in India, 1946-1947,' *International History Review*, Vol. 4., No. 4, (1982).

– 'Keeping India in the Commonwealth: British Political and Military Aims, 1947-1949,' *Journal of Contemporary History*, Vol. 20, No. 3, (1985).

– 'Post Imperial British Attitudes to India: The Military Aspect, 1947-1951,' *Round Table*, No. 296 (1985).

Singh, Daljit, 'Military Education in India,' *Journal of the United Services Institute of India*, (July-September 1974).

Sinha, Brigadier B.K., 'Career Prospects for Officers in the Armed Forces,' *Journal of the United Services Institute of India*, (July-September 1968).

Sinha, Lieutenant General S.K. (retd), 'Preserving the Army Ethos,' *Indian Defence Review*, (July 1992).

Spangenberg, B., 'The Aitchison Commission: an Introduction,' in *Report of the Public Service Commission 1886-1888*, (New Delhi: Concept Publishing Co, 1977) [reprint].

–   'Social Affiliations of the British Army Elites,' in Jacques Van Doorn (ed.), *Armed Forces and Society: Sociological Essays*, (The Hague: Moutan & Co, 1968).

Thapan, Lieutenant General M.L., "The Army as a Career,' *Journal of the United Services Institute of India*, (July-September 1977).

Wavell, A.P, 'The Army and the Prophets,' *Journal of the Royal Services Institute*, No. 75, (November 1930).

Index

Addiscombe, 54, 55
Aden, 37, 124
Afghan tribes, 11
Afghanistan, 118, 126
Africa, 118, (East), 37, 138, 140, (South), 142, 143, (North), 137, 144, 145, 146, 147, 148, 151
Afrika Korps, 137, 139, 141
Ahir, 94
Ahmednagar, Machine Gun School, 100
Aitchison College (Lahore), 15, 17
Aitchison, Sir Charles (Lt. Gov Punjab), 27
Aiyer, Sir Sivaswamy, 38, 41, 46, 48, 51, 116
Akali, 98
Alamein, 140, 141
Alanbrooke, General Sir (CIGS), 141, (Lord), 165
Aldershot Command, 127
Allahabad, 99, 105
Allahabad Club, 105
Allied Forces Netherlands East Indies (AFNEI), 152
American, 161
Amery, Leo (Secretary of State India), 106
Andaman Islands, 167
Anderson, Sir Harvey (Lt. Gov Burma), 22, 26
Anglo-Sikh, Wars, 8
Armed Forces Reconstruction Committee (AFRC), 168
Armed Forces Nationalization Committee (AFNC), 166
Army in India Committee (Esher Committee/Report), 116, 117
Army Service Corps (ASC), 102, 103
Army Reorganization Committee (1879), 15
Aryan, 29
Asia, South-East, 144
Atal, Major General Hira Lal, 174
Attlee, Clement (Prime Minister), 165
Auchinleck, Lord, 95, 97, (DCGS India), 121, (General), 127, (C-in-C Middle East), 140, 141,142, 144, 146, 148, (C-in-C India), 161, 162, 163, 165, 166, 168, 169, 170, 171, 192
Aurora, Jagjit Singh, 82, (General), 92, 93, 103

Bombay, 10
Baghdad, 94

Baig, M.R.A., 78, 100, 102
Baig, Mirza Sikander Ali, 83
Baig, Osman, 102
Bangalore, 50, 84, 92
Bangladesh, 177, 192
Banihal Pass, 170
Baramulla, 170
Barrow, General Sir Edmund (C-in-C Southern Army), 20, 76
Batavia, 152
Beasant, Annie, 29
Belgaum, 50, 84, 92
Bengal, 10
Bengal Club (Calcutta), 105
Bengali, 68, 96
Berkenstead, 63, 64
Bewoor, Gopal Gurunath, 83
Bhadwar, Captain, 148, 149
Bhagat, Brigadier 'Tony', 92
Bhagat, Permindrah Singh, 146, 148
Bidwell, Brigadier R.G.S., 139
Billimorai, Brigadier N.D., 174
Billimoria, Cadet, 71
Bir Hachiem, 146
Bishop Cotton School (Bangalore), 67, 68
Black, Major General, 98
Bofors, 195
Bolaram, 100
Bombay Sappers, Royal, 146
Borneo, 154
Brahmins, 105
Britain, 25
British General Staff, 122, 124
British Cabinet, 122, 125
Brown, Stuart Kelson (Joint Secretary Military Dept India Office), 61
Brownlow, General Sir Charles, 20
Bucher, General Roy (C-in-C India), 169, 172
Burma, 50, 95, 96, 97, 101, 137, 138, 145, 149, 150, 151, 153, 154, 167
Burnett-Stuart, General, 126, 127

Cab Ranks, 145
Cabinet Committee on Political Affairs (CCPA), 196
Calcutta, 18, 27, 68

Camberly, Staff College, 10, 126, 139, 166, 192
Cambridge, 63, 67, 72
Carden-Lloyd light tank Mk.1, 129
Cardwell system, 9, 115, 122, 123, 126, 127
Cardwell, Edward (Secretary of State for War), 9
Cariappa, K.M., 64, 65, 66, 97, 98, 99, 102, 164, (C-in-C India), 172, 173, 174, 175
Celebes, 153
Central Asian Treaty Organization (CENTO), 127
Ceylon, 153
Chamberlain, General, 14
Chamberlain, Austen (Secretary of State India), 23, 37
Chatfield Committee/Report, 120, 121, 129, 130, 161
Chatfield, Lord (Admiral of the Fleet), 120
Chaudhuri, Jayanto Nath, 68, 69, 70, 71, 72, 73, 77, 79, 91, 93, 96, 97, 98, 102, 103, 104, 105, 106, 107, 151, 164, 175
Chelmsford, Lord (Viceroy), 37, 38, 117, 123
Chesney, Sir George, 13, 15
Chetwoode Hall, 48
Chetwoode, General sir Phillip (C-in-C India), 46, 47, 48, 52, 127, 128, 199
Chetwoode Committee, 49
Chief Royal Artillery (CRA), 138, 142
Chief of Imperial General Staff (CIGS), 116
Chiefs Colleges, 17
Chillianwalla, 8
China, 161, 167, 194
Chinese, 144
Churchill, Winston S., 106, (Prime Minister), 137, 141, 144
Clifton, School, 78, 100
Club Culture, 105
Cobbe, Lieutenant General Alexander, 41, 51
Cold War, 161
Collins, Brigadier, (Commandant Indian Military Academy), 81
Collins, Mrs ('mommandant'), 81
Columbo, 195
Committee for Imperial Defence (CID), 116, 118
Commonwealth, 37, 129, 137, 139, 144, 145, 147, 148, 151, 161, 162, 165, 167, 175, 191
Congress party, 38, 194
Connought, Duke of, 9
Cooch-Behar, Maharaja of, 9, 10

Coorg, 65, 66, 68, 94, 98

Corbett, General T.W. (8th Army Chief of General Staff), 141

Cork, 125

Corkran, General (Commandant Sandhurst), 73, 74

Cox, General Sir Herbert (Military Secretary India Office), 64

Cranwell, 54, 69

Crawford, Lieutenant Colonel, 81

Creagh, General Sir O'Moore (C-in-C India), 20, 21, 27

Crewe, Lord (Secretary of State India), 22, 27

Croydon, 55

Cunningham, General (8th Army Commander), 139

Curzon, Lord (Viceroy), 17, 18, 19, 28, 203

Daily Mail, 52

Daly College (Indore), 17, 64, 65, 98, 99

Darwinism, 29

Das, Major General M.N., 103

Davies, Major General, 95

Deccan, 122

Deccan Horse, 151

Dehra Dun (Indian Military Academy), 19, 38, 39, 42, 43, 48, 50, 54, 65, 67, 79, 80, 84, 163

Delhi, 19, 97

Delhi, New, 161, 163, 195

Deolali, Staff college, 10

Deverell, General Sir Cyrill (Chief of Imperial General Staff), 124

Dhargalkar, Captain, 148, 149

Dhillon, Joginder Singh, 83

Dillon, Brigadier, 174

Dimoline, Brigadier, 142, 143

Director of Military Intelligence (DMI), 165, 166

Distinguished Service Order (DSO), 146, 147, 153

Divide and Rule, 7

Dominions, 37, 44, 56, 165, 168

Doon School, 68

Dormer College, 48

Dorsetshire, 106

Dragoon Guards, 100

Drigh Road, 84

Duff, General Sir Beauchamp (C-in-C India), 23, 25

Dutch, 152

Dutt, Captain Som, 106

East India Company (EIC), 27, 54, 55
Eden Commission, 9
Egypt, 37, 127
Eight Units Scheme, 48, 84, 106
El Adem, 147
El Mekili, 147
Elgin, Lord, 15
Emergency Commissioned Officers (ECO's), 50, 163
England, 15, 16, 27, 28, 50, 51, 66, 68, 78, 107
Esher, Lord Reginald, 116
Eton, Public School, 75

Far-East, 129
Fitzsimmons, Major General (Fortress Commander Singapore), 94
Forward Observers, 145
France, 24, 37, 63, 151
Franks, Colonel, 98
Free French, 143
French, 153

Gallipoli, 37, 64
Gallipoli Division, 63
Gandhi, 1, 73, 153
Gandhi family, 196
Garran Tribunal, 118
Germans, 140, 141, 142, 143, 145, 146, 147, 148, 151
Germany, 137, (West), 195
Gerrard Street, 79
Goakhle, 27
Gort, General, 124
Gour, Sir Hari Singh, 45, 46
Government of India Act, 38
Gracey, General Douglas (C-in-C Pakistan), 169, 170, 171, 172
Great Depression, 48
Great War, 3, 24, 26, 64, 106, 115, 118, 126
Greece, 137
Gujerat, 8
Gurkhas, 7, 25

Hamilton, Lord George (Secretary of State India), 15, 28

Hamilton-Britton, Colonel, 94
Hannoverians, 16
Hardie, Kier, 29
Hardinge, Lord (Viceroy), 22, 27
Harrow (Public School), 75
Hayyauddin, Lieutenant Colonel M., 171
Henderson, Colonel G.F.R., 9
Highland Light Infantry, 92
Himalayas, 194
Hindi, 104
Hindu, 7, 68, 78, 137, 171, 177
Hobart, General Sir Percy ('Hobo'), 115, 126, 127, 139
Hong-Kong, 144, 153
Hore-Belisha (Secretary of State for War), 118, 124
House of Commons, 124
Hyderabad, 100, 172
Hyderabad Regiment, 19th, 93, 95, 100

Imperial War Conference, 37
Imperial Defence Council (IDC), 164, 166
Imperial Service Corps, 24
Imperial Defence College (IDC), 41, 97
Imperial Cadet Corps (ICC), 17, 18, 19, 22, 61, 62, 63, 64, 76, 91, 203
Inchappe, Lord, 118
Indian Corps (France), 25
Indian Expeditionary Force (IEF), 24, 26
Indian Military Academy (Dehra Dun), 38, 48, 49, 50, 51, 55, 56, 80, 81, 82, 84, 91, 101, 106, 108, 197
Indian Military College (IMC), 47, 48
Indian Civil Service (ICS), 27, 28, 29
Indian Sandhurst Committee, 71, 73, 79
Indian Councils Bill (1909), 29
Indian Councils Act, 38
Indian Commissioned Officers (ICO's), 84, 107, 146
Indian Ait force, 84
Indian National Army (INA), 96, 148
Indian Armed Forces Naturalization Committee, 96
Indian General Staff, 127, 128, 129
Indian Cabinet, 196
Indian Emergency Commissioned Officer (IECO), 152, 167
Indian National Congress, 137
Indianization, 2, 3, 7, 30, 38, 40, 41, 42, 44, 46, 48, 51, 52, 53, 54, 55,

56, 61, 62, 63, 84, 91, 98, 102, 103, 104, 106, 162, 191
Indo-China, 137, 151
Indonesia, 152
Inskip, Major General R.D., 81
Insurgency, 10
Iraq, 98, 153
Ireland, 16, 125
Irish Free State, 125
Irish Ulcer, 125
Italians, 140
Italy, 137, 143, 154

Ja, Captain Khalid, 106
Jacobs, General Claud W., 41, 42, 54, 67
Jacobs Committee, 41, 43, 68
Jaipur, 77
Jakarta, 152
Jallianwallah Bagh, 1
Japan, 137, 153, 167
Japanese, 95, 96, 101, 102, 138, 144, 145, 148, 149, 150, 152, 153
Jat, 94
Java, 153
Jawaharlal Nehru University, 198
Jinnah, Muhammad Ali, 74, 170
Jitra, 101
Jock Columns, 138
Jodhpur, 77
Joint Defence Council (JDC), 168
Juin, General Alphonse (Commander Free French), 143

Kandhar, 126
Kangaw, 96, 145, 150
Kashmir, 170, 174, 176
Kaul, Lieutenant General B.M., 102, 103
Kaula Lumpur, 97
Keren, 138
Kerry, 125
Khadakvasla (National Defence Academy), 197
Khan, Agha, 77
Khan, Sahebzada Yakub, 83
Khan, Sir Zulfikar Ali, 45
Khan, Gul Hasan, 82, 153

Khan, Lieutenant Colonel Akbar, 171
Khan, Nazir Ahmed, 171
Khan, Faiz Mohammed, 100
Khan, Mohammed Asghar, 83
Khan, Agha Mohammed Ayub, 68, 73, 83, (Colonel), 171
Khanna, Captain K.C., 106
Kim, 1
Kimberly, Lord, 13
King's Commissioned Indian Officer (KCIO), 62, 63, 64, 76
King's Commission, 23, 27, 30, 38, 39, 40, 52, 62, 63, 98
Kirke, Major General, 54
Kirkee (TNT factory), 121
Kitchener, Lord, 10, 20, 21, 24, 28, 29
Kitchener College Nowgong, 101
Kodava, 65
Kohima, 150
Koi-Hai, 94
Kotah, 100
Kumaon Battalion, 153
Kumaramangalam, Major P.P., 146, 147, 148
Kunzru, Pandit, 161

Labour Government, 161
Lahore Division, 25
Lahore, 98
Lansdowne, Lord, 16
Latin America, 203
Lawrence, Sir Henry, 12
Leopard-I (Main Battle Tank), 195
Lewis, Lieutenant Colonel, 94
Liberal Reformers, 13, 24, 29, 30, 37, 45, 51
Lidell Hart, B.H., 122, 126
Limerick, 125
Linlithgow, Lord (Viceroy), 118, 137
Liverpool, 55
Lloyd George, David (Prime Minister), 37
London, 68, 79, 97, 165
London Evening News, 44
London Indian Society, 26
Loring, Brigadier (Military Adviser U.K. High Commission India), 172,
    173, 174, 175
Lucknow, 122

Lyall, Sir Alfred (Chair Political Committee), 16

Macasser, 153
Machiavelli, 13
Madras University, 98
Madras Presidency, 125
Madras, 10, 12, 126
Malaya, 97, 101, 137, 144, 149, 150, 151, 153, 167
Maldives, 176
Mamdot, Nawab of, 13
Manekshaw, Jemi H.F., 83
Manekshaw, Captain S.H.J.F., 149
Maratha confederacy, 12
Marathas, 21, 54
Marsh, Lieutenant Colonel, 98
Martel, Sir Giffard, 126
Martial Races, 7, 11, 25, 66, 177, 198
Masters, John, 91, 102
Mayo College Ajmer, 17
Mayu range, 95
Medan, 153
Medjerda, 143
Meerut, 13, 99, 122
Meerut Division, 25
Menon, Krishna (Defence Minister), 195
Mersa Matruh, 146
Mesopotamia, 37
Messervey, General Sir Frank, 104
Messervey, Colonel, 96, 97, 103
Mhow Division, 5th, 76
Mhow, 48, 50, 84
Middle East, 129, 137, 153
Mills, James, 13
Monro, Sir Charles, (C-in-C India), 123
Montagu, Edwin (Secretary of State India), 27, 37, 38, 39, 62, 117
Montagu-Chelmsford Reforms, 45, 51
Montgomery, General B.L., 127, 141, 143, 146, (CIGS), 165, 166, 173
Montgomery-Massingberd, Lieutenant General, 49
Monywa, 154
Moplah Rebellion, 125, 126, 127
Morley, John, 29
Morley-Monto reforms, 29

Mountbatten, Lord Louis (Supreme Allied Commander), 96, (Viceroy), 168, 169
Mungadaw, 95
Munro, Sir thomas, 12, 29
Muslim, 68, 78, 131, 171
Muspratt, General (Military Secretary India Office), 121

Naoroji, Dadabhai, 26, 28, 29, 63
Naoroji, K.A.D., 63, 64
Napier, Field Marshal Lord, 14
Nasirabad, 91
National Defence Academy (NDA), 197
National Defence Council (NDC), 163
National Liberal Federation, 42
National Security Council (NSC), 196
Native Indian Land Forces (NILF), 20, 39, 61, 62
Nehru, Jawaharlal, 166, 168, 194, 196
New Zealand, 143
Nibeiwa, 138
Nicholls, Colonel, 94
Nina, 94

Officer Training Course (OTC), 40, 64
Operation Gibraltar, 169, 176
Oxford, 67, 72
O'Connor, General, 138
O'Dwyer, Sir Michael (Lieutenant Governor Punjab), 44, 45

Pachamari (Small Arms School), 100
Pakistan, 4, 99, 154, 161, 168, 169, 170, 173, 175, 176, 177, 192, 193
Pakistan, East, 149
Pakistani Air Force, 171
Palel, 152
Palembang, 153
Palestine, 37
Palit, Dharti Kumar, 83, 102, 104, 105
Pathan tribes, 10
Pathania, Mohinder Singh, 83
Pathans, 21
Patton Tank (M-47), 193
Pedang, 153
Peel Commission, 9

Peel, Jonathan (Secretary of State for War), 9
Peoples Liberation Army (PLA), 194
Peshawar, 84
Pethick-Lawrence (Secretary of State India), 153
Platt, General, 138
Polish, 171
Polk, General, 94
Ponappa, C.B., 98, 99, 100, 102
Poona Division, 6th, 76
Pownall, Major General H.R., 118
Pownall Report, 120
Prasad, Niranjan, 83
Presidential Armies, 9, 10
Prime Ministers Office (PMO), 196
Prince of Wales Royal Indian Military Academy (PWRIM), 40, 42, 43, 47, 48, 49, 51, 65, 66, 67, 68, 79, 82
Probyn's Horse, 151
Provincial Civil Service, 30
Public Schools, 17, 75
Public Services Commission, 27
Punjab, 12, 193
Punjab Club Lahore, 105
Punjab Regiment, 14th, 92, 101

Quetta (Staff College), 10, 65, 94, 96, 97, 106, 126, 127, 128, 139, 149, 164

Rahman, Mohammed Attiqur, 82, 83
Railway Staff College, 48
Raina, Major T.N., 153
Rajendrasinjhi, Major, 147, 148, (General), 172, 173
Rajkumar College Kathiawar, 17
Rajputs, 25
Rangoon, 96, 97
Rawlinson, Lord (C-in-C India), 39, 40, 45, 117, 123, 125, 127
Raza, Brigadier, 99
Reed, A.H., 171
Rees, Pete, 103
Reorganized Army Plains Infantry Division (RAPIDS), 193
Revolt of 1857, 13
Ricketts, Major R.L.(Commandant Imperial Cadet Corps), 22

Ritchie, General (Commander 8th Army), 139, 140
Roberts, Lord, 10, 17, 20, 24
Roberts, General Sir Frederick (C-in-C India), 14, 15, 21, 22, 23, 29
Robertson, Sir Benjamin (Chief Commissioner Central Provinces), 23
Rommel, General Erwin, 139, 140, 141
Round Table Conferences, 46
Royal Air Force (RAF), 54, 129
Rudra, Major General, 63, 64, 65
Rugby, 75
Russell, Lieutenant General Dudley, 174
Russia, 118, 167

Sainik Schools, 197, 198
Salonika, 37
Sandhurst Committee, 45
Sandhurst (Royal Military College), 15, 21, 22, 24, 39, 40, 41, 42, 43, 44,
    47, 49, 52, 54, 55, 56, 63, 64, 65, 66, 67, 68, 69, 70, 71, 72, 73,
    74, 75, 76, 77, 78, 79, 80, 81, 82, 83, 91, 100, 102, 108, 197
Sarkar, Captain B.N., 152
Satara, chp.48
Saugor, Cavalry School, 100
Scotland, 16
Second World War, 2, 3, 30, 103, 104, 105, 107, 152, 161, 192, 203
Secundrabad, 96
Semarang, 152
Sen, L.P, 96, (Colonel), 149, 150
Settlement of 1790, 16
Shafi's Restaurant, 79
Shah, Lieutenant Sgha Casim, 20, 76, 77
Shea, Lieutenant General Sir John, 40
Shone, Sir Terence (U.K. High Commissioner India), 172, 173, 174
Shrinagesh, Captain, 106, (Lieutenant General), 174
Sicily, 137
Sidi Rezegh, 140
Sikhs, 7, 8, 12, 21, 25, 68, 72, 78
Simla, 67
Simon, Sir John, 45
Simon Commission, 45
Sindhia, 54
Singapore, 94, 118, 144
Singh, Sukhwant, 83
Singh, Mohan, 101, 102, 148

Singh, Sartaj, 83
Singh, Gurbax, 83
Singh, Sheodatt, 100, 151
Singh, Kanwar Daulat, 100, 101, 102
Singh, Brigadier Nathu, 163
Singh, Kanwar Amar, 20, 21, 22, 62, 63, 64, 76, 77, 102
Singh, Dhuleep, 15
Singh, Major General Lakhinder, 174
Sinha, General S.K., 83, 152, 153
Sinjhi, General Rajendra, 172, 173
Skeen Committee, 42, 44, 45, 47, 68
Skeen, Lieutenant General Andrew, 42, 44
Slim, General Sir William, 144, 145, 149, 154, 164, 166, 192
Smith, General Sir Arthur, 166
Smith Dunn, Cadet, 81
South East Asia Treaty Organization (SEATO), 177
Sri Lanka, 176, 194
Srinagar, 170
St. Joseph's College Conoor, 66, 67
St. Pauls, 75
St. Alysosis College, 98
Staffordshire Regiment, North, 91
Stephenson, Brigadier, 171
Stewart, Sir Donald (C-in-C India), 13, 14, 15
Stooks, Colonel, 71, 72
Stuart, Brigadier N.J.B., 175
Sturgess, Colonel, 70, 72
Subadar, 12
Sumatra, 153
Sundarji, General K.S., (Army Chief India), 199
Surabaya, 153
Swedish, 195

Tamil Tigers, 194
Tekrit, 98
Thapan, Kroshna Lal, 83
Thimmaya, Kodendera Subayya, 66, 67, 68, 69, 70, 72, 73, 77, 79, 92, 93, 94, 95, 96, 97, 98, 99, 100, 102, 103, 105, 149, 150
Thorat, S.P.P., 72, 73, 92, 96, 149, 150
Tibet, 194
Time on Target (TOT), 143
Tipperary, 125

Tuker, General Sir Francis, 142, 143
Tumar, East, 138
Tunis, 143
Turkey, 100

Umedwar (hopeful), 11
United States, 177
Utilitarians, 12, 13, 24, 28

Verma, S.D., 70, 91, 147, 148
Verma, Brigadier, 174
Viceroy Commissioned Officers (VCO's), 67, 82, 101
Viceroy's Commissions, 41
Viceroy's Corps, 17
Victoria Cross, 37, 138, 146
Victorian, 28, 30
Viet Minh, 153
Vietnam, 11, 153

Wainwright, Major John, 104
Walker, Brigadier J.F.(Military Adviser U.K. High Commission Pakistan),
    171, 172
War Cabinet, 23, 24, 27, 37
War Office, 16, 21, 23, 24, 30, 37
Ward, General Dudley, 127
Washington, George, 106
Watson, Colonel E.E., 81
Watson, Colonel H.D., 30, 41
Wavell, General A.P., 127, 128, 153
Waziristan, 62
Weber, Max, 53
Western Front, 106
Western Front, 30
Whitehall, 26, 30, 115, 116, 161, 165
Willocks, General Sir James (Commander Indian Expeditionary Force
    France), 25
Wilsom, Sir Arthur, 16
Wilson, General, 13
Wogs, 91, 104
Woolwich (Royal Military Academy), 54, 55, 69, 74, 75, 80

Yacht Club Bombay, 105